FRANK KNOPFELMACHER

SELECTED WRITINGS

Published by Connor Court Publishing Pty Ltd.

Copyright © Andrew Knopfelmacher (as a collection)

ALL RIGHTS RESERVED.

This book contains material protected under International and Federal Copyright Laws and Treaties. Any unauthorised reprint or use of this material is prohibited. No part of this book may be reproduced or transmitted in any form or by any means, electronic or mechanical, including photocopying, recording, or by any information storage and retrieval system without express written permission from the publisher.

CONNOR COURT PUBLISHING PTY LTD
PO Box 7257
Redland Bay QLD 4165
sales@connorcourt.com
www.connorcourtpublishing.com.au

ISBN: 978-1-923224-00-1 (pbk.)

Cover design by Maria Giordano.

Front cover photo courtesy of Andrew Knopfelmacher.

Printed in Australia.

Dedicated to the memory of Frank Knopfelmacher

1923-1995

DR FRANK KNOPFELMACHER (1923-1995), philosopher, sociologist and psychologist was born in 1923 in Vienna and educated in Czechoslovakia and in England. During WW2 he worked in an Israeli kibbutz, then fought with the Eighth Army in the Western desert and the British liberation Army in Western Europe. After the war, he lived and studied in Prague at Charles University where he experienced the communist takeover. Returning to England in 1948, he attained high academic distinction at Bristol University and University College London, from where in 1955 he was appointed to the University of Melbourne. There he combined academic teaching as a lecturer with activities as a publicist and controversialist in political affairs, was a frequent contributor to the weekly and quarterly press and a media personality. In 1965 he was the centre of a heated academic controversy when a unanimous recommendation by an academic selection committee to appoint him to a post in political philosophy at Sydney University was overruled in an unprecedented manner by the University's Professorial Board. An incisive critic of political parties and social institutions, he took a prominent part in the Vietnam controversy, supporting Australia's commitment. He lived to see the collapse of the Soviet Empire and returned twice to Prague in 1990 and 1991. In 1991 as a distinguished guest lecturer for a three month period at Charles University Prague where he had formerly studied under leading philosopher Professor Jan Patocka, a founding member of Charter 77.

TABLE OF CONTENTS

Preface		9
Acknowledgments		11
1	My Political Education *Quadrant,* July-August, 1967	13
2	What's in My Name *Nation Review,* June 4-10, 1976	45
3	Fellow Travelers At Fault *Quadrant,* No. 5, Summer, 1958	51
4	A False Equivalence Between East and West *Quadrant,* No. 13, Summer, 1959-1960	57
5	The Catholic Church and Totalitarianism Published in *Catholics and the Free Society,* ed. Henry Mayer, 1961	61
6	The Situation in the University of Melbourne *Twentieth Century,* No. 4, 1964	69
7	'There But For The Grace of God...' *The Bulletin,* 7 March, 1964	81
8	The Consequences of Israel *Quadrant*, No. 50, Nov-Dec, 1967	87
9	There Are No Youth Movements *Quadrant,* No. 54, July-August, 1968	105

10 America The Bad Society
    The Australian, May 3-5, 1971   111

11 The Parasite as Revolutionary: The Fleecing of America
    Intercollegiate Review, Summer, 1971   127

12 What Makes Australia Tick?
    News Weekly, November 17, 1971   141

13 Wilhelm Reich, the Founder of Porno Politics
    News Weekly, February 14, 1973   145

14 Modern Australia British to the Core
    Nation Review, March 8-14, 1974   151

15 The Case Against Détente
    Nation Review, July 19-25, 1974   157

16 Manhattan Versus the Vatican
    Nation Review, August 29-September 4, 1975   163

17 The Murky Origins of the Russian Revolution
    National Times, August 9-14, 1976   167

18 A Quiet Scholar Dies Hard: Jan Patocka
    Nation Review, April 6, 1977   173

19 Terrorism and Reason
    Nation Review, October 22, 1977   179

20 Among the Flesh Pots: Solzhenitsyn and the West
    Quadrant, October, 1978   185

21 No Breaking Ranks If You Weren't in the March
    The Age, January 12, 1981   191

22	Arthur Koestler: The Mole of God *Quadrant,* October, 1982	197
23	In (Mild) Defence of Karl Marx *Quadrant,* July, 1983	221
24	*Nineteen Eighty-Four* *Quadrant,* January, 1984	227
25	The Multicultural Enterprise and Its Consequences *Quadrant,* May, 1984	235
26	Second Thoughts on Muggeridge *Nation Review*, 1984	243
27	Boring For Women *Quadrant*, October, 1984	249
28	The Vietnam Debate Revisited *Quadrant,* October, 1989	255
29	Bangs and Whimpers: The Soviet Crisis *Quadrant,* March, 1990	263
30	The Crown in a Culturally Diverse Australia *Proceedings of the Second Conference of the* *Samuel Griffiths Society,* 30 July-1 August, 1993	273

PREFACE

The essays and articles in this volume are the written and spoken words of a fearless fighter. Not an armchair academic or ivory-tower scholar, but someone who was from the late 1930's to the end of his life a 'participant observer', as my father described himself. A man who was many things through intellectual interest and academic endeavor; social theorist, political philosopher, analyst and commentator. Least, as far as he was concerned, an academic psychologist – philosophy and social theory being the great intellectual loves of his life.

Personal knowledge and loathing of totalitarianism through necessity not choice, was the great motivating factor in his political activities. Experiencing the Hitler and Stalin regimes 'on the skin of his back' (Solzhenitsyn) in his formative years, was to mark him for life. It has been said of Hannah Arendt that she wrote as 'someone who hasn't only suffered but has also thought'. This applies equally to my father. He may certainly be remembered as an anti-communist 'cold war warrior' but more than that – as this largely chronological collection shows, a broad-ranging incisive social commentator admired and respected from near and far, by friends, fellow fighters against the left and ordinary people who understood his message. Devoid of false modesty on the one hand, and pomposity on the other – too much self-irony for that – in John Carroll's words (as my father himself often said of the great Max Weber) there was about him an 'unconditional sobriety': or as FK would have put it, 'no bullshit'.

A penetrating speaker, he drew students from all over the university to his public lectures, and to classes where it has been said 'you could hear a pin drop'. Famous for his lucidity, cutting wit and humour, he was a great conversationalist and teacher and a delight to have as a father. He lived to lecture, write and teach. For decades, large numbers of ordinary people interested in ideas were drawn to his WEA and CAE classes. In his own words to an interviewer, '...I educated a generation, a whole generation, if I have a lasting achievement it is that'.

Whether alerting the public to the inherent dangers of the Soviet Empire – externally, geopolitically and militarily or internally, through subversion – or to various threats to social cohesion, such as a 'multiculturalism' which 'breeds ethnic furies and hostilities' or post-marxist political correctness – above all, based on his own experiences and insight, my father felt he really had one duty: to warn.

Andrew Knopfelmacher, Melbourne 2023

ACKNOWLEDGMENTS

First of all, to my mother Susan whose constant love and support has been the driving force behind my work on this extensive project. Not to mention her tireless help in making its publication possible, and her generous subsidizing of my time to put the collection together. Also, to my sister Stephanie for all her support.

Secondly, I want to thank Patrick Morgan, student, friend and long-time ally of my father over many decades. Many thanks Patrick for all your help in selecting and editing the pieces here into a publishable format. There would be no volume before you without Patrick's help.

Finally, but not least, to Anthony Cappello, a most patient publisher. Anthony has allowed me the time and space to work in my own way at getting this volume together, despite passing a number of potential 'due by' dates. Thank you, Anthony.

1

My Political Education

(*Quadrant*, July-August, 1967)

A talk given to an Association for Cultural Freedom seminar on personal experiences of Communism.

As a psychologist, I cannot take autobiography seriously, except as a datum about a person, not as a true story. Autobiographies are webs of self-deceptions, defences, rationalisations and repressions. I shall therefore not attempt here a story in depth. I may as well introduce my story in the style in which Communists used to give their confessions at their trials. I come from a Jewish bourgeois family. It had lived in Bohemia and Moravia for centuries. I was brought up in a provincial city in Moravia, though I was born in Vienna, where my uncle, Professor Knopfelmacher, a leading paediatrician, helped bring this event about at a clinic where he worked.

My family tended to be German speaking (unlike my wife's which was super-patriotically Czech, as only Jews can be super-patriotic), a fact connected with the social history of Bohemian and Moravian Jews. A condition of their emancipation by the Emperor Joseph II was that they adopt German as their language. Joseph was, of course, not a nationalist but an enlightened despot with a purely administrative outlook who wanted to introduce German as the one language of the Empire for reasons of administrative convenience. In his days the Czechs were almost extinct as a nation, Czech being pretty much in the position of Welsh in the Victorian era: a language of peasants studied by academic eccentrics. An unfortunate consequence of this fact became apparent with the upsurge of the Czech *risorgimento* in the nineteenth century: The Jews tended to form German enclaves in purely Czech regions, and some of them (both my grandfathers, for example) became suspected trusties of the Habsburg administration in a sea of Czech nationalism. I myself was brought up a as a Czech, and became a fierce Czech nationalist at the age of seven, deeply ashamed of my 'German' antecedents. In this manner anti-Semitism and anti-Germanism tended to merge: to be a Jew was doubly suspect, in that it meant also to be a 'Germanizer' of Czech lands.

My first political experience was of the tremendous hatred between Czechs and Germans and of anti-Semitism. This first experience coincided with the bankruptcy during the depression of our family factory, a distillery. The bankruptcy almost resulted in the break-up of my family.

Another very strong early impression was the impact of the Catholic Church on the life around me. The town where I spent the first ten years of my life and from where my father's family comes is Kromeriz, which is the centre of Hanakia or Hana, an extremely fertile part of Moravia. It was also the residential city of the Archbishop of Olomouc, one of the oldest archbishoprics in Europe. There was a curious link between Catholicism, Czech nationalism and anti-Semitism, which led me, when I was still under the age of ten, to a rejection of Judaism as something cumbersome which separated me from my mates. I did not realize at that time that I was experiencing a very common, phenomenon, Jewish self-hatred. But I also truculently refused to give in to anti-Semitic pressures and tended to emphasize my Jewishness at most inappropriate opportunities. Some of my nannies were very pious Catholics, in the manner of Czech peasant women, and it was under their influence that I received my first truly religious impressions in a vague sort of way. (As a matter of fact an experience very similar to mine has been described by the author Franz Werfel in his book *Barbara oder die Frommigkeit*[1] which is about the impact of a religious peasant nanny on a young – perhaps Jewish – man in the Czech lands.)

In 1933 when I was ten, my family moved to the industrial city of Ostrava in the northern part of Moravia. A year and a half later we moved from Ostrava to Brno. My father's career was on the upgrade. He was a Freemason and, after the bankruptcy of our factory, through his Masonic contacts he was very quickly placed in an insurance business and rose rapidly to an executive position.

I might perhaps say one or two things about my families. My father was very much a conventional middle-class Jew, assimilated in a Germanic direction. He studied law, he was a member of duelling fraternities; he still had scars on his face; he was a very good horseman; he played in the tennis championship for Moravia in 1929 and almost won; and his values were generally those of a young gentleman in the old Austro-Hungarian monarchy. He made a point of associating socially (riding, tennis) with members of the nobility. Later when he entered the insurance business, he insured quite a number of them. He had a very good war record in the old Austro-Hungarian army and he was decorated on a number of occasions. He spent three years on active service in the Dolomites on the Italian front. He was basically anti-intellectual and was a bit worried about my predominantly intellectual tendencies. My relations with him were on the whole good and to this day I still regard him as a sort of paradigm of what a manly man should be like. My mother was a great beauty in her day, yet she became quite domesticated and conventional. My two grandfathers were in many ways more interesting, because they were contrasting types. The grandfather from my father's side was a typical cavalier, a country gentleman frequently on horseback who used to drive out to the villages where he had many mistresses. He was a tall, handsome man, with a Bismarckian moustache, an easy going, irreverent

---

[1] *Barbara or the pious*

wencher. My maternal grandfather was almost a textbook case of a Puritan. He too was very tall, a magnificent figure, but he was cold, detached, calculating and contemptuous. He gave up the pleasures of life very early and devoted himself fully to business. He despised his predominantly 'barbarian' Czech milieu. Unlike my paternal grandfather, who was completely identified with Vienna and the Austrian monarchy, and obtained the title *Kaiserlicher Rat*[2] from the Austrian Government, my maternal grandfather took the Protestant, puritan, up-and-coming, modernizing Germany as his model. He was a supporter of the German National Liberal party, his ideal was Bismarck, and his hero was Emperor Wilhelm II. In 1930 when our family went bankrupt, my paternal grandfather rather characteristically lost all his property whereas my maternal grandfather actually made more money and managed to buy our family out. Both grandfathers were 'liberal' Jews. They attended the synagogue but did not keep the dietary laws.

My awakening and my puberty, as it were, started at the age of about 12. Very soon I became a voracious reader of philosophical and religious literature and I fell under the influence of a very brilliant teacher in the Jewish Gymnasium in Brno which I attended. It was under his influence that I became very briefly an orthodox Jew. Between 1934 and 1938 I lived the comfortable life of a precocious Jewish kid, mainly interested in philosophy, religion and metaphysics. But I couldn't help noticing, vaguely, the Nazis in the background. Brno was a mixed city with a strong German minority, who were under Nazi influence. I saw them as a bunch of barbarians wearing white stockings, leather shorts and Tyrolean hats.

Then in 1938 the blows began to fall. Hitler invaded Austria and occupied Vienna. Many of my relatives lived in Vienna and the first dramatic contact I had with reality was when my father had to wrangle visas for them to enter Czechoslovakia. I suddenly saw a number of aunts, uncles and cousins, whom I knew as

---

[2] Member of the Imperial Council

happy human beings, turned into shaking and broken wrecks. Professor Knopfelmacher and two cousins committed suicide. The war scare was almost continuous. In May, 1938, the Spanish Government organized an exhibition in Brno of Fascist atrocities in the Spanish Civil War. The exhibition showed the effect of air raids, mangled bodies, disembowelled soldiers, killed babies. It was an exhibition, as I have subsequently found through my reading, organized by Koestler and Munzenberg and partly based on faked material. But witnessing that exhibition started a new chapter in my life. I still remember the day. It was beautiful and sunny, and the exhibition was held in a cinema on one of the main squares of Brno, with a baroque church in the middle. As I left the exhibition I looked into the sun; I breathed the spring air, and suddenly I had the feeling of a curious kind of Being, which was somehow whispering to me that there is going to be violence and death. It is very difficult to describe what it was exactly, but suddenly I was saddled with the awareness of violence and death, which has never since left me. I also realized that what I saw may occur in the next few minutes in Brno. The Czech army had just started to mobilize.

The experience connected with the 1938-9 crisis led to a collapse of my orthodox religious Jewish beliefs. I found that the people around me behaved in a manner which did not show any correlation between their avowed religious belief and their personal courage. The teacher under whose influence I became an orthodox Jew, became frightened, bewildered and physically scared. Another shock was the dreadful behaviour of many Gentiles. The first major tragedy occurred for us in October, 1938, when the town where my maternal grandmother had her property was occupied by the Germans as a part of the Sudetenland – though it was actually a Czech city. The grandmother and a number of aunts (one of them a total cripple) were expelled by the Germans within 24 hours and were not admitted into the rump of Czechoslovakia. We had to pick them up on the border, from a no-man's-land zone, bribing the customs officials, and smuggle them in to rump Czechoslovakia. Before they were expelled, the son of their

German neighbours who had known them for about 60 years, came with a bucket of paint and a brush, and painted the word 'Saujude' on the shop windows.

Another experience was the behaviour of the Western powers, particularly of the British government. The men of Munich, Chamberlain, Lord Halifax, Lord Runciman and the rest, imprinted themselves on my mind as the representatives of a certain kind of English gentlemanliness which I have never ceased to suspect. I have since become an Anglophile but I still associate at times Englishness, Britishness and treachery. I know this is an irrational prejudice but I mention it here only because it is one which is shared by many people of my generation from Central Europe and because it has also had political consequences.

It was at that time that I more or less independently worked out the basic propositions of Marxism for myself under the impact of these experiences. I discovered a link between human conduct, human culture and the character of the socio-economic base: I saw proud human beings with distinguished political and cultural records reduced to wrecks by the destruction of their socio-economic base, and normally decent people turned into beasts by changes and opportunities in the socio-economic base. The notion that culture and even spirituality are linked with the socio-economic machinery of society was utterly destructive of my religious and metaphysical views. I met a Marxist who drew my attention to the fact that my 'discoveries' were not very original and I began to read Marxist literature and Communist newspapers. I was also particularly impressed by what I thought was the fearless conduct of individual Communists and Communist organizations. While everybody else was scurrying for cover, the Communists alone appeared to be standing out like rocks of decency and resistance.

Under the impact of those experiences, the Soviet Union, about which I knew very little, became a symbol of life and civilization for me. I became convinced that the culture in which I had been brought up and which could collapse so easily must be rotten; that in order to destroy and to prevent Nazism a total reconstruction of society was necessary; that civilization had to be based on a foundation quite different from the rather fragile one of bourgeois capitalism.

This basic conviction remained with me for the next six years. I knew, of course, that the methods of the Soviet government tended to be rather drastic – I was ignorant of the details – but I did not disapprove of it. I felt that society required radical and drastic changes which could only be carried out with a mailed fist.

When the Germans finally occupied Czechoslovakia I insisted that I should be allowed to leave the country and go virtually anywhere. My father tried to persuade me to stay, but I insisted that I did not want to. I was convinced, as I told him, that the Nazis were going to exterminate us all. I remember that my father became very upset about this statement. He tried to explain to me that I was immature, that I saw things in much too lurid colours. He used the German proverb: *Es wird nie so heiss gegessen wie gekocht*.[3] But I felt that I had an intuitive understanding of the Nazis. I was convinced that they were going exterminate us. This conviction was based on a sort of intuitive apprehension of their mental and political make-up which I just felt when I looked at them. Risking boastfulness I want to add that I regard this intuitive understanding of the totalitarian mentality as one of my intellectual assets. I think I have never been wrong on anything connected with totalitarianism. The only opening for emigration was to go with the Youth Aliyah (which in Hebrew means emigration to Israel). Before being deemed eligible for 'Aliya' one had to pass through a preparatory camp, called 'Hachsharah' in Hebrew. These camps were run by the Jewish Agency under strict supervision of the Gestapo. I spent several weeks in such a camp in Moravia at Blansko, near the famous Macocha caves. Time was evenly divided between work at farms, ivrith [Hebrew] and Zionist propaganda. After work we donned

---

[3] You never eat the food as hot as it is cooked, i.e. things aren't as bad as they seem.

our uniforms – white shirts, riding breeches and jack-boots – and sang patriotic (Hebrew) songs. There were frequent marches with torches. I was profoundly nauseated by the whole process, which reminded me of the Hitler youth. Years later I understood that what I witnessed was 'identification with the aggressor', a key to concentration camp psychopathology. There were frequent visits of inspection by the S.S. Gestapo people, usually unannounced. At one such visit, the place was found to be in a mess. We were lined up, and the S.S. man gave us a dressing-down, the key sentence of which was: *'wo Jud, dort Sauhaufen'*.[4] He spoke in a strong wheedling Saxonian dialect. Suddenly a tall lanky girl collapsed – fainted. *'Abtragen und weitermachen'*[5] commanded the SS man. The girl was orthodox in a predominantly 'left wing' camp without kosher food and refused to eat most of our food. This and the shock of the S.S. man's insults were too much. She was very ugly. I spent the rest of the day repeating to myself stereotypically: *'Ceterum autem censeo Carthaginem esse delendam'*.[6] Only I meant Germany and I hoped that the avenging sword would come from the East, from the USSR.

Meanwhile my mother tried to get out to England on a domestic servant permit but the official permit from the Ministry of Labour in London reached her on the day England declared war on Germany and she couldn't leave the country. I managed to get out in November, 1939. Italy was still neutral and we travelled via Trieste, quite legally. I, with other youngsters, got a certificate of immigration from the British Mandate government and I was on one of the last youth transports from central Europe to Palestine. I must add here, that I went to Palestine purely to get out. I rejected Zionism utterly. I accepted the official Comintern doctrine on Zionism that it was a tool of British Imperialism. We were put into a kibbutz where we were supposed to be turned into agricultural labourers, into *halutzim*, under the expert guidance of instructors

---

[4] 'where there's a Jew, there's a mess'
[5] 'Review and carry on'
[6] The Roman public figure Cato the Elder's exhortation during the Punic Wars: 'Moreover I consider that Carthage must be destroyed'.

(one of whom was Mr Arie ben Gurion, a nephew of the former Israeli Prime Minister). I rejected the kibbutz and its collectivism completely and a number of others and I behaved in a silly way. We felt we were acting in defiance of something or other, but I realize now that we were behaving like spoilt middle-class brats. Hard physical work combined with collectivism and a general atmosphere of collectivist conformism was not the kind of life that I wanted to live. But the kibbutz, like most of the older kibbutzim in Palestine, had a very good socialist library and I spent every moment I could spare reading socialist, Marxist and Leninist classics. After nearly a year I was shifted to a settlement which was less collective – a so-called Moshaf Ovdim – where I was put up with a German family. It was a kind of centre for political malcontents who were not prepared to accept the discipline of a kibbutz and it was there that I first met a Communist who was deeply involved in Communist Party work. He is now a high official in Czechoslovakia. He became what is known, since Arthur Koestler coined the term in relation to the Communists, my guru.

I read a great amount of philosophy then but I kept on reading Marxist-Leninist classics; I think there is very little in that field which I did not read at that time. The village had enormous private libraries which belonged to formerly wealthy German Jews who became farmers and who brought their libraries with them. I read a great amount and discussed politics and sociology with my guru. Like me my guru rejected Zionism very violently. I had two doubts in connection with Communism. I felt that the Soviet Union should join in the war against Germany, and I could not fully accept dialectical materialism as a philosophy. But I finally decided to join the Communist Party in January, 1942, and became affiliated with the Communist Party Youth Movement (I was not yet nineteen), I moved from the village where I was, first to Tel-Aviv then to Haifa. (During my brief sojourn in Tel-Aviv I saw my first Australians in uniform. As a porter in a small Tel-Aviv hotel catering mainly for Australians on leave from Tobruk I cleaned up the vomit after the drinking parties).

In order to be able to study I joined the Auxiliary Settlement and City Police in Haifa which was then being set up by the British and the Jewish illegal defence authorities to extend defences against German paratroopers (periodic paratroop scares were current in those days). I became an Auxiliary Constable, a Gaffir. Dressed in an Anglified Turkish uniform and equipped with an ancient Colt revolver (manufactured in 1890, I believe), my job was to guard public buildings. Our instructor told us that we were allowed to shoot only if our lives were in danger, but that if we did shoot, we would wish that we had never been born. I continued to read a great deal. My doubts concerning the Soviet Union were dispelled because now the Soviet Union was fighting against Germany. I accepted the spirit of the anti-Fascist front and in May, 1942, I joined the Czechoslovak army in the Middle East. In joining the army I graduated from the Communist Youth Movement to the Communist Party proper and became a member of the illegal Party Organization in the army.

The Czechoslovak army in the Middle East was a curious outfit – most of its men were Jews recruited from Palestine. The officers, however, were not and some of them tended to anti-Semitism. The situation was further complicated by the fact that the Czechoslovak officers were trained to command armies of workers and peasants. Yet the private soldiers with which our officers were confronted were Jewish businessmen and intellectuals. This created very serious misunderstandings. It helped to reinforce the feeling among the Jews that the officers were anti-Semitic Fascists, and among the officers to stiffen such anti-Semitic prejudices as they had.

At that time the Communist line changed from an internationalist one into one which stressed the solidarity of the Slav nations and the Germanic character of the Nazis. The war against fascism was presented increasingly as a war between Slavs and Germans. We were also forbidden to speak German in the army. I made a point of always speaking in German to German soldiers, pointing out that the language of Marx and Goethe was good enough for me. In the end I was caught speaking German to an anti-Fascist German and was confined to barracks. I refused to apologize and as a result of this breach of discipline the Communist Party decided to sever connections with me temporarily. By that time I was fed up with the unimaginative and stupid Party bosses in the army. As I subsequently found out, I was not the only one expelled at that time; three others were thrown out. One of them was a cousin of the girl who eventually became my wife. We formed a little group of our own and, knowing that soon we were to be shipped to England, we were determined that we were going to put matters right and that we would be able to explain our case to the top party bosses in London.

Physically I felt well. We took part in the Desert Campaign. A light anti-aircraft regiment, we were on active service for seven months in North Africa. The climate and the air in the desert were good and I really enjoyed myself. But in June a decision was reached that our unit would be transferred to England where it was to be fused with the main Czech unit under British High Command, a unit which had been in England since the fall of France.

We were assembled in a dismal camp in El Cassasino in Egypt and we embarked on the liner *Mauretania* for the journey to England via the Cape. The U-boats were busy at that time – but the *Mauretania* sailed without convoy apparently because it was fast. We never knew where we were and the ship proceeded in quite fantastic zigzags. The journey was uneventful. We reached the Irish coast after six weeks, and it was nice when two Spitfires came out to greet us as we were approaching Liverpool. We were put on a train in a compartment which, in Europe, would be first or second class. I remember noticing that it was upholstered! The custom in all European countries (and in the Middle East) is to transport soldiers in goods trains which bear the inscription '8 horses or 40 men'. Here, in imperialist England, we were not only put into a passenger train but into one with upholstered seats and plenty of room for everybody! We also had tea and good meals served to us in a civilised manner. We came to Colchester and our military camp. The first place I looked up was the Communist book shop. I also started to attend meetings of the British Labour Party.

England was a great surprise for me. It was not all what I had expected. It was completely different from what my Marxist upbringing had led me to expect. I found it increasingly difficult to regard people I met at Labour Party meetings as agents of Imperialism. There was no servility in their conduct; as a matter of fact they were much less servile in those days than the few English Communists I had met – of course the Communists had been instructed to observe the electoral truce and get on with the Tories. I was amazed by the fantastic tolerance in English public life, by the enormous freedom and by the almost uninhibited freedom of discussion. Czechoslovakia was a democracy before the war, but I could never think of a period where freedom and civil liberty were as completely uninhibited as I saw it in wartime England. What had happened of course, was that, a provincial, I encountered for the first time in my life a major democratic metropolitan culture. I met new and interesting people. One of them was my friend Dr Koerner (now Professor of Philosophy at Bristol). He had just got his doctorate at Cambridge and he joined up shortly afterwards. Another man who influenced me was Joseph Doppler, a former Communist who had left the Party in 1934. He was the first strongly anti-Communist left-winger I had encountered.

I also started to read very widely English newspapers and periodicals and the one paper I was particularly keen on was Aneurin Bevan's and Jennie Lee's *Tribune*. There was one name which caught my eye very soon in *Tribune*. It was a name which was unknown to the English people I talked to, including Labour intellectuals; a man called George Orwell, whose weekly column, 'I write as I please', had a peculiar effect on me. Here was a man who understood the thinking of a soldier like me, who knew what it meant for a young intellectual to be in the army and in the war in the paradoxical way in which we were in it, and who understood our particular requirements. I also noticed that he had had all the things I was looking for in the Communist Party, but did not have a number of liabilities associated with being a Communist. He was anti-Fascist and totally opposed to Capitalism, but at the same time undogmatic, reasonable, frank, and he was prepared to call a spade a spade. I also kept up my philosophical interests. I had long philosophical debates with Koerner and I began to study mathematical logic. I still remember, once on guard duty, trying to fight my way through Russell's *Introduction to Mathematical Philosophy*.

I was also increasingly repelled by Soviet jingoism and I became, particularly under the influence of *Tribune* and other socialist magazines, increasingly critical of Allied policy towards Germany, and especially the Allied bombing of German cities, the working-class districts in particular. My rows with my comrades were becoming more frequent. I somehow did not bother any more to rehabilitate myself with the Communists. I became increasingly nauseated by them. The kind of people who were running the Party in London were utterly objectionable scoundrels, adventurers, opportunists and shirkers. Yet somehow I was still maintaining a basically pro-Soviet position. My new English friends and my new intellectual friends in the British-Czech army began to play a more important role in my life. Under the influence of talks with Doppler I began for the first time to study the shadier parts of Soviet history and became familiar with some of the background concerning the Moscow Trials. By the beginning of 1944 when I met my future wife my beliefs were thoroughly shaken, although I still tried to maintain a basically pre-Soviet position. I still remember specifically when I finally decided to cease to be what was called 'a friend of the Soviet Union'.

There occurred a crisis. I believe it was early '44 or late '43, when the Allies recognised the government of Marshal Badoglio; Moscow at that time made great play of the fact that they would not recognize a government headed by a Fascist general. I remember having a discussion defending the Soviet line in the barracks. Then in the evening at nearby Kettering with my cousin, I bought an evening paper and there it was on the front page headlined: 'Soviet Government recognizes Badoglio'. I still remember saying to my cousin: 'They're a bunch of bastards. They can't be believed, they are no better than the others.' Anyhow it was the first time that I had freely said it.

I was married in August, 1944, and a week after my marriage had to leave for France. In November I began to experience the realities of the European war. Normandy was a distressing place. The air stank with the smell of the rotting cattle lying all about. There were also occasional corpses lying about. I remember once we came to a burnt-out tank which stank terribly, as if it had been filled with rotting corpses. One of our people crawled into it and all he found was a rotting middle finger with a ring on it. That middle finger for some reason seemed to have emitted a terrible kind of stench. Then one day, when we were in tents in Normandy waiting to be sent to the front, I had an experience which became very important for my subsequent political development. I was on guard duty and a friend of mine, a young economist, who was also on guard duty had left a book lying on his bunk in the resting tent. I had no books with me, so I picked this up and started to read through it. I read it. I just could not put it away. I went out on sentry duty. I thought about it and I returned to the tent and read I again. When I finished reading it – within the 24 hour period I was on guard – I found that all my beliefs were shattered. My defences were broken, and the suspicions which I had harboured for a considerable time seem to have been particularly confirmed. The book was *Darkness at Noon* by Koestler. I knew at once that this was the true account. It was not a kind of religious intuitive knowledge, but I felt that this was an account which put all the disconnected and inexplicable pieces with which I had been struggling into their proper place. I also knew that Czechoslovakia after the war would be under Stalin's rule and I did not want to live there. Shortly afterwards we were transferred to the front.

The front was rather an odd one. By that time the Allies were already crossing into Germany, but there were a number of ports in France, including Dunkirk, which the Allies had decided to bypass and not take. Our armoured brigade was dumped around Dunkirk in order to lay siege to the beleaguered German garrison there. The object was probably to prevent us having too many casualties so that we might be available at the end of the war to counter the Russians. If that was the reason we were dumped there, it was not a very good one, for it soon turned out that our casualties were sometimes greater than those of the units operating on the main front. Dunkirk was mined; the Germans had naval artillery there which they turned around on us; we were constantly engaged in patrols, in raids and raiding parties. Many of my friends were killed. Doppler, my ex-Communist friend, was killed by a sniper the second day we were in Dunkirk.

The German garrison was haphazardly assembled under the command of Rear-Admiral Frisius. We were told by German prisoners that he had only one hand, had lost all his family in a bombing raid, and behaved like a man who had nothing to expect from life any more. I saw a number of things which one expects normally to see only in grade B war movies. For instance, after an artillery bombardment I suddenly heard cries coming from the other side – the Germans were about a hundred yards away from us. They were desperate cries which were getting weaker and weaker, then gradually changed into groans and sighs and then they stopped altogether. Obviously, a man had been hit and was slowly dying. Then I saw a stupid young fellow who had decided to be a hero and go after a German post being gradually pinned down by rifle fire and shot to pieces with us standing around not being able to do a thing for him. Then a patrol brought in a young German naval officer who was shot in the lungs by one of us and who was slowly suffocating and expiring under terrible conditions. The next day I saw his corpse under a blanket with his boots sticking out. I saw people being torn to pieces – a friend of mine had half his body blown off. My former battery commander from the Middle East had his head blown off. Generally speaking I experienced the realities of war, and as I was experiencing them, I became increasingly nauseated at another aspect of the

Communist Party, its crass and loudmouthed war mongering which the Party in general and the left intelligentsia in particular went in for at that time. Again, it was only Orwell who shared my sentiments.

The week when the war ended I went on leave to England, and the announcement that Germany had surrendered reached me in the middle of the Channel. I hoped to stay in England and be demobilised there. However, the Home Office told us that while those who had joined the army in England could be demobilised there, those who had joined the army elsewhere had the option of being demobilised in Czechoslovakia or in the country where they had joined. This left me with the choice of Palestine or Czechoslovakia. I decided to risk Czechoslovakia for I just did not want to live in Palestine. I was not a Zionist although I am a bit more sympathetic towards Zionism now than I then was. (I can now see that much of my opposition was of a rather silly kind.) I just wanted to live in Europe in a European kind of society and I knew and felt that sooner or later Czechoslovakia would be integrated one way or another into the Soviet Union. I knew too that if I became a political refugee from Czechoslovakia I would be admitted into England. At that time I had a fairly adequate knowledge of the working of the English mind and I knew that the Home Office would have to let us in if we got into trouble again. There would be such public pressure that they would have to grant us visas. In the event this is what happened. Not much pressure was necessary – the Labour Government behaved very well towards us, when the trouble really started. In those days the Labour Party was much more anti-Communist than the Tories.

When my wife and I returned to Czechoslovakia, what we saw surpassed our expectations. The behaviour of the Red Army in Eastern Europe is well known. There was rape, pillage and unspeakable conduct particularly in the eastern part of the country. The Red Army's behaviour evoked strong echoes of an 'archetypal' kind. It brought back memories of atrocity stories preserved in folklore and legend about horrors of Tartar and Mongol invaders of the Czech lands. I still remember the shudder which I felt on seeing mongoloid, pock-marked, gun-toting Red Army men – bandy legged, short and wiry – walking against the background of the St Nicholas Church in Prague, one of the treasures of the Czech baroque. The Russians were by that time as hated by the general population as the Germans. The regime which was set up in Czechoslovakia was corrupt. People who had collaborated with the Nazis were flocking into the Communist Party and anti-Semitism was rife. Insults were thrown into your face, and you were told that it was a pity that so many Jews had survived. The best people, particularly among the intelligentsia, had been killed.

I enrolled at the Charles University Prague, as a student of psychology, philosophy and English and tried to make the best of a bad job. The property which I still had was not returned to me, on the grounds that my Jewish grandmother, gassed in Poland, was German. I would have been prepared to put up with the loss of the property, if it had been socialized, but it had been handed out as a graft to a Czech gentile who had collaborated with the Germans and who was in with the local Communist National Committee. I managed to outfox him in the end. I hired myself a top lawyer who was also a top civil servant with Communist connections. I promised him a cut, if my property were restored. He managed to outsmart the gentleman in question. My two houses were returned to me about a week after the *coup d'etat*. I could still dispose of them and I had lots of money in my hands which I could use to bribe my way out of the country.

The Czech students (I became one), were the best section of the population. They had a bit more courage than the others and they also resisted the increasing Communist encroachment. In 1946, the I.U.S. [International Union of Students] had a conference in Prague and I observed American so-called progressives and Communists in action. It was interesting that amongst them there was a man who later became famous as a victim of McCarthyism; he committed suicide during the McCarthy period. He was on an exchange visit and while in Prague he made no bones about the fact that he was a Communist though in the USA he would deny it strongly. I suspect that he committed suicide because most of his friends were either sent to jail or executed during the Slansky trials. It was probably more than he could bear. Despite the fact that the man was a conspirator and a Communist I could not help liking him. He was obviously a nice man who was inspired by generous motives. I experienced something for the first time which has been with me ever since: meeting rather immature Englishmen, Americans and Australians, whose political postures reminded me in a vague way of my own early political adolescence. It is somehow odd to see one's own political adolescence re-enacted by people who are around fifty.

Two and a half years in Prague gave me a priceless opportunity to study Communist techniques and a Communist takeover under what I might call laboratory conditions. I would not trade this experience for anything in the world. It was my political university. I watched the process from the storm-centre which was the University. The only part of the population which resisted in February, 1948, were the students.

The experience which changed me finally from non-Communist into an anti-Communist was the general conduct of the Russians and the Communists in Czechoslovakia, but there was one event which stands out – the trial of the Bulgarian Communist leader Kostov; one of the first of the great frame-up trials of Communist leaders in Eastern Europe. Kostov belonged to the old Bulgarian Communist Party, the so-called Tesniaky, and he was critically involved in the Stambousky uprising after the first world war. That uprising was quelled by the Bulgarian Whites with the utmost cruelty. People were flung into ovens by the Bulgarian police. Kostov himself was inhumanly tortured, and in order to escape torture he jumped from a top-floor window. He injured his spine, and became a hunchback. When he was being tried by the Communist regime in Bulgaria, cartoons of him appeared in the Communist Press which stressed two things – his Jewish appearance and his hunchback – in other words the terrible physical injury which he suffered in the service of the Party was used by the Party hangmen to ridicule him and to help to destroy him. I felt that to do this was such an act of human bestiality that a regime which did it was on a par with the Nazis. After the Kostov trial I became, emotionally, in my attitude to the Communists, as committed as I had been in my attitude to the Nazis. I had at that time come to the conclusion that Communism in its current form – I kept on calling them Stalinists for a long time – was as evil as the Nazis, that it is a new Nazism.

At Prague University there was one other person whose attitude towards the Communists was a bit different from the common attitude amongst the students. This was my friend Hayek who is now at Radio Free Europe. There was a curious unwritten rule in Czechoslovakia at that time that whilst it was proper to criticize the Communist Party, it was somehow taboo to criticize the Soviet Union. This taboo, which was promulgated by President Benes himself, did in fact paralyse anti-Communist activity, because of course the Soviet Government was the principal source of Communist activity in Czechoslovakia. Both Hayek and I simply ignored this taboo, and we were the only two at that time who were freely talking about features of Soviet life such as slave labour camps and the Moscow purges. When the *coup d'etat* came both Hayek and myself expected to be expelled from the university but instead we were treated with extraordinary politeness. People very much more innocuous than the two of us were kicked out quite ruthlessly, but we were treated with an oily kind of deference. I have often wondered why this was so. I think it was because both Hayek and myself made no bones about having English contacts. We were reading English newspapers. We had English visitors. I think the Communists had come to the conclusion that we were in some way British agents and they may have felt that touching us may have involved them in international complications. There was also the war in Israel and if you were able to persuade the government that you wanted to go to Israel and were prepared to pay for a passport you got one. You were stripped of your possessions but you were given a passport. The reason presumably was that the government wanted to maximise trouble for the British government in Palestine at that time.

I invested what I got for my two houses in the bribing of a long series of officials, paying the necessary taxes (the bribes were usually paid in the form of American cigarettes), and I ended up with a passport and an exit visa. The operations were carried out by professional 'contacts' who took a lot for their services. In those days there was a curious ritual. In order to go to Israel you had to be in possession of a South American visa. I got myself a fake Bolivian visa and on the strength of that faked visa I obtained a transit visa to Paris. The understanding was that the transit visa was a façade and that one was really going to Israel. I feel, however, that the authorities probably knew that we were going to England. At one of my last official visits for some kind of bureaucratic stuff, a little and unimportant looking official came to me and said: 'Now look, we know that you are going to England. Don't cause any trouble there.' It is quite possible that the whole business was just make-believe and that the regime wanted to get rid of as many middle-class Jewish survivors as possible, provided it could strip them of their possessions.

In August 1948, my wife and I flew to Paris. It was a nice flight. In the morning we were still in the nightmare which was Prague; at five o'clock in the afternoon we were having a wonderful meal in the Latin Quarter of Paris. My visa for Britain came in due course and we sailed to Newhaven six weeks after arrival in Paris. At that time my friend Koerner was Assistant Lecturer at Bristol University. My plan was to study as an external student at the University of London and work during the day. Koerner persuaded me not to do this but to enrol in a full-time course at Bristol where the Professor of Philosophy was the distinguished Plato scholar, G.C. Field. At that time it was hard to get into the universities, as there was a queue of ex-servicemen waiting to be admitted. Field was not only head of the Philosophy Department but also pro-Vice-Chancellor of the University. Koerner asked him if it was possible for me to get into Bristol. Field asked Koerner if he thought I would be good. Koerner said yes and that more or less settled matters – there were no further formalities.

I was in, but the question was how to get money to support myself. A friend, whom I met in the Labour Party during the war, gave me a loan and after a few months the Czech Refugee Trust Fund opened again and started to support Czech refugee students in London. This is how my studies were paid for. The course, which was in the special school of Philosophy and Psychology, modelled on the Oxford special school of the same kind, led to graduation in both philosophy and psychology. Professor Field was strongly opposed to the idea that people should study philosophy only. He maintained that philosophy could be fruitfully studied only if the person who was a philosopher was simultaneously developing an expert interest and skill in a non-philosophical subject, to which skill in philosophical analysts could then be applied. From what I have seen since among philosophers I agree with this, though unfortunately it did prevent me from getting my post-graduate training in philosophy. Field was opposed to people getting their post-graduate training in philosophy and no amount of pleading would move him. In an odd kind of way, this outlook was devised from the Platonic scheme of educating an elite. It was perhaps Field's one shortcoming that he tended to apply Platonic precepts rather uncritically and perhaps sometimes unsuitably to the social milieu of Bristol. Field was one of the finest men I have ever met, a gentleman and scholar in the best sense of the words. He was a man whom I respected without reservation and my acquaintance with him helped me to balance my initial dislike of the English upper classes – a dislike I had developed during the Munich period. Field was a socialist. He was involved in debates on Guild Socialism after the first world war and was strongly anti-Tory though he looked like a *Punch* cartoon of the Tory military gentleman. He had a fairly good military record from the first world war and was a descendant of Oliver Cromwell, though it seemed that the family had settled down to manufacturing soap.

He was strongly opposed to Pacifism. His little book on the

subject is a classic, since it is based on his wartime service on C.O. tribunals. Yet it was typical of the man that he went out of his way to assist former C.O's in their academic careers. I myself at that time was very sympathetic towards pacifism. Field's little book opened my eyes to the fact that English Pacifism is a phony, immoral movement, quite different from my own image of Pacifism. Orwell did the rest. For all I knew this may be an accident, but all the Anglo-Saxon Pacifists I have met to date were intellectually dishonest people with a shady character. I know of 'Good Anglo-Saxon Pacifists only from literature and, yes, there is an exception – Vincent Buckley – but he is I believe no longer a Pacifist and is an Irishman anyhow.

From Bristol I went to London to do my Ph.D. I chose experimental psychology of the rigorously experimental and biological kind, because at that time I felt the best way of getting into the philosophy of science, which interested me most, was by way of developing a complete expertise in a scientific subject. I also attended philosophical seminars, particularly those of Professor Ayer at University College, where I was enrolled as an internal student, and also, occasionally, seminars of Professor Popper.

Throughout my stay in England I was not really involved in politics at all, apart from occasional sallies. I spent almost every minute of my time studying and preparing myself for what I thought would be my future profession as an academic teacher. My relations with my teachers were extremely good. Despite the fact that Bristol was a liberal and progressive University (it had Communist and left wingers on the staff), it was non-corrupt and properly run. This was I think largely due to the presence of Professor Field who as pro-Vice-Chancellor exerted the decisive influence. I have seen some other universities since leaving Bristol and I am always astounded at the fact that the term University can be used for such diverse institutions, both morally and intellectually. It is like calling both a Pekinese dog and a St Bernard dog, dog.

In 1955 I was invited to a lectureship at Melbourne University and

I took the opportunity. I had always planned to emigrate to one of the Commonwealth countries rather than stay in England. I did gradually begin to feel the pinch of English class society. As long as you are a foreigner it does not really affect you very much, but once you become accepted into the population, once you cease to be an exotic presence and are regarded as a potential competitor for jobs, then if one has any other background one has to start at the lowest rung of the social scale, which in England is pretty low. The salaries for junior academics, assistants and assistant lecturers were shocking. At that time in 1955 the post-war Labour Puritan atmosphere which I liked (I liked England particularly during the war, when it was at its Puritan best), had started to wear off and the Macmillanish 'You've never had it so good' stuff started to come up. Social snobberies began to reappear and much of this I did not like. I found it very difficult to put up with the one-upmanship games which were constantly being played in university circles. The ritual of graduate common-room membership was comic. Even the kind of lavatory you were allowed to visit was apparently an important social problem. A short time before my departure, I was graciously given permission to use the same cloakroom as senior members of the staff and the key to the cloakroom was sent to me in a special envelope, by the secretary of the College. It was really only in Australia that I became involved in organized politics. I have described this elsewhere and I don't want to repeat the story here.

Since leaving Prague I have spent much time trying to digest my political experiences and integrate them into my general philosophical and sociological outlook. I am still doing that. It will probably take the rest of my life. Have my basic beliefs changed since my brief late adolescent period as a Communist? As I have said, I had come early to the conclusion that our culture is fragile and our institutions are vulnerable. It was this Hobbesian insight which had made me into a Marxist in the first place. My road to Marxism was not via working-class politics of socialism, despite the fact that in my family there were socialist politicians. It was prompted by personal experience of a total collapse of the society in which I was living. I thought at first, when I was a Communist, that the Soviet Union was adopting the proper way of securing for men a more adequate institutional and socio-economic basis for culture, but my experiences in Prague taught me that the USSR embodies not the hope but the threat.

Between 1944 and 1950 my philosophical views changed considerably and I became a liberal progressive pragmatist. Philosophically I was brought up thoroughly, I would say almost unconditionally, in the tradition of empiricism and logical positivism. I was never keen on dialectical materialism and Continental philosophy filled me with boredom and disdain. Anglo-Saxon institutions struck me as durable and good to live in. In other words, I felt that the type of society that existed in Anglo-Saxon democracy might be the kind of society I would like to see everywhere, that the tradition-based skill-rooted institutional know-how which is the basis of Anglo-Saxon democracy is relatively immune to the kind of collapse which I had experienced in Europe in the 'thirties. But I also could not help noticing that these institutions by their very openness were capable of being permeated by totalitarian agents, that whilst they are sociologically secure they are politically insecure in a mechanical sort of way.

I also became aware that in societies without the special type of Anglo-Saxon political tradition the danger of totalitarianism was acute; that if the spread of totalitarianism was not halted, the Anglo-Saxon powers could find themselves to be democratic enclaves in a totalitarian sea. This perception has been highlighted by the peculiar geographical situation of Australia. I feel it much more strongly here than I did in England. Somehow, even in moments of great political crisis, I always felt in England that when the chips were down the Americans would bail us out, I have not got that feeling in Australia. A gentleman in the academic world here has recently written an article where he calls me and the people like me threat experts. I am rather proud of this description. I am quite happy to be called a threat expert. In fact I am a threat expert.

During the years between Prague and now I have been trying to put my experiences on a theoretical foundation, developing a link between politics, philosophy and the social sciences. I have had quite a number of scuffles with the left-liberal fellow-travelling intelligentsia. I do admit that there is something about these people which irritates me personally. I think it has an interesting personal root. When I see some of these long-haired middle-aged gentlemen of fifty who are still behaving like adolescents, I am somehow irritated by the fact that there are people around who are as I was at the age of fourteen and who have been able to remain like it. Incidentally, there are fellow-travellers or pro-Communist left-wingers in Australia who are not of this kind and whom I do not dislike personally. An example is Dr Cairns. He is obviously not an overgrown adolescent. He is very much a mature man with a puritan streak. I could never dislike him personally. It is the boyish, Angloid academic that gives me the creeps.

My philosophical views are changing. As I have said I had been brought up rather dogmatically in the empirical logical positivist tradition – that is, the spirit of Cambridge in the 'thirties of this century and the logical positivism of the Vienna Circle, Prague and Weimar Berlin. Since the early 1950s I have become strongly interested in Kant, to some extent under the influence of my teacher Koerner.

My political experiences in Australia and the gradual reflection on my experiences in Prague, and the severe limitations which I could not help perceiving in experimental psychology in which I have specialized, have led me to a fundamental restructuring of my philosophical outlook. I have found myself indulging in what I would call irresponsible metaphysical speculation more and more. Whenever I sit down to write something official and responsible I feel the old positivist habits taking hold of me – I'll probably never shake them off – but I have come to the conclusion that physicalism and behaviourism cannot be adequate bases for the social sciences, and I have tried to supplement positivist methodology by certain concepts in neo-Kantian philosophy. I have published a summary of my speculations in a recent number of the *Australian Journal of Psychology* (December, 1965) under the title of 'Types of Behaviour Theory'. That article roughly represents my current philosophical position.

I was brought up in a place permeated with Catholicism, and Catholic imagery, architecture and ways are part of my personality make-up. I am used to Catholics. My childhood experiences are connected with Catholic churches, Catholic nannies, the sound of bells with archbishops, St Nicholas, devils and angels and all sorts of pagan superstitions which in the countryside of Moravia were inextricably linked with Catholicism. Catholicism in Central Europe was much less severe than the Irish variety, but it had much deeper popular roots than in a country such as Australia. It was also thoroughly bowdlerized by paganism and its piety was permeated with ordinary superstition to an extraordinary degree. My religious beliefs at the age of four were beliefs in God, Child Jesus, in Santa Claus or St Nicholas as he was called, always dressed up as an archbishop with a mitre on his head. Even today whenever I see an archbishop in full regalia my first reaction is – there goes St Nicholas. I also believed in water spirits, in witches, in Judah Maccabeus, in the devil and that Moses brought the children of Israel from Egypt. (When on St Nicholas' Day, December 6, St Nicholas visited us, the Devil and the angel – they were actually officials of the local town council, who played the roles and visited various children at invitation – I fell on my knees and intoned a Hebrew prayer which I had been taught by my father '*Baruch Ata Adonai*'.[7])

When I came to Australia I was confronted for the first time in my life with an intellectually coloured variant of Catholicism. For me Catholicism has always been a way of life, a milieu rather than a body of propositions. I never took Catholic doctrine seriously as doctrine. I never knew very much about it. Today 'most of my best friends are Catholics'. I found very soon that the people

---

[7] '*Blessed be the Lord God*', a Jewish prayer of blessing.

who understood what I was talking about – Bob Santamaria, Jim McAuley, Vincent Buckley – and who sympathized with my political position here were not left wingers and liberals (who tended in the first place to brush them off as amiable eccentricities of an otherwise acceptable and even respectable person), but Catholics.

When I came to Melbourne my first social contacts were with philosophers who were on the whole left-liberal and accepted me as one of them. They felt I was a good philosopher and psychologist unfortunately burdened by certain political eccentricities which ought to be disregarded. They kept on disregarding them until the 1960s and then of course I was dropped. It is interesting that my political views and prognostications, which I felt to be based on empirical and rational considerations, were brushed off by the local spokesmen of the rational and empirical culture and taken seriously only by people whom I at that time still regarded as the protagonists of superstition and obscurantism. But my attitude had an undertone of emotional sympathy which is traceable to my early milieu and there were times in Australia when I was seriously thinking about Catholic propositions, God, society and the universe in general. I must say that I am now probably quite immune to conversion and the people to whom I owe this intellectual protection against Catholicism (and to whom the Church perhaps owes an insurance against the presence of an embarrassing member) are the so-called Catholic progressives in the university. Whenever I feel sympathy towards Catholicism I think of them and they nauseate me so thoroughly that my sympathy is immediately dissipated. In so far as I find Catholicism attractive it is as an alternative to the obvious inadequacies of liberalism. If it were to become liberalized, that is, if it were to fall into place with prevailing liberal progressive superstitions, it would lose whatever intellectual and emotional attraction it has for me and I would simply view it with utter contempt. Catholic progressives and Catholic fellow-travellers give me the creeps. I prefer the McMahon Balls of this world without incense. I also find that religious hypocrisy, self-seeking under the guise of religion, is prominent among the Catholic liberal progressives and to lubricate the machinery of Irish upward social mobility in the universities with holy water – which is what the activities of Catholic progressives in the universities really amount to – disgusts me. The potential Catholic in me – the religiously musical man in me – prefers to remain potential. If holy water can be used for that, it is perhaps not so holy after all.

Summing up, I may say the fundamental beliefs I had about society which I had when I became a Communist sympathizer and eventually a Communist Party member have not really changed. What brought me into the Communist Party was the perception that our institutions are fragile and that human personalities and ideas are very much a function of socio-economic circumstances and of the institutional set-up which conserves them.

When I became a Communist, I felt that the existing institutional set-up had to be radically changed. I felt that under the impact of Fascism, which I had experienced in a personal way. (It led to the total destruction of my family. I might perhaps add that both my own and my wife's family were liquidated by the Nazis, mothers, brothers and all. I do not actually know where my own family perished – I think it was Maidanek rather than Auschwitz – and they may well have been machine-gunned rather than gassed. If they were gassed it would have probably been with carbon monoxide rather than cyanide, because it occurred in the early stages of the process). Since then I have made the acquaintance of major metropolitan democratic cultures and I feel that Anglo-Saxon democratic institutions are viable. My present political outlook is based on the proposition that the democratic world centring around the Anglo-Saxon powers has to maintain itself by adopting a tough military and political posture, which would make it impossible for it to be conquered and possible for it to spread its influence.

So, whilst I have completely changed my political allegiances the basic discovery in 1938-9 which led me towards Marxism is one which I still regard as valid. It is essentially a Hobbesian type of discovery; that human persons are what they are because of the institutional context in which they are enmeshed; that institutional context can at times be very fragile and there is no point in moralising about the qualities of persons unless you are translating your moral fervour into policies and reform proposals aimed at institutions.

When I read Arendt's *Eichmann in Jerusalem* I was very impressed by it because I felt that that book reproduces to some extent my belief about the fragility of human institutions. Arendt's main thesis is that Eichmann was not a monster but an ordinary human being where moral restraints collapsed when the institutional framework in which he was brought up collapsed; his moral inhibitions survived the destruction of the institutions which enforced his inhibitions by roughly six weeks. In other words, an ordinary chap like Eichmann can be a monster, which militates against the thesis that ordinary human chaps are perfectible, a myth deeply ingrained in left-liberal thought. Secondly, it indicates that there are no real demons among men; in other words, that the Freudian notion of the irruption of elemental impulses as the explanation of Nazism is partly phony because Eichmann was just an ordinary chap. In other words, Eichmann's behaviour is not exceptional and demonic, it is the kind of behaviour which can be expected from ordinary chaps when the institutional restraints which hold them on leash are severed. This is a basically 'anti-progressive' attitude which is why I found myself so much in sympathy with the book.

From my Marxist days I have retained a distrust of moralising – an additional reason by the way why the Catholic left irritates me and why I tend to be sympathetic towards the more tough-minded kind of Catholic, who is on the whole conspicuous for his non-moralising attitudes. I have also retained a rather irreverent attitude towards social philosophies and moral ideas. The old Marxist habit of asking '*cui bono*' has remained and although I know that this is obviously not the only question to be asked about ideas I think that it is a question which ought to be asked and there are some ideas about which it is pointless to ask any other kind of question.

I like Australia because it shares the high standard of living of America, without American competitiveness, and it has all the good characteristics of an English society without the English system of class snobbery. The general level of Australian intellectual discourse is at times depressing, although it is still more pleasant than the extremely fierce competition which one would have to face in New York or London and the hysteria of the alienated, which is damped locally by a healthy kind of philistinism. What depresses me most about Australian academics and intellectuals (and I have often been misunderstood on this) is not so much their left-wingery but their general provincial and colonial outlook. To be colonial and provincial is not to be in any conspicuous way nationalistically Australian or Aussie; on the contrary, Australian provincialism manifests itself by the fact that Australians tend to discuss ideas and cultural products not in terms of their merit but in terms of their legitimacy. And legitimacy is bestowed on the ideas and products when they are okayed by an overseas mandarin. We are told that because 750 American professors have signed a resolution against the war in Vietnam the war in Vietnam must be bad. We are told that the policy of involvement in Vietnam must be bad because General de Gaulle, the Pope and other prominent Europeans have said it is bad. Donald Horne, in *The Lucky Country,* has given the best account I have seen of the business when he criticises Australian intellectuals for the derived, borrowed nature of their pursuits. One reason why I have such great admiration for Bob Santamaria is that he strikes me as perhaps the only truly metropolitan Australian in public life. There is absolutely no overseas equivalent for his type of organization and political activity, and no overseas model for his type of political thinking. It is based on Australian needs, whilst at the same time it is completely free of any self-conscious Australianism and indifferent to what the mandarins overseas may say. (One reason for that may be sought in Santamaria's origin.

As a person of Italian descent he is detached from prevailing Australian shibboleths, taboos and folklores. He has none of the Irish, English or Scottish millstones and servilities around his neck). Within the rather provincial atmosphere of Australia, including the rather provincial atmosphere of Australian Catholicism, Santamaria seems to represent an older and grander tradition of political Catholicism of which men like Adenauer and de Gaspari were representatives.

Postscript:

I gave the above talk before the recent war in the Middle East. I am, of course, utterly delighted with the fact that the Russians suffered a monumental defeat, and I would have 'barracked' for Israel even if I had been an Eskimo, for this and for a number of other 'objective' reasons. Yet I must confess that, to my own surprise, I felt more deeply touched by this affair than it warranted on purely 'geopolitical' grounds. It seems that it is now very hard for any Jew not to be concerned with the future of Israel. It is not only a State that has been created and that has asserted itself in the traditional manner of States, but a new Jewish 'self-image'. The fact of knowing all the psychoanalytic and related social science low-down on 'national pride' did not protect me against feeling it a little myself. Like that of many other foreign-born Jews in Australia my own 'loyalty' seems to be not dual but triple. To Australia, to the Jewish State and to my country of origin. I hope that the happy coincidence of all three having the same principal enemy will last.

The six-day Arab-Israeli War took place in early June 1967.

2

What's in My Name

(*Nation Review,* June 4-10, 1976)

A self-explanatory musing on the family surname written in a light-hearted vein.

An Australian-Irish friend of mine charged me recently – indulging his Calvinistic 'moral' sadism, so characteristic of the stern Irish daughter of Mother Church – with self-indulgence in my writing. The charge is, I believe, untrue, yet for once I shall indulge myself a little.

Like all last Mohicans, ageing survivors of an extinct tribe, I am, from time to time, given to daydreaming about the past which yields to a half-hearted resolve to churn out some sort of autobiography. My method is to carry a notebook and pencil and write down the next bout of recollections, or yell them out into the mike of a cassette recorder. I have made several lame starts from time to time, being utterly disorderly in my habits I either lose the notebooks or mislay or louse up the tapes.

Ms Vassilieff-Wolf's extremely brilliant puns about my name triggered off another such case of lost times.[8] It is, incidentally, rather odd that displays of wit about my name tend to come from people with names like Vassilieff-Wolf, rather than from men with names like Jones. Vassilieff sounds nice – like a ballet dancer.

---

[8] Elizabeth Vassilieff-Wolf, an author and painter, was a peace activist in Communist front organizations.

Much nicer than Vasiliev which makes me think of the things the bore Solzhenitsyn goes on about. They are also frequently people unlike Vassilieff, of my own race – Jews. One such jester, a Jewish solicitor, used to send me signed 'anonymous', i.e., obscene, letters fairly regularly, addressing me as Kakelmacher, which means 'baby-shit-maker'. A long pause in writing induced me to inquire of his health, since his style was rather hypertensive, and the information I received was distressing; his new address was Pentridge, the charge was fraud.

Before delving into linguistics and old days, may I correct a few mistakes? I am supposed (according to the letter [in *Nation Review*] by Ms Vassilieff-Wolf) to have 'inveighed' against something or other in 1952-53, here in Australia. At the time mentioned I was a student at University College, London, (I arrived here in April 1955) and my knowledge of Australia was then restricted to flying doctors, kangaroos and the dictation tests, having read as a boy E. E. Kisch's Czech report of his experience in Melbourne – a city whose existence was known to me, incidentally, only from Kisch's book.[9]

My name is KNOPFELMACHER. The 'k' is pronounced, a near impossible feat for Anglo-Saxons, and the 'o' is an umlaut 'ö' which turns it into a vowel equal to the 'e' in the French 'le'. There are two ways of writing an umlaut o; either by putting two dots over the o, or the archaic one of adding an e to the o. There are a few spelling fanatics in Australia who are prepared to dot an umlaut o. One of them is James McAuley, who (as editor) actually dotted my umlaut o in the second most fascist article I ever wrote ('The Threat to Academic Freedom', *Quadrant,* Issue no. 6, 1958). The object of the article was to argue that the only significant threat to academic freedom in Australia came from the totalitarian left. The article enabled me to meet a man of destiny; John Kerr (as he was then) who, as a member of the

---

[9] Egon Kisch *Australian Landfall* (1937). Kisch, a Czech Jew like Dr Knopfelmacher, was a journalist and Comintern activist, whom the Australian government tried unsuccessfully to deport in 1934.

executive of the Australian Committee for Cultural Freedom, took strong exception to the article being published in *Quadrant* (with some others). Those interested in *umlauts* and the recent past may find the article still interesting. May I add that I regard it now as outdated and largely irrelevant. Yet it was appropriate in 1958.

Being afflicted with a feudal-reactionary pride in family and name I refused to distort my name with an archaic 'e' and insisted on my two dots. Australian telephonists and editors refused to indulge my feudal whims, so I was left with the option of a bare dotless 'o' under protest or an archaic 'oe' which no member of my family ever used. I chose, eventually honourable deprivation, under protest, to distortion. It also met the spelling requirements of the name which my Australian relatives actually use, namely 'nofelmahker'. Senator Frank McManus (as he then was), who found it difficult to believe that a man of my fortitude in the struggle against the common foe can be anything but Irish or, at least have an Irish streak in him, used to refer to me as Knopfel-Maher.

My name, registered at birth in Wien (Vienna) in 1923, was Franz Peter Knopfelmacher (*umlaut* ö), Franz being chosen not after the two saints Xavier and Assisi but the unofficial third St Francis, Kaiser Franz Joseph. My realistic father insisted that, with a Czech republic to live in, a nice Jewish boy cannot remain a German-speaking freak and he turned Franz into its Czech equivalent Frantisek, commonly called Franta.

In November 1939 the Gestapo insisted that all emigrating Jewish children had to add Israel to their given names when boys and Sarah when girls. (The Gestapo, while nice from a progressive standpoint – it was the Stalin-Hitler pact – was however hopelessly sexist). I have developed an allergy ever since to long strings of forenames and dropped the Peter (which I now regret). On arriving in a British port Frantisek was unviable and had to be translated into the vernacular. At first I used Francis, a name which evokes in my mind for a reason or reasons unconscious and therefore unknown, an association with pigtails. So I made it Frank. And there it is. My BA certificate has Francis on it, my doctoral one Frank. My father's name was Paul Knopfelmacher, my mother's name Steffi nee Höllander (with an *umlaut*). Grandfather Joseph Hollander of Breslau was a hardware wholesaler. Grandfather Ignatius Knopfelmacher of Kromeriz made the best slivovitz in the world.

Other claims to family pride: in 1956 I was appointed fire officer of the Melbourne University Psychology Department; my instructions did not include saving the then Head of the Department from the blazing building. My paternal grandmother Haas was very bright. Her three brothers were all MPs for the socialist party as well as being party officials. One, Victor, designed and administered the Czech miner's Medibank in Ostrava, the other, Rudolf, was a pioneer of social paediatrics among Ostrava miners and the third a bit of a duffer, just a lawyer politician. On my father's side, a great uncle was Professor Wilhelm Knopfelmacher, a pioneer of modern pediatrics at Vienna University, and teacher of the above Rudolf.

The Hollanders were depressives and musical. A surviving uncle, Hans, published a book on Janacek recently, and some others were in the musical kitsch trade in Vienna. One is, I believe, still around somewhere in California. Hans is a musicologist of note, a former director of music in the Czechoslovak German section of music broadcasting; he taught musicology at a British university and is now retired. A younger Haas is Professor of Linguistics at Manchester. Distinguished ancestors are largely on my late father's side: a lawyer of Austro-military habits, a thoroughly decent man, whose main interest was women. To wit, Rabbi Low ben Bezalel who was in the 17th century a court Jew for Emperor Rudolf II. He had a job not unlike Kissinger's but he, my ancestor, had some real abilities – apparently a brilliant physicist, he constructed the robot Golem. Another was the 18th century Talmud scholar Makhsit Hashekel – meaning, literally, a halfpenny. So there!

Why Knopfelmacher? German for 'button' is not Knopfel but

knopf. Knopfel is 'little button' in several regional dialects. Thus, anglicized, I'd have to be Littlebuttonmaker. During the period of enlightenment under the rule of enlightened despots such as Joseph II, Jews were forced – without malice I believe – to adjust their Oriental names (e.g., Simon ben Yitzhak) to the administrative requirements of a regime which asked for a given name and a family name in intelligible language, for purposes of orderly administration. In many cases the imperial officials simply gave the names out, naming the Jews after their presumed trades – eg. Knopfelmacher, Farber etc – or their place of origin – Wiener, Warchauer, Berlin(er) etc. – or just in jest.

Why did I not change my name? It's too late now. Once I tried and drew up a long list. Carefully selecting from it I was left with a short list of two: Abraham Salzmann and Terence Sacheverell Thistlethwaite. And I decided there and then that mine sounds better. In a recent linguistic article on names I read that there exists another Knopfelmacher in Australia who renamed himself Kent. May I use this opportunity to ask Kent-Knopfelmacher to step forward or at least send me a note? We might meet for a shadow swapping session.

Vassilieff-Wolf letter – *Nation Review,* June 1976

3

Fellow Travelers At Fault

(*Quadrant*, No. 5, Summer, 1958)

A review of Victor Wallace's *Paths to Peace* (1957)

The book is a collection of articles, compiled and edited by Victor H. Wallace, who claims in the preface that each chapter is 'written by an author who is recognized as a competent specialist in his particular subject...' A similar assurance is repeated on the dust jacket. There are first of all purely technical contributions such as the chapter by Sir Samuel Wadham on 'Population and food production in relation to world peace', which are politically neutral, fairly interesting summaries of reports on specialized researches and might have appeared in technical journals. Then there are articles of a highly political kind which determine the general tendency of the book. These are typical United Front stuff, even if written, as some of them are, in academic jargon: a hard Stalinist and Stalinoid core blurred and camouflaged by a haze of lofty and more or less dishonest pseudo-liberal irrelevancies. If we followed the advice of the book we should set out on a path to a very special kind of peace: the Pax Sovietica of Kadarized Hungary.

The hard core of the book is contained in F. E. Emery's chapter on 'Economic conflict in relation to war' and in G. Sharp's chapter on 'Social structure and war'. Both authors are by training psychologists, but their contributions are Stalinist propaganda tracts on foreign policy and East-West relations. Mr Emery's chapter, by far the less paranoid of the two, elaborates the familiar Lenin-Stalinist myths that the ultimate causes of modern wars are conflicts between metropolitan financial and industrial monopolies for markets and colonies. The 'socialist' bloc is, on the other hand, a bulwark of stability and peace, free from colonial ambition and exploitation, and without any conceivable vested interest in conquest. I have it on Mr Emery's authority that the views expressed in his chapter on the 'socialist' bloc are, since October 1956, no longer his.

Mr Sharp's chapter is an intellectual horror comic, yet it is more honest than some others in that the Stalinist propaganda line is stated openly. Written in turgid *djugashvilese* it reproduces the torturous doctrine of the bosses in all its reality-defying brazenness: '...the antagonism within and between imperialist countries will determine their inevitable progress towards socialism. The exposure of past misrepresentations of the Soviet and socialist bloc (sic) and the rapid development of the socialist countries added to the moral support they lend will facilitate that process.' Mr Sharp quotes approvingly not only Zhdanov but Former Personality himself as if nothing had happened during the past two years. All this is of clinical significance since it is obvious that the chapter was written or at least was accessible for revision *after* publication of the Khrushchev speech and the Hungarian revolution. It shows that Stalinist intellectuals have been falsely diagnosed as mere human loud speakers: they are in fact tape-recorders.

Professor Partridge's chapter on 'Conflict of Ideologies' makes a sharp distinction between ideological and power motivation. The conflict between the democracies and the totalitarian bloc is represented as a struggle for power pure and simple. Both protagonists cherish power with equal zeal. Ideologies are relatively unimportant in the whole matter. The forced and very artificial distinction between quest for power and dedication to ideology is only in part responsible for the unreality which permeates everything that Professor Partridge says. 'Communism, of course, resembles the revolutionary doctrines of France of 1790 in this respect,' namely 'because of its appeal to the peoples of autocratically governed European states.' The opposite of the truth could not be stated with greater precision. But then, we are told, 'it does not seem that the propagation of the classical ideology of liberal democracy in Asia or in those parts of Europe (e.g. Poland) where the Communists have already gone a long way with agricultural reform and other phases of political and social reconstruction is likely to have much effect'. The 'classical ideology of liberal democracy' presumably means freedom, and Professor Partridge makes it quite clear that 'underdeveloped' nations such as Poland or China are neither ripe for it nor interested in it. His views are fairly typical for a group of upper-middle-class British left intellectuals in whose *Weltanschauung* racist arrogance and Stalinoid mythology blend into a curious new version of the White Man's Burden: the totalitarian horror inflicted by Communist bosses is necessary and even proper for lesser breeds such as Poles or Chinese, but of course quite inappropriate for The Race and its overseas offshoots. The Poles do not seem to agree with Professor Partridge; they have done enough loud thinking recently to expose his views as a heap of absurdities.

Mr R. S. Ellery's chapter on 'Frustration and Aggression in Relation to War' is likely to increase the already very large and steadily growing number of professionally competent judges who view psychoanalytic theory with extreme skepticism. Mr Ellery's is a third-hand version of German pacifist writing of the 'twenties which he reproduces with an almost bizarre disregard for the concrete realities of his own environment. Germans such as Reich[10] and Hodan made an attempt in the early 'twenties to combine Freudism and Marxism into a new theory with which to fight German militarism at what they correctly perceived were its roots; in the German Youth Movement. Their theories were proved wrong by almost every subsequent event. Mr Ellery has produced a lifeless caricature of these exploded theories.

---

[10] See the article 'Wilhelm Reich, the founder of Porno Politics' in the present volume.

Mr Glanville Cook in his chapter on 'Propaganda and War' exposes the war-like machinations of *Reader's Digest* and the Catholic Church. Yet, he leaves us comforted with the assurance that the Communists and the mighty socialist bloc led by the USSR are 'wholly for peace' both in intention and propaganda. Good. Mr Cairns has a chapter on 'Economic Policy and the Prevention of War'. All major powers should renounce their imperial ambitions and combine to develop the underdeveloped territories and generally promote a New Jerusalem. This should be quite easy, since Communism is, you see, just a 'system of economic production in which control has been taken away from present owners and acquired by departments of government'. Its other characteristics are apparently so unimportant for the success of Mr Cairns' scheme, that he does not deem them worth mentioning. It is like saying that Belsen was just a place where everything was government owned and where most people did not smoke.

Mr Wallace's chapter on 'A world population policy as a factor in maintaining peace' ranges over a large variety of subjects, from the menstrual cycle of women to Mr Corliss Lamont who is described as an 'American Liberal', a description which Lamont himself explicitly denies. Corliss Lamont's phantasies glorifying the Stalin-Yezhov-Beria regime are recommended as 'well balanced objectively written books on Russia'. There is a vast array of disconnected technicalities intermingled with platitudes and occasional unintended comic relief ('family limitation is practiced for a great variety of different reasons well known to workers in this field'), but the cat slips out of the bag completely when Mr Wallace makes his one concrete policy suggestion: the intake of migrants to Australia should be restricted to people from Great Britain and Asia. 'There is greater social harmony within the state when there is racial homogeneity', and 'miscegenation is not desirable in the interest of world peace'; yet an annual quota of Asiatics would be a token of 'goodwill and friendship'.

The most depressing are, however, the contributions of authors who unlike Mr Wallace are genuine progressive liberals. One has a right to expect good and stimulating thinking from people who honestly claim to be 'spokesman' of a great intellectual tradition. Uniformed toddlers are taught to chant the glory of the Soviet Fatherland; the insolent luxury of the boss's 'dacha' accentuates the misery of overcrowded working-class slums and the unspeakable horror of the Arctic concentration camp; rebellious Hungarian workers and intellectuals are sold into slavery at £3 a head. Yet Professor Sawer can write: 'Communism has a predominantly civilian and equalitarian ideology'. We have therefore nothing to fear. The world is getting better. The dominant powers are in most important respects 'satisfied'. Satisfied. What a revealing term! The postprandial smugness with which so many liberals are trying to ignore the nasty features of life is perhaps the main reason why people are turning away from them.

Some practical reflections are prompted by the book as a whole. The first concerns some of our accredited spokesmen of what Sidney Hook calls 'ritualistic liberalism'. It can be stated briefly: the sooner they disappear from the public scene, the greater are the chances that liberal values will survive in the uncongenial climate of the corporate-managerial era. The second relates to 'communists' and fellow-travelers: it is now quite obvious that the decisive class struggle of our time is fought between the hardcore of the reactionary Stalinist bureaucracy who defend their privileges with the usual savagery of a cornered ruling clique, and the downtrodden masses in the Communist orbit whose aspirations are expressed in a somewhat confused and guarded but clearly perceptible manner by men like Nagy, Djilas, Harich, Dudintsev, and many others in and outside the 'Communist' parties, whose names have not reached us. Most of these men would probably be classed as belonging to the 'extreme left', and as being 'Marxist', by the average Western observer, but any attempt to apply our own principles of classification to an utterly alien milieu such as the Soviet orbit is bound to be misleading. On the outcome of this struggle depends the main chance of peace. Intellectuals who still persist in their flirtations with the Stalinist machine must know that they are accomplices in a grossly anti-social racket. The consequences may be unpleasant, but, unfortunately, not only for them. The justified fury of the public at having been made game of by some 'eggheads' may all too easily degenerate into an upsurge of generalized anti-intellectualism, never too deeply under the surface in countries with vigorous 'plebeian' traditions, such as America or Australia. A book on how the silliness of some American intellectuals contributed to the rise of McCarthyism still remains to be written. The poisonous myth of The Treacherous Professor, now part of American folklore, may easily gain roots here when the news gets around that some of us are infatuated with a system which employs phosphorous bombs, firing squads, and mass deportations against striking workers and their unfortunate families.

An introductory chapter to this book was written by his Excellency the Prime Minister of India.

This article announced the presence of Dr Knopfelmacher on the Australian scene as an adversary of the pro-Communist left.

4

A False Equivalence Between East and West

Quadrant, No. 13, Summer, 1959-1960

A review of C Wright Mills *The Causes of World War* (1958)

C. Wright Mills knows – and hates – the American social landscape for reasons which are on the whole honourable. His analysis of the American social structure, contained in *The Power Elite* and briefly restated in the present volume is misleading only in so far as 'ideal type' social theories (in Weber's sense) are bound to be misleading: things fit in too neatly, mobile and hazy borderlines and contours are sharpened, and latent trends are treated as if they were glaringly obvious social realities. And, as Weber knew only too well, an 'ideal- type' social theory in the hands of a pamphleteer writing for an unsophisticated public may be used to disseminate half-truths and to distort the picture of reality by over statement and by suppression of negative evidence. Some chapters give one the uncomfortable feeling that the author is doing just that.

While Mills' knowledge of American society is intimately and oppressively personal, his picture of Communist societies is indirect, schematic, abstract and, therefore, unreal. The result of an uneven perception of society is the following disastrously inaccurate picture of the world situation: American pluralism is a sham restricted to subordinate positions of social power. A 'power elite' consisting of top brass and the top controllers of the privately incorporated national wealth have acquired history-making power in the US. They are in undisputed political command and they make decisions in a manner calculated to override the formal constitutional structure of America. The traditional social basis of American democracy – small businessmen and independent farmers – have been liquidated as an independent political force and absorbed into the amorphous world of militarized monopoly capitalism. American society has been turned into a callous mass of politically helpless and indifferent ciphers, drugged by the massmedia and by consumer goods into passive acquiescence with the irresponsible rule of the high and mighty. There is no basic difference between the USSR and the USA. If anything, the USSR is a shade preferable, because its mode of economic planning acts as a safeguard against the chaotic irresponsibilities of a privately incorporated economy. The American and the Soviet power elites (the American more so) are obsessed by an inhuman and relentless military metaphysics which drives the world towards thermonuclear destruction. The intellectuals on both sides have abdicated their responsibilities as critics and have become willing tools of the warlords. Yet there is a way out of all this. American intellectuals must take the lead, use the formal freedoms still at their disposal and formulate programmes of survival. These include unilateral disarmament, the unconditional moral as well as diplomatic recognition of all Communist regimes, and an increased measure of state control over American science and industry. The present military and political leaders of the nation ought to be subjected to relentlessly hostile campaigns and hauled, if possible, before congressional committees to be exposed as illegitimate usurpers. A suitably transformed and disarmed America will, eventually, enter into peaceful competition with the USSR, organize exchange visits of intellectuals in luxury airliners and flood the under-developed countries with atomic generators.

It is quite obvious that Mills' basic recommendations – unilateral disarmament and moral as well as political neutralism – are in substantial agreement with the policies proposed by the spokesmen of the Communist bloc in our midst. Yet it must be stated as strongly as possible that Mills is not one of them. Some of his incidental observations on American life and manners are devastatingly accurate and his most important charge against the American upper class – the charge of irresponsibility – is largely justified. The valetudinarian who played golf while Soviet tanks were crushing the bodies of working-class boys in the streets of Budapest[11] – 'I did not ask them to rise' – has come to be regarded by many as a highly significant symbol of America's high society, together with nymphomaniac heiresses and the rest.

Mills' indignation is intelligently analytical and sincere, qualities for which one would look in vain among the stereotyped, callous and dishonest half-wits who, nowadays, make up the fellow-travelling livestock. How then can a man of his calibre advocate policies which would result, if adopted, in global Communist conquest in a very short time? Mills' basic error seems to be this: he has correctly perceived that all modern societies have totalitarian trends and America is, of course, no exception. Yet he seems to be incapable of distinguishing between a fully developed totalitarian dictatorship and the mere presence of potentially totalitarian trends in a vigorously pluralistic society. Even if his claim that American society is multi-centric only on the middle levels of power could be substantiated, it would still not follow that it resembles a totalitarian dictatorship. Pluralism on the middle level limits the degree of freedom of the power elite very severely and makes total social control impossible. Mills' restricted range of personal experience and his extraordinary lack of imagination, coupled with a sophisticated yet highly abstract and schematic social theory, have conspired to make him say things which border,

---

[11] President Eisenhower

occasionally, on delusions. Thus, he seems to equate himself and other American left-wing liberals with the 'dissenters' on the other side, with men like Kolakowski and the Hungarian writers. It appears that he has hallucinated himself into a perception of social reality which obscures the difference between himself – a well-paid, recently appointed academic celebrity with unlimited access to the platforms of the American cultural establishments – and men like Djilas and the rest, who are, literally, walking with death.

Mills' book has already been used profusely by those who would like to goad us into a position of military helplessness. The organizers of Communist 'Peace' fronts whose retinue of phony parsons, political swindlers and professional bores has become somewhat shopworn will hope that here, at last, they have acquired an honest and brilliant front-man. They may be in for a severe disappointment: the art of frontmanship and the type of integrity which Mills possesses do not go hand in hand. It remains to be seen for how long Mills' sensitive stomach will stand the unsolicited compliments now coming to him in large numbers from the Partisans of Peace, both in and outside the Communist bloc.

5

The Catholic Church and Totalitarianism

Published in *Catholics and the Free Society*, ed. Henry Mayer (1961).

Issues arising out of the Catholic 'Movement' and the split in the ALP in the mid 1950s.

The chief characteristic of fully developed totalitarian movements – and there have been only two, National Socialism and Bolshevism – is their unconditional reduction of the human person to a mere organism, and the concomitant belief reflected in action that, like tractors, manure and space-dogs, human beings are expendable. Totalitarian elites are not inhibited in their actions by any moral taboos. As power is manipulated, the pseudo-moral norms of the totalitarians, based on the promise of chiliastic ends in an unspecified secular future, become identified with a demand for absolute power pure and simple. The obsession with power – vertical over the total human personality, and horizontal over all human beings – increases as the incompatibility between reality and the chiliastic ends becomes more and more apparent. The 'ideal type' of a totalitarian state was drawn in Orwell's unforgettable *1984*, a utopia which has been widely misunderstood. It is now generally assumed that Oceania is an extrapolation of trends existing in the

USSR, and that it is related to the latter as a fully- grown monster is to a mere embryo. Yet all that Orwell did was to describe in an imaginative way the essential features of Soviet social organization as it then existed, cleansing it of irrelevant contaminations due to local peculiarities and technical inefficiencies. In so far as totalitarian states deviate from the 'ideal type' drawn by Orwell, they do so in the sense in which say, a triangular object deviates from an 'ideal' Euclidian triangle, or in which real stock exchanges, churches and business corporations deviate from the formalized pictures drawn of them in economic and social theories.

It is difficult to imagine a body more unlike a totalitarian organization than the Catholic Church. The Church is, above all, a traditionalist depository of moral taboos – some of them an obstacle to social improvement but most of them protective devices against physical and psychological violations of the human person – which are utterly incompatible with the totalitarian quest for total power and its instrumentalist and manipulative image of man. Quite irrespective of Catholic theology and social doctrine, which are open to a large variety of conflicting interpretations and *logically* consistent with any state of affairs whatever, Catholic behaviour is circumscribed by a variety of restraints enforced by the Church with the utmost determination under all circumstances. No Catholic can advocate or practice birth control, abortion or divorce without getting into trouble, but neither can he become a protagonist of genocide, brainwashing, and the disruption of family life by permanent conscription of labour and by intra-family pimping. While Catholic opposition, say, to abortion may aggravate the population explosion, it ought to be realized that it came about as an extremist extension of the taboo on murder. It should be remembered that the truly remarkable organizational and technical achievements of the Nazis and the Bolsheviks, so much admired at various times by our 'progressives', were made possible only by a systematic and institutionally endorsed disregard of this and of other taboos expressed in the Decalogue.

The current misconception about the Catholic Church being

totalitarian seems to be reducible to two basic confusions. The first confusion arose from the very wide acceptance of the Stalinist theory of fascism, which the Communists succeeded in selling to the liberal public in England, America and Australia during the Popular Front days of the 1930's. According to that theory Nazism is nothing but an extremist mode of enforcing capitalist-conservative social policies in a period of acute imperialist rivalry. The Catholic Church and the political organizations under her influence are on the whole conservative in the sense of being opposed to revolutionary solutions of social problems, particularly if a revolution might disrupt a social organization such as ours, which is moderately hierarchical, multi-centric, private property based and built around the patriarchal Western type of family. Once the false premise is granted that Nazism is extremist conservatism, it is easy to see that non-Nazi conservatives, including Catholics, can be classified as pro-Fascist to the extent that they cling to their conservative social principles. Even if it was conceded that the Nazis and the Bolsheviks may employ similar administrative methods, it could still be argued that they 'represented' different class interests in a sense in which the Nazis and the Vatican, despite superficial differences, did not. This 'dialectical' *tour de force* is still believed by many 'progressive' liberals in Australia in an indirect way, despite the fact that the Church was persecuted under Hitler and that the Nazis violated almost every Catholic principle. As a matter of fact, despite some differences in terminology, it is almost impossible nowadays to distinguish the political program of reformist Social Democrats and Laborites from that of most Catholic political parties. Political coalitions between Social Democrats and Catholic organizations are, therefore, quite common. The Bolsheviks, on their part, have always been keenly aware of the fact that there is no 'real' difference between the 'clerical fascists' and the 'social fascists'.

The second confusion about the Catholic Church is due to the fact that the Church is a doctrinaire and tightly hierarchical organization, which is opposed to *laissez faire* attitudes in matters of belief and morality. Those among the liberals who are addicted to moral and philosophical relativism in a sense in which the classics of liberalism such as Locke, Rousseau, Kant and Mill were not, are bound to look askance at any organization which proclaims and enforces, by education, propaganda and political pressure, strong ethical and metaphysical beliefs. Since totalitarian organizations, too, are strongly committed to specific doctrines the conclusion is easily drawn that all strongly and explicitly doctrinaire 'authoritarian' groups, including, of course, the Catholics, are totalitarian. There is some evidence that the opposite may very well be true. People whose traditional beliefs have been destroyed by social scientism – a shallow mixture of popular anthropology, Marxism and psychoanalysis so dear to the hearts of 'progressive' liberals – are morally emptied out as it were, and ready to receive the totalitarian instruction. The systematic debunking of morality as 'bourgeois' and 'clerical' among the Russian and German *illuminati* paved the way for the 'armed bohemians' of the Bolshevik and Nazi revolutions who translated the teachings of Verkhovensky and Nietzsche into durable and appalling social realities.

It is obvious from her record through the ages that the Catholic Church is not attached to any particular mode of social organization. Prelates and organized Catholic laymen have supported at one time or another almost all identifiable forms of government, except totalitarian ones, ranging from plutocratic autocracies e.g. Franco's regime - to egalitarian republics. The reason for this is neither diabolical cunning nor ruthless opportunism, but simply the fact, apparent in theological doctrine, that the Church does not expect too much from changes in social organization as such. Despite an unparalleled political intelligence which they display when they are defending their political interests, Catholic elites, unlike totalitarian ones, have essentially limited secular aims. These aims are *in principle* attainable under any non-totalitarian form of government. Totalitarian dictatorships are unacceptable because they claim control over those parts of the human personality which the Church regards as her own domain, and because totalitarian regimes cannot tolerate the existence of independent Catholic institutions. The basic, theologically grounded limitations of secular aims are a part of the world as Catholics see it. Strong, institutionally vested beliefs of this kind are as much a part of social reality as the means of production and the means of violence. To ignore them is to ignore an important part of reality. A superficially cynical, 'materialist' theory, according to which Catholic elites are fighting for purely secular objectives hidden behind an otherworldly, theological smokescreen, fails to explain and to predict Catholic behaviour and is, therefore, unscientific.

At the present time Catholic organizations in most parts of the world support liberal democracy, for the simple reason that the limited secular aims of the Church can be appropriately realized within the framework of a free, multi-centric society. The practical alternatives are totalitarian dictatorships or corrupt autocratic governments which merely usher in the former. It is quite pointless to brandish papal encyclicals from days gone by in order to prove the obvious, namely that this has not always been so. No sincere Catholic could possibly claim that it was and that the Church has consistently supported the same type of government or that it is *doctrinally* committed to support liberal democracy. The *basic* political opportunism of the Catholic Church, far from being a symptom of Machiavellian cynicism, is, in fact, a product of her fundamental otherworldliness which dictates a coolly dispassionate, instrumentalist attitude to forms of government. And it is precisely her 'holy' opportunism in politics which makes nonsense of the claim that the Catholic Church is or could ever be totalitarian.

In Australia interest in Catholic politics is tied to the persistent controversy about the nature of Mr Santamaria's 'Movement'.[12] The controversy is really about two separate issues of which only one is of general political interest. The other is a purely intra-Catholic affair. The general political issue arose, in part, from the belief that the Catholic Church is totalitarian, and that, in using pressure group tactics to achieve their ends, members of 'the Movement'

---

[12] Catholic organization formed by B.A. Santamaria to rid the ALP of perceived far left influence; it became a secular body, the National Civic Council (NCC), after the Labor split of the mid 1950s.

have been guilty of the same offences against Australian democracy as the Communists. The arguments are usually supported by more or less lurid stories about penetration, dossiers, secret meetings, etc. The arguments seem to be bogus and the supporting evidence, even if true, is irrelevant. Whether the leaders of 'the Movement' use dossiers, smear opponents, and conduct secret meetings or not, is totally devoid of political interest. If they do, they are merely adopting normal methods of political strife which are in fact used with varying degrees of success and consistency by most political groups in all pluralist democracies. People who feel that these methods are contra-democratic and totalitarian ought to study the history of any one American presidential election campaign, or the internal history of any major political party or clique in England or America. The Communists in Australia are dangerous not because they, too, are using these universally popular methods of political warfare, but because they are using them in conjunction with other more sinister ones, such as espionage and industrial sabotage - for the purpose of promoting the political interests of a hostile military power bloc, in order to destroy our political independence and our pluralist institutional set-up. The worst one could possibly say about the leaders of 'the Movement' if all the tales of political 'immorality' concerning them were true, would be that they too are behaving like politicians. It is difficult to see why tough-minded agnostics and atheists, many of them professed admirers of the apocalyptic concentration camp known as People's China, should get steamed up about the fact that some Catholic politicians and prelates do not seem to take the Sermon on the Mount to heart as much as they might.

The intra-Catholic controversy about 'the Movement' is a variant of the old ends-means dilemma. Some Catholics maintain that the use of political pressure group methods by organized Catholic laymen under episcopal guidance or inspiration is intrinsically incompatible with Catholic principles. It is not easy for an outsider to judge the legal and theological rights and wrongs of the case, but one cannot help noticing massive historical precedents for the use of pressure group tactics by organized Catholic laymen and for the participation of bishops in secular politics. It seems that Catholic principles lend themselves to a politically activist, as well as to a relatively quietist, interpretation. An argument from historical precedent is, of course, *ad hominem* but it is difficult to see what other argument could be valid in a field where the decision procedures of empirical science do not apply.

The issue which divides the Catholics of 'the Movement' from other Catholics is, in fact, not a specifically Australian one and seems to be as old as otherworldly religions with a foothold in secular politics. If the Catholic is to participate successfully in the political struggle he may have to violate certain norms which demand of the Christian an absolute ethical purity of means. On the other hand, if he refuses to participate, say, in effective political operations against Communist influence in trade unions on the grounds of absolute ethical purity, he may be accused of conniving at evil. It seems that the dilemma is real and that it reflects a fundamental doctrine of the Christian faith according to which all man's works are, by necessity, tainted with corruption.

At the present time the activities of Australian anti-Catholics are a greater danger to our democracy than anything Catholics could possibly do. The professional anti-Catholic contributes to the political de-education of the Australian public by diverting attention from our genuine social problems and from the very real danger of gradual Communist conquest, to what is essentially a red herring. It should also be added that Australian anti-Catholicism, with the partial exception of the politically uninfluential Andersonian variety, is of a shamefully low intellectual calibre, using sources and arguments which no serious American or European intellectual would touch. The politically influential and malignant variety of Australian anti-Catholicism stems mainly from two sources. It emanates, in part, from elements in some Protestant churches who have lost or watered down most of their positive beliefs but who still retain the traditional hatred of the 'Romish' Church, and from a distaste for the Irish, an interesting reflection on the psycho-social basis of Christian zeal among some Calvinists. The other source is the Stalinoid liberals who hate the Catholics for their anti-Communism. It is interesting to note that in the USA where the position of the Catholic Church is to some extent similar, the two strains of anti-Catholicism have not merged. The 'nativist', Puritan, and racist[2] anti-Catholic is usually an extreme right-winger in politics, anti-Labor and in an unintelligent way vigorously anti-Communist. The American Stalinoid 'progressive' or genuinely liberal anti-Catholic would have no truck with him. It seems to be Australia's unique contribution to political synthesis that her Labor politicians succeeded in bringing the two together on one political platform. When one listens to some Australian Labor supporters discussing Catholicism, one never quite knows whether one is attending a Klan meeting or a tea-party of the Soviet friendship society.

As for the future, all one can say is that as long as there are groups in positions of political or academic influence who, for reasons better known to themselves, are prepared to offer tangible social rewards to the professional anti-Catholic, his deplorable racket, so similar to that of the professional anti-Semite, will continue to confuse our politics and to befog our thinking.

Author's Notes

1 For a brilliant treatment of this topic Max Weber's 'Politics as a Vocation' in H. Gerth and C. Wright Mills (eds.), *From Max Weber* (London, 1947) is strongly recommended.

2 The most prevalent expression of racism in Australia is hostility directed against New Australian and Asian minority groups. In a recent survey conducted by the author among fourteen-year-old Australian school boys in denominational schools it was found that the Catholics were significantly more tolerant towards ethnic minorities than the others.

6

The Situation at the University of Melbourne

(*Twentieth Century*, No. 4, 1964)

Interrelated political feuds among students and academics, and their ideological backgrounds.

In recent months, public attention has been drawn to the deterioratting moral and political situation among students at the University of Melbourne. Things came to a head over some issues of the student newspaper *Farrago* which contained grossly offensive and repulsive material. The Student Representative Council intervened, inviting the editor of *Farrago* to resign and an inquiry by the University Council was instituted. In situations such as the present, people are tempted to seek simple explanations based on their own favourite moral generalizations. Yet the situation is, in fact, very complex, and in order to unravel it one has to go into the past of the afflicted institution.

Five years ago, I wrote an article 'The Threat to Academic Freedom' (*Quadrant*, No. 6. Autumn, 1958) in which I drew attention, among other things, to the fact that the University had been even until very recently effectively dominated by the Communist Party, through Party members and fellow-travellers on the teaching staff. I had not the slightest intention of 'exposing' anything in that article, since I assumed that the blatantly obvious facts of the matter would be generally known. I wrote for the purpose of contrasting the very real threat to academic freedom from a totalitarian organization entrenched *inside* the academy, with alleged dangers to academic freedom from the government and from conservative bodies which have been and still are being highlighted by 'liberal' academics in an exaggerated way. Evidence for my claim that the Communist Party was the paramount influence at the University is also contained in a number of sources, from people who are either partly or completely hostile to my point of view. The most important of these is a recent remarkably frank public admission, made by a group of Melbourne University communist staff members to the effect that, until the advent of *Quadrant*, the new *Bulletin* and activists associated with the Congress for Cultural Freedom, they had the intellectual field completely to themselves. May I add that I myself regard this communist claim as exaggerated for Melbourne and largely false for Sydney. In Melbourne there was always some resistance from Catholic intellectuals, and in Sydney Professor Anderson and his followers channeled radical trends away from the Communists.

Yet the historical fact of *past* communist domination of Melbourne University and the moral and intellectual corruption which it engendered are still the most important factors to be considered if one wishes to understand our present discontents. It must be borne in mind that communist influence at the University reached its peak in the late 'forties and early 'fifties, at a time when Communism was at its most depraved - in the period of zhdanovism, lysenkoism, state sponsored genocide against the Jews, and at the height of Stalin's campaign against Tito. For an Australian academic to have sympathized with such a movement then must surely seem either a symptom of intellectual incompetence or of moral depravity. And the presence of influential persons with inadequate intellects or eroded characters in an educational institution cannot produce good results quite irrespective of the communist issue *per se*. The causally relevant intellectual and character inadequacies are likely to outlive attachments to communism and produce other morally undesirable effects.

I should, perhaps, add that by 'Communist Party domination'

I do not understand acceptance, holus bolus, of marxism-leninism, or Communist Party mass-membership. In a University within a pluralist society, it simply means the imposition of the main tactical objectives of the Communist Party as social and intellectual orthodoxy in matters such as foreign policy, Labor Party structure, education, and on such other issues as the Party may choose to highlight at a given moment. All this may go hand in hand with beliefs and practices explicitly repudiated by the marxist-leninists. These included, at Melbourne, the toleration by the communists of politically useful variants of religion, and the toleration and encouragement of excessive sexual licence and promiscuity. The latter provided the Melbourne Left with one of its principal selling points, despite the fact that sexual promiscuity is explicitly discouraged and repudiated inside the communist bloc. Contrary to a view widely held, there is no *causal* connection between sexual promiscuity and communism, yet there is mounting evidence that in countries of predominantly Puritan and Irish-Catholic formation an assault on sexual mores functions as a lever to 'get' at the rest of the person's and nation's character.

The hegemony of the Communist Party at Melbourne University was broken in circumstances with which I was very closely associated, and I cannot avoid using the first person singular in what follows, even at the risk of sounding pompous or boastful. It so happens that I was brought into close contact with what was, by 1955, the most important centre of communist influence in the University, and through it, with leading communist intellectuals. In those days, communists in the University were still accustomed to have things pretty much their own way, and it was, perhaps, a mistake on their part that they attempted to interfere with the content of my academic teaching, a branch of experimental psychology on which there existed at the time a strong Lysenkoist-Pavlovian party line, using standover tactics. Faced with the alternative of resigning my job or fighting, capitulation or connivance being out of the question, I decided to accept the challenge, to stay and to try to change the intellectual climate of the University. A chance combination of factors, time and place of birth in Central Europe, social origins, and a professional interest in social philosophy and sociology, have given me a reasonable working knowledge of communist theory and practice. I entered into ceaseless arguments and polemics with the communists and prepared them to some extent for the crisis which started in 1956, when Khrushchev made his secret speech to the 20th Congress of the CPSU and which culminated in the exodus of intellectuals from the Australian Communist Party after the revolt in Hungary.

My contacts with communist and ex-communist intellectuals were widened as some of the principal defectors became my good friends. I tried to achieve their full organizational and spiritual emancipation from the Party, but not only that. I hoped to ensure their active co-operation in the struggle against the remainders of Party influence throughout Australian society. At the same time I began to take an active interest in the rather somnolescent ALP Club of the University, working on the assumption which was then in harmony with my own political beliefs, that a strong social democratic organization is not only intrinsically desirable, but that it is also the best operational basis against the communists. Three years later, at the time of the Melbourne Peace Congress of 1959, the political objectives which I had set myself were almost achieved. The Communist Party had, by then, virtually disappeared as an intellectual force among students at the University, and a powerful ALP Club had become the dominant social force on the campus. I also had, by that time, a number of influential allies among the students, and some among the staff. The powerful muckraking '*Mugga*' articles in the *Sydney Observer* of 1959 and 1960 which exposed the corruption in the Victorian ALP on a national scale, were the major contributions to adult politics made by the ALP Club in those days. This, and the breakup of the 1959 Peace Congress, were no mean achievements for a group of intellectual activists, operating from an institution which only a few years earlier had given a hero's welcome to the reverend communist agent Hromadka. By 1961 the ALP Club was in a position from which it could plan the overthrow of the Victorian

Central Executive of the ALP. The plan failed, unfortunately, and I wish to put it on record that it was not due to any failings of my colleague, Mr. James Jupp, one of the chief organizers of the operation, that the plan fell through.

Yet, despite a fair measure of success, there remained some shortcomings which proved, if not fatal, at least very damaging in the long run. They were due to structural features of the ALP and of the Australian academic establishment, over which neither I nor any of my allies had any control. Thus it came about that the social democratic movement which I helped to shape in the university lacked an effective social base with which it could link itself up, to become a lasting social force. The young and often very gifted intellectual activists generated by our network of Club lecturers, seminars, tutorials and literature-distribution centres had nowhere to go outside the University to apply their talents, and this had a profoundly demoralizing effect on some of them. The DLP and the NCC complex of organizations, with their strong attachment to some Catholic social doctrines traditionally at loggerheads with socialism, and with their concern for controversial Catholic objectives (e.g. State Aid, opposition to divorce legislation, etc.) could not provide political anchorage for what was a motley collection of Protestants, freethinkers, Jews, and liberal-progressive Catholics. The choice fell by necessity and inclination on the ALP. This may seem quixotic in 1964, but it was not so in 1959. Yet while the communists were being defeated on the intellectual front, they proceeded to entrench themselves deeper and deeper in the trade unions, thereby consolidating their well-known present-day stranglehold on the ALP. And as the ALP continued its downward path of collaboration with communists, the hope that the new crop of progressive anti-communist intellectuals could be absorbed by it dwindled. As a matter of fact, ever since the ALP Club helped to expose and to destroy the communist-led Melbourne Peace Congress of 1959, it had been in a state of almost uninterrupted guerilla war with the Victorian Central Executive of the ALP.

The other great impediment to our success was the persisting influence of what may be called, for want of a better name, the Old Melbourne Left. At the time when the Communist Party constituted the nucleus of intellectual and social life at the University of Melbourne, it operated through a system of concentric circles of sympathizers entrenched in academic organizations which it either created or captured or influenced. These organizations included such diverse bodies as some university departments, the University Staff Association, the Labor club and at one time the SRC and the student newspaper *Farrago*. Not even some religious clubs escaped Party influence and penetration. When the Party branch at the university was shattered in 1956, the nucleus of Party activists almost vanished, at least for a few months, but the system of sympathizers remained. Unlike many Communist Party members proper, the old non-party 'lefties' were not affected by the events of 1956, and they continued to be available, in varying degrees, for Party manipulations inside the University. From positions of importance on the professorial board, in the Staff Association, and elsewhere, and always acting in a concerted and intelligent manner, the Old Melbourne Left continues to wield the whip-hand, or at least to exercise significant veto powers in matters of academic preferments and sinecures. It maintains close informal contacts with Left-wing ALP parliamentarians, with trade unionists and with communists. Unlike conservative academics, the old 'lefties' have no real respect for genteel academic properties and they do not hesitate to use their powers in a politically corrupt and corrupting manner. Around them there is an amorphous soft cushion of ignorant 'liberals' avid at displaying 'liberal' reflexes in the old way, on good terms with the old left, and 'nice' to the communists. The conservative element which makes up the bulk of the University Council, much of the University administration and a part of the professorial board adopts the outlook of essentially un-political officials whose paramount desire, characteristic of bureaucracies through the ages, is 'not to rock the boat' - almost at any price. The conservatives are anti-communist in a traditionalist and sometimes confused manner, yet they are also by tradition, upbringing and by inclination incapable of understanding the subtleties of the contemporary social scene among left-wing intellectuals, and, therefore, incapable of countering modern communist operations. This, rather than outright corruption or culpable connivance, may explain their extraordinary conduct during the scandals in the Social Studies department before and after the *Bulletin* exposures. ['Melbourne University Communists at Work', *Bulletin,* April 19, 1961 and 'Melbourne University Communists Again' *ibid,* May 3, 1961].

The situation as it existed at the end of 1961 when the power of the ALP Club reached its zenith, can be summarized thus: the communists were totally defeated in the intellectual field by groups of students and junior academics and they had lost all political influence on the campus. The climate at the University in those days was radical, intellectually stimulating and completely anti-totalitarian. An unusual air of brotherhood, good fellowship and intelligent hope pervaded the place and found boisterous expression in the student action movement against the White Australia policy. Yet a politically and morally ambiguous Old Guard of 'lefties' on the staff with contacts in the Communist Party, in the ALP Central Executive, and with a stranglehold on the careers and job prospects of their younger adversaries, held the fort and prevented the translation of an intellectual victory into institutional changes. A 'conservative' administration, consisting almost entirely of supporters of the present government, stood by and watched 'impartially'.

At the beginning of the academic year 1962, it became apparent that a counter-attack from the Left was in the air. Senior academics of the Old Left launched a strong and determined campaign against prominent individuals in the ALP Club, stand-over methods against student leaders and against myself assumed blatantly open features, and associates of the Victorian Central Executive of the ALP and Left-wingers on the staff proceeded to encourage Club members to shake off 'Dr. K. and his fanatical anti-communism'. Perhaps the most obscene incident of the period was the shameless expression of relief which resounded throughout University House at Easter 1962, while students, relatives and friends were gathering in stunned grief to pay their last homage to Bill Thomas, the Club's outstanding president, killed in a car crash on Easter Monday, in the twenty-second year of his life. Thomas' death created a vacuum which has not yet been filled, the enemy felt a weakness, and the counter-attack began in full earnest. The tactic chosen was internal disruption and the devices were sectarianism and sex. They were cleverly selected; the organizers of the Hitler Youth had shown the way. To paralyze a hold on the young which had been based on rational arguments and pride in intellectual and cultural achievements, one fans and exploits racial or sectarian prejudice and the kind of sexual restlessness and curiosity which characterize normal adolescence and early maturity. By the end of 1962 and the beginning of 1963, a flood of sectarian rubbish and pornography – ranging from 'scientific sex talks' to ordinary smut – were flooding the University and the student press, tearing up and destroying like a muddy torrent educational achievements attained through years of patient academic work in extra-curricular lectures, tutorials and seminars. Free-thinkers and Catholics who had worked, fought and studied side by side for a better Australia in the past, were now tearing each other to pieces. Student parties, formerly centres of earnest discussion and healthy fun, became sordid arenas of debauchery. The communist-dominated Labor Club grew in leaps and bounds under a professional Soviet-trained organizer newly dispatched to the campus, communist academics launched a new theoretical magazine, *Arena,* under the general supervision of Rex Mortimer, editor of the Communist *Guardian* and a Melbourne graduate from the period of Party dominance at the University. Party academics who, for years, did not dare to show their hand, now appeared boldly in print and on platforms again. There is adequate political evidence contained in several issues of Communist Party publications which indicates that the Communist Party had a partly hidden but directing hand in what was happening at the University in 1963. Inside the ALP Club, the disruptive operation was encouraged by an ambitious student politician with an eye on a key job at the Victorian Central Executive of the ALP, by a lecturer who hoped to earn parliamentary pre-selection and academic preferment if he destroyed 'right-wing influences', and by a prominent campus politician operating through the SCM.

The Catholic element in the University played a crucial role throughout all this. Bill Thomas, the outstanding leader and organizer of the ALP club, was an active Catholic lay apostle, and the Newman Society provided a steady stream of activists. Things went well as long as the hope could be maintained that a link-up between the ALP Club and the ALP could be brought about. Yet when signs began to multiply that the ALP would not sever its link with the communists, and as relations between the Club and the ALP grew worse, an element of moral ambiguity began to paralyze members of the Newman Society. The most important political experience of senior Newman Society leaders had been what they conceived to be their victory over the Movement in the University. Yet events tended to bear out Santamaria's gloomy prognosis about the ALP, and Catholic activists were faced with the unpleasant alternative of having to concede that, at least in the field of secular politics, Santamaria had been right, or else shut their eyes to reality and adopt an attitude of connivance towards a major social evil.

There are, roughly, three types of response to this challenge among members of the Newman Society. One group concedes that at the present time the DLP is right and ought to be supported, but that, inside the Church, opposition not so much to the Movement but to 'Movement attitudes' ought to be continued. Another group simply decided to follow the ALP and the Old Melbourne left through thick and thin, and whilst maintaining an apolitical, moralizing, pseudo-opposition to 'all evils including totalitarianism', it has in fact, if not in terminology, abandoned opposition to communism. The third group, which may be the largest, seems to be predominantly motivated by an impulse towards upward social mobility which is characteristic of Irish-Catholic minorities throughout the contemporary Anglo-Saxon world. This means in practice, social assimilation, and acceptance of prevailing social mores. In the context of Melbourne University it means accepting quietly the hegemony of the pro-Communist left, and, of course, adopting an attitude of 'not rocking the boat'. A central feature of the struggle against the Movement at the University was its inspiration by an intensely personal variant of religious devotion which is in fact, if not in principle, hostile to *any* form of political organization. It is an outlook which contributes to greatness and saintliness in a few outstandingly gifted individuals. In the mass, its upshot is political indifference, withdrawal from social issues and the mouthing of an esoteric 'spiritual' jargon. The cult of disdain for 'mere' politics which this outlook engenders, and which pervades the Newman Society at the present time, generates political ignorance. And political ignorance helps to smooth over the moral scruples of those Catholics who choose to maintain the traditional path of loyalty to the ALP at all costs, or who take the new path of loyalty to an emergent middle-class status: they must be innocent because they do not know.

The reaction of the ALP Club leadership and of the Newman Society throughout the period of assault was disappointing. Worried about their prospects in the ALP and about their academic careers, and generally unable to resist pressure in an organized manner as a result of years of misleading indoctrination about the evils of organized politics through the Newman Society, they did next to nothing and scuttled for cover. Vincent Buckley and some people under his most direct personal influence recognized the danger and fought back, but they were the exception which proved the rule. Had it not been for support from the DLP Club, from *News-Weekly* and from Catholic commentators, the rampant coalition of communists and moral degenerates would have become dominant, and my own standing in the university would have been completely destroyed. The episode itself is, for me, adequate evidence that my original program of attempting to build a viable social democratic organization - progressive but anti-communist and based to a large extent on the 'liberal-pluralist' segment of the Catholic laity in the University - has turned out to be a failure based on a misreading of the Australian social situation, and on an unduly optimistic estimate of the moral and intellectual capabilities of the 'liberal pluralist' Catholics. Some good has been achieved, but future efforts will have to be based on a broader basis, more closely attuned to the distribution of concrete political interests among the major social forces outside the University, which will have to be persuaded to press for structural changes in University administration. The present situation is not a very happy one despite the fact that the outcome of the Federal Election has dealt a blow to the Left in the University no less than elsewhere. The ALP Club has picked up some of its old zeal, a new society for the study of defence and foreign policy has been formed, and the shattered ALP Club seminar program has been successfully reconstructed. Yet the Old Left continues to maintain its crippling stranglehold over the academy, linked to the sectarian communist coalition which still rules the ALP in this State. There is no reason to assume that in another showdown the same weaknesses would not again become manifest.

It must be clearly understood that what the 'left' in universities is striving for is not the acceptance of an explicitly *political* program which can be publicly defended. There is now next to nothing in their repertoire which they could publicly acknowledge. Like rats, they wish to operate in the dark. Their aim is, therefore, total intellectual *stagnation*, certainly not 'dissidence' or 'rebellion'. Their wish is to eliminate altogether intelligent discussions of political issues from the campus. The outspoken command is: be a fellow traveller, or a neutralist, or else keep quiet. The fact that the struggle for academic freedom has to be waged not against oppressive governments and an obscurantist clergy, but against an academic junta whose members have been corroded by totalitarianism and against their psychologically disturbed and delinquent student progeny, is very damning. It must lead, sooner or later, to a fundamental re-examination of our current notions about the structural guarantees of academic freedom in Australia.

The original footnotes to this article have not been included here. This article was used as evidence against Dr Knopfelmacher when his appointment to a position in Political Philosophy at the University of Sydney was overturned by the University's Senate in 1965.

7

'There But For The Grace of God'

(*The Bulletin,* 7 March, 1964)

A review of Hannah Arendt's book 'Eichmann in Jerusalem' (1963). The publication of Arendt's book provoked a storm of controversy, especially from many quarters of the Jewish community. Arendt's use of the phrase 'the banality of evil' to describe Eichmann's actions, and her claims about the extent to which European Jewry were complicit in their own destruction, were found by some commentators, but not by Dr Knopfelmacher in this review, to be offensive.

The dead cannot argue and they have no will. A sense of fairness, some kind of piety, and perhaps a residual belief in spirits make us recoil when the living try to manipulate the dead for their own worldly purposes. The sight of politicians attempting to swell their 'numbers' with dead souls is not a pretty one. For some reason this revolting custom has grown since the war, particularly among Jewish politicians both in and outside Israel. Nowadays, in almost any Jewish faction fight – be it about the Suez Canal, the proper allocation of welfare funds, or the propriety of employing Jewish baby-sitters on the Sabbath – someone will, sooner or later, invoke 'the holocaust' and 'our martyrs' to score a point and to humiliate or silence his opponent.

The fact that this type of blasphemy is particularly painful to the survivors of Hitler's genocide and to the close relatives of the dead does not seem to worry the perpetrators, usually American, British,

Australian or Israeli Jews with little or no personal experience of what they are talking about. The very term 'holocaust' is now being used as an emptied out verbal symbol, a part of Zionist and Israeli 'officialese', and uttered post-prandially by after-dinner speakers, politicians and bureaucrats in pretty much the same tone of voice as 'football' or 'Mount Scopus College'. It is not really surprising and it is even to some extent defensible that the State of Israel should attempt to derive tangible material benefits from the cluster of attitudes and guilt feelings which Hitler's genocide has generated among Jews and gentiles alike, and that Israel's spokesmen and ideologues should be busily engaged 'adapting' history and creating uplifting simple morality tales and myths suitable for school books and at variance with the sordid, grey and degrading mess which was the reality of the Final Solution.

A Zionist 'realist' might argue that, after all, history is about the dead, and the State of Israel is the hope of the living, and there is, therefore, no good reason why the dead should not be conscripted to do a chore for the national renaissance. Yet among the living, there are a few who maintain the final heritage of the Hebrew prophets that 'the truth shall make you free'. Devotion to truth in action almost at any price and incisive self-criticism (sometimes degenerating into self-hatred) are among the noblest parts of the Jewish intellectual tradition, and they stand in sharp contrast to the populist-Babbitish clichés of official Zionist propaganda. And from time to time, the two must clash. For this, and for some other reasons not at all connected with Jewish politics, one should not be really surprised at the flood of distortions and character assassination which greeted an outstanding book about the Eichmann trial written by one of the finest Jewish intellectuals alive.

From the moment the work made its first appearance (initially as a series of articles in the *New Yorker*) it has been quite apparent that powerful and influential groups were incensed by it, and that they were determined to crush it. The book is being discussed in Australia yet most people who pass judgment on it here have not yet read it and they merely repeat and embellish some of the misleading nonsense which has been written about it in America. Rarely, if ever, has it been so difficult to estimate the content and style of a book by the reviews of it. To counter the cruder kind of distortion it is, unfortunately, necessary to restate what must be obvious even to the most superficial kind of reader: Arendt supports the capture and trial of Eichmann to the hilt. She dismisses legalistic squabbles about 'violation of Argentinian sovereignty' and related stuff as irrelevant, and, unlike some other Jewish liberals who pleaded for commutation of Eichmann's sentence, comes down squarely in favour of the gallows.

Her comments on the conduct of the trial and on the demeanour of the judges is favourable in the extreme, though she does not gloss over the conceptual and procedural difficulties and irregularities which a fairly unique trial like this must generate. Her analysis of the legal issues is, perhaps, a bit too pedantic and tedious yet she does accept the competence of an Israeli court to sentence Eichmann to death. The state prosecutor emerges from her description as a simple-minded publicity-seeking ham who did not really understand the nature of the Eichmann problem, and who tried to turn a trial for crimes against the whole corpus of humanity into a parochial Jewish revenge-festival. Yet the judges, particularly the great Judge Landau, countered the prosecutor's antics quite firmly, and, what is more, they resisted successfully Ben Gurion's attempts to use the trial as a platform for transacting Israel's quarrels with the Arabs.

Why was it then that her book stirred up a hornet's nest? What were the exposed nerves which she touched? It seems that she offended two different yet overlapping interests: those of the official Zionist establishment in Israel and in the USA, and the interests of the more fatuous section of the liberal establishment. The Zionists were offended by the icy and cliché- free objectivity of her style, by the remorseless frankness with which she discussed the failings of the Jewish leadership in Europe, and by some skeletons released from cupboards in the course of her narrative, such as a description of Israel's semi-fascist marriage laws. Yet it would be a mistake to assume that Arendt's book is merely an exercise in self-criticism. We read about Father Tiso, an un-excommunicated priest and quisling Premier of Slovakia who delivered converted Jews, including baptized babies, to Eichmann. (Pope Pius XII interceded on his behalf after the war to save him from execution). We also read about Catholic Italy, where resistance fighters, fascists and the clergy co-operated in keeping the Jews out of Eichmann's clutches. Ruritanian Bulgaria and liberal progressive Denmark alike saved their Jews. The ex-Socialist radical and free thinker Laval offered 4000 Jewish children under sixteen, separated from their parents, for Auschwitz. (Some between two and four years of age did not survive the transport to the gas chambers and their corpses were *returned* from Auschwitz in empty carriages, presumably so as not to interfere with the perfect auditing system of the concentration camp administration. The corpses were found by Belgian railwaymen). The Croat Ustashi leaders delivered their Jews but saved their wives - who were predominantly Jewish.

Arendt reminds us again and again that mass-murderers are now in positions of great social respectability in Western Germany and that the much-vaunted German guilt feelings are psychological devices to avoid responsible action, particularly against the ridiculously low sentences passed by German courts against SS murderers. It is easy to 'feel guilty' and to announce it to all and sundry. It is somewhat more difficult to endanger one's career within the *Wirtschaftswunder*[13] and to fight. Yet the scandal which her book caused in some liberal quarters is due not only to her objectivity, but has to be sought in her interpretation of events. Thus, Arendt shows quite conclusively that Eichmann was not a monster. He was an ordinary, very conventional, slightly shoddy semi-intellectual in pursuit of a job and in search of prestige, with sentimental attachments to Franz Josef and 'gay Austria' - averse to cruelty and emotionally not involved in anti-Semitism.

---

[13] The miracle of the economic recovery of West Germany after the Second World War.

Always 'objective', he despised rabid emotive Jew baiters like Streicher. When an Israeli guard gave him a copy of *Lolita,* he expressed shock and dismay at the book. Now if Eichmann was not a monster but an ordinary chap, two conclusions follow: there are no demons among men, but only rather murky fallen creatures, mixed-up, lazy and arrogant little fools, pretty much the sinners conceived by orthodox Christianity. And if this is all that Eichmann amounts to, and if evil, even supreme evil is indeed in Arendt's words 'banal', then where Eichmann walks there but for the grace of God are you and I. Arendt's image of Eichmann contradicts the two incompatible beliefs of many contemporary liberals, the Manichean, transmitted by Freud, that civilization is a thin crust covering irreducibly demonic instinctual forces which, if repressed too much, will erupt and turn men into types like the Nazis, and the Gnostic derived from Marx and the Enlightenment, that human beings are perfectible. If Adolf Eichmann, the man who participated in a near ultimate crime – the deliberate extermination of a part of the human race – was a non-demonic ordinary fellow, then there are no Princes of Darkness among men, yet it is scarcely conceivable that ordinary fellows could be perfected.

Arendt argues convincingly, though her evidence is not conclusive, that the Jewish Councils set up by the Nazis were instrumental in accelerating and expediting the extermination programme. Since the Jewish leaders presumably knew what they were doing, some blame must attach to them. And she concludes that the only correct policy would have been total non-co-operation. In the absence of possible armed resistance, this would have amounted to passive resistance. The thesis is in line with Arendt's more general proposition that totalitarianism must be met by uncompromising defiance, since totalitarians yield only to courage and determination. Their favourite victims are the innocuous and the weak. In an age of 'peaceful co-existence' and organized deals with moral equivalents of the Nazis, Arendt's message cannot be expected to cause much enthusiasm.

Hannah Arendt concludes the book by passing her own verdict on Eichmann:

> You... said that your role in the Final Solution was an accident and that almost anybody could have taken your place, so that potentially almost all Germans are equally guilty. What you meant to say was that where all, or almost all, are guilty, nobody is...This is indeed a quite common conclusion, but one we are not willing to grant you. And if you don't understand our objection, we would recommend to your attention the story of Sodom and Gomorrah, the neighboring cities in the Bible which were destroyed by fire from Heaven because all the people in them had become equally guilty. This, incidentally, had nothing to do with the newfangled notion of 'collective guilt' according to which people supposedly are guilty of, or feel guilty about, things done in their name but not by them - things in which they did not participate and from which they did not profit. In other words, guilt and innocence before the law are of an objective nature, and even if 80 million Germans had done as you did, this would not have been an excuse for you... there is an abyss between the actuality of what you did and the potentiality of what others might have done... Let us assume, for the sake of argument, that it was nothing more than misfortune that made you a willing instrument in the organization of mass-murder; there still remains the fact that you have carried out, and, therefore, actively supported a policy of mass-murder. For politics is not like a nursery; in politics obedience and support are the same. And just as you supported and carried out a policy of not wanting to share the earth with the Jewish people and the people of a number of nations – as though you and your superiors had any right to determine who should and who should not inhabit the world – we find that no one, that is, no member of the human race, can be expected to want to share the earth with you. This is the reason, and the only reason, you must hang.

In view of the controversy over the war crimes trials in Australia in the years around 1990, Dr Knopfelmacher republished (News Weekly, January 18, 1989) these earlier 1964 comments, as his views on the topic had not changed.

8

The Consequences of Israel

(*Quadrant*, No. 50, Nov-Dec, 1967)

Written in the aftermath of the six-day Arab-Israeli War of June 1967, mentioned in a postscript to the article 'My Political Education'.

It seems that it is very difficult for the Jews to get away from the doubtful blessing of being a chosen race. They are condemned to transact mankind's business in a big way, and often against their explicit will and intention. No matter how hard they try, the benefits of provincialism and triviality appear to be forever denied to them. The war in the Middle East, between Israel and the Arab States, is an event of immense consequence in a number of diverse ways, and it is perhaps best to start with the purely political aspects of the affair. The Middle East has been for some time the major area of confrontation between the USSR and the West. The Russians are angling for oil in two ways – trying to get it for themselves, or at least deny it to the West – and they are out to get aero-naval bases on the Arab peninsula with access into the Indian Ocean. To achieve their objective they seem to have put most of their eggs into the Nasser basket, though in Syria they have set up a relatively independent satellite regime of their own, and they exercise much direct influence in Iraq and in Algiers. Yet it would be wrong to assume that their anti-Israeli policy is merely a device to get on side with the fanatics and adventurers who pass as 'leaders' in the Arab world. It is that, of course, but not that alone, as I shall try to explain later on in this article.

The legal and moral position of Israel is unimpeachable: for 20 years the Jewish state has been treated unilaterally as an object of war by the surrounding Arab states. Nasser and the rest kept on repeating *ad nauseum* that they were in a state of war with Israel whenever challenged on one or other of the many acts of political gangsterism which were being committed against the Jewish state with impunity by her Arab neighbours, and certainly without any serious resistance from the United Nations; and the programme announced by the Arab leaders in relation to Israel was formulated in a manner exceeding in ferocity Rome's famous *esse delendam*. The programme, as we know it from innumerable official and semi-official statements, was 'annihilation'. It is difficult for Jewish political leaders familiar with recent Jewish history, as well as with the treatment of minorities in the Middle East and the Levant, instanced by the fate of the Armenians, not to take the programme seriously. Too many Jews have been reduced to 'nihil' in the gas ovens of Auschwitz.

Israel's *causa belli* on June 5, 1967 was morally and politically unchallengeable: (a) the port of Eilat, Israel's principal outlet for its trade with Africa, Asia and Australia, was subjected to an illegal blockade: the U.N. proved either unable or unwilling to honour its obligations and keep the port free. (b) Israel's vessels could not pass the Suez Canal. (c) For the first time, all Arab states surrounding Israel, including the British satellite Jordan, were united under Nasser for the explicitly proclaimed purpose of launching a Holy War of extermination against Israel. (d) Soviet military hardware of the most sophisticated kind, including rockets, accompanied by Soviet instructors, was made available in massive quantities to both the Syrian and Egyptian armies. (e) Jewish settlements in the north of Galilee were subjected to frequent artillery bombardment from the privileged sanctuary of Syria. (f) Nasser and other Arab leaders went on record stating that the hour to annihilate Israel 'had come'. (g) Israel has virtually no hinterland and cannot possibly wage a successful defensive war in depth.

As it turned out, the new emergent forces led by Nasser proved to be a paper tiger, and the military hardware supplied to his warriors as wasteful as bicycles supplied to kangaroos. Yet the strategic model which fits the brief campaign is not always clearly understood. True, the war was an Arab-Israeli duel, but this could have happened only because the presence of the American Sixth Fleet in the Mediterranean made Soviet intervention on behalf of her clients impossible. Nasser's 'Big Brother' was held in check by Israel's 'big brothers' so that the small boys could fight it out between themselves. In this sense, U.S. protection was essential even if merely implicit, since direct Soviet intervention would have turned the scales against Israel. The situation was in some way analogous to what happened in Indonesia in 1965. There, too, it appeared that the P.K.I. was defeated without American help. Yet had it not been for America's unchallengeable military and naval presence around Indonesia, thereby preventing intervention on behalf of the P.K.I. from outside, things might have turned out differently, quite apart from the fact that America's then already visible determination to stay and fight in South East Asia had given heart to anti-Communists whilst demoralizing the Communists.

The Israeli 'model' is based on two postulates: (1) you maintain a strong and independent military machine of your own which is capable of defeating the combined military forces of your 'underdeveloped' hostile neighbours; (2) you maintain a 'strong friend' but you do not rely on his advice or initiative. Within the great power vacuum created by the nuclear stalemate in which your 'big friend' is deadlocked with your 'big enemy', you take the military initiative and gain hegemony in the disputed area. The 'big friend' is maintained in two ways: by one's obvious strategic usefulness to him, and by a massive propaganda apparatus on his home ground. Zionism is now so deeply entrenched in American public opinion of almost all shades that it is virtually impossible for any American administration to adopt an anti-Israeli foreign policy. It can be seen that the key feature of the Israeli model is that it is not your 'big friend' who takes the initiative and 'handles' you, but it is you who 'force' the policies of a hesitant 'big friend' by decisive preemptive action.

It is, I suppose, barely necessary to point out that the Israeli 'model' is in almost every respect the opposite of the current Australian one. Australia has no independent military force capable of decisive action, it has no independent foreign policy, and it 'responds' rather sluggishly to American initiatives. And there is, of course, no Australian lobby in Washington. If the Americans were to contemplate withdrawal from South East Asia tomorrow, there is absolutely nothing an Australian Prime Minister could or would do to preempt such an American decision, except perhaps plead with the Queen to intercede on Australia's behalf. Israel has demonstrated what a small nation, surrounded by hostile and underdeveloped societies, can do in self-defence. It has exploded both the arguments of Australian defeatists, who believe that our own European enclave must bow to the New Emergent Forces or perish, as well as the arguments of the colonial provincials who see Australia's salvation in following blindly the biddings of the protecting power. In this context it must be noted that the official argument in favour of Australia's commitment in Vietnam – all the way with LBJ (or rather, behind LBJ) – is totally inadequate. It seems to be based on a curious kind of legalistic moralizing reasoning, namely that if we 'help' the Americans in 'their' wars they will somehow be bound to help 'us' in our future troubles. The corollary of this childish belief is the enormous assumption that such American 'gratitude' for help received would be forthcoming even if it exposed American cities to nuclear retaliation. It is sufficient merely to state this belief explicitly to appreciate its absurdity. Absurdities such as this and others will continue to befog Australian thinking about strategy until the doctrine of military and strategic self-reliance penetrates the skulls of her people, conditioned to an attitude of provincial dependence on 'overseas' signals in almost anything.

The war in the Middle East has exposed the United Nations for the sham they are. This system of incarnated legal fictions will now perhaps join the League of Nations and other ghostly entities of the shadowy world of the liberal non-imagination. For the time being the U.N. continues to act as a stage for a curious schizophrenic farce. The projected victim of annihilation who had the temerity to survive is treated to stern moral reprimands by the unsuccessful bullies. Such residues of reality which occasionally penetrated U.N. debates in the past have been abandoned, and the world is treated to purely psychotic transactions which can no longer be regarded even as propaganda with some claim to credibility.

Soviet behaviour throughout the crisis has been 'traditional'; that is, true to Soviet form. The Soviet Union continues to penetrate areas of weakness but pulls back when challenged. This has been so for the past 25 years. The pattern of confrontation followed by withdrawal emerged in Persia in 1945, in Greece in 1948, repeatedly in Berlin, and in Cuba during the missile crisis. The myth that Soviet foreign policy has in some way 'changed' is based on two legends. One is that Stalin's foreign policy was in some extra special way aggressive, or at least more aggressive than that of his successors. The other is the notion that there is a simple one-to-one relationship between Soviet internal nastiness and aggressiveness in foreign policy, in that Stalinist methods of internal rule tend to be related to aggressive foreign policies, whereas liberalization is linked with 'peaceful co-existence'. Events do not bear out either legend. Stalin's foreign policy was cautious and defensive, much more so than Khrushchev's, but perhaps no less so than the one of the present ruling combination (which may not last). It would have been quite unthinkable for Stalin to get himself entangled with the Americans in the Caribbean or in the Congo, or to support free-booting revolutionary movements such as the various new emergent forces in Africa, Asia and Latin America. Stalin never co-operated with any revolutionary movement which was not rigidly controlled by the old Comintern secret police apparat. When offered a gift, such as Eastern Europe, Stalin grabbed it but he took no risks whatever in acquiring disputed territories. Khrushchev, who was willing to take much greater risks than Stalin, overextended Soviet power, and he entered into commitments with revolutionary demagogues of the Nasser-Soekarno variety, thereby sacrificing a great deal of Soviet control over events.

The present Soviet leadership is saddled with the consequences of Khrushchev's over-extension and seems to be intent on retrenching and reverting to the more prudential methods of the Stalin era. As for the significance of the process of liberalization on foreign policy, it is of a 'long trend' kind. If the Soviet Union does indeed transform itself from a totalitarian society into a 'normal' sluggish autocracy, as it seems to be doing, the overall style of Soviet behaviour is likely to change in that the USSR may lose her auxiliary pressure levers represented by the Communist parties, which are still wholly or partly under Soviet control, but contested areas will remain, and they will continue to be contested. With growth of popular veto over policy still a long way off in the USSR, certain acts of raving lunacy characteristic of all autocracies may in future be avoided, such as supplying sophisticated weaponry to Nasser's barefoot warriors. As for those who still maintain lingering illusions about the motivation of Soviet foreign policy, the brutal and stupid cynicism of their support for Arab fanatics against an orderly and progressive nation in the Middle East highlights the fact that in the last analysis what matters is the old chestnut of popular control over rulers. The USA is a democracy administered by representative government, her leaders are checked by the normality of the masses, however partially, indirectly and inadequately, and criminality *cum* paranoia among the rulers can therefore not escalate beyond a certain point. The USSR remains a despotism where the common man has no say in the running of affairs. It is as simple as that. Neither the Soviet Jew whose relatives were being shelled by Soviet shrapnel in the Northern Galilee, nor the Soviet housewife who sees her dreams of consumer goods littered all about the Sinai Desert, can exert any pressure on their incompetent rulers. If those rulers go, it will be for the wrong reasons and as a result of intrigues restricted to a circle of roughly ten men. They will be replaced by other, equally remote, despots.

Why is it that the rulers of the USSR find it impossible to establish good relations with Israel? Why is it that they support the Arabs, despite the fact that their military weakness must have been obvious. The whole answer cannot be found in purely power political factors pertaining to the Middle East, such as oil and bases. True, only the Arabs can give them those - in principle. In fact, however, the Arabs can give nothing to anybody at present. They are impotent, and Israel rules the roost. The Soviet government is notorious for its ability to change sides rapidly and to jettison allies and supporters. It has done so repeatedly in the past, the paradigm case being the Stalin-Hitler Pact, the only instance of a treaty which the Soviet government implemented with the utmost scrupulousness and loyalty, perhaps because of Stalin's personal admiration and respect for the Germans in general, and for what he deemed to be the most highly developed form of capitalism in particular. Somehow the Soviet government finds itself unable to accept the Jewish state. The official doctrine of the Comintern, never repudiated and still officially valid, is that Zionism is a tool of Western Imperialism. In 1948 it appeared for a brief period as if the ice were breaking. Stalin supported the creation of Israel, and the Jews in Eastern Europe (though not in the Soviet Union) were given exit visas if they wished to emigrate to Palestine. Arms were reaching the Israelis from the Soviet bloc.

The idyll did not last. A few months later Stalin turned with the utmost ferocity not only on all Jewish organizations, but on individual Communists of Jewish descent and on all individuals who were in any way instrumental in implementing his own pro-Israeli policies of 1947-48. The Slansky trials in Prague added Zionism to the most heinous of crimes; Jewish cultural institutions throughout the USSR were wiped out overnight and their active members murdered. The 'doctors plot', Stalin's parting gift to the world, was seen by most competent observers as a preparatory move to liquidate Soviet Jews as a minority by deportation and slaughter. After Stalin's death, the minority rights of the Jews were not restored, and anti-Semitism as well as anti-Zionism continue unabated. The charge of Zionism is frequent in the trials of 'economic criminals', many of whom are obviously framed innocents. All this does not provide the Soviet government with any military or political advantage, and it contributes a fatal flaw to the Soviet image among Western 'progressives'. Since no explanation based on a rational model of Soviet behaviour appears to be adequate, it looks as if one were faced with an instance of phobic behaviour, a kind of ritualized compulsive hatred. Those who value sincerity above all other virtues should be pleased by the fact that Soviet policy towards the Jewish state is not based on any ulterior 'motive', such as lusting after oil or Arab territories, but on plain, sincere and compulsive hate. It is, of course, irresistible at this stage, particularly if one's aim were simple 'red baiting', to excommunicate the Soviet government from the ranks of decent humanity by declaring it anti-Semitic and leave matters at that. True, anti-Semitism exists on all levels of Soviet society and is particularly strong on the 'radical right' of the party, among secret police hardliners; and yet it is anti-Semitism of a new kind with a strongly theological constituent rooted in the sacred history of the Russian revolution.

It is a well-known fact that contemporary Jewish political life of almost any kind has its origins in Czarist Russia. Czarist Russia was the cradle of modern Judaism, both politically and culturally. The basic institutions of American, Israeli, and (in a very minor way) of Australian Jewry are largely imported offshoots of Czarist and post-Czarist East European political and cultural organizations. On the eve of the Russian revolution the allegiances of the Russian Jews were distributed across the Centre and the Left of the Russian political spectrum. Since the right was anti-Semitic and favoured retention of anti-Jewish laws, it was 'out of bounds' for the Jews. The Jews participated in Russian political life either directly, by joining Russian political organizations (revolutionary as well as legal ones), or they frequently formed their own Jewish variants of Russian parties. The most famous one was the Jewish Socialist

Bund, an organization within the Russian Social Democratic Party; what was true about the Bund was indirectly true about other Jewish parties as well, including Zionist ones. Thus Jewish middle class parties and groups, Liberal, Orthodox and Zionist alike, worked with the Russian Kadet Party (the constitutional democrats). Within the Russian Social Democratic Party, the prominence of Jews among the Mensheviks and their relative scarcity among the Bolsheviks was so marked that it induced Stalin to make his famous jibe about the best way of getting rid of Mensheviks: by organizing a pogrom inside the Party. As for the men and women of Jewish descent in the Bolshevik party apparatus, they were hard-boiled renegades who viewed any form of Jewishness with hatred and scorn. As a matter of fact, the strong self-hatred of Jewish Communists has contributed not a little to the incorporation of uncompromising anti-Zionism and anti-Judaism into the official Bolshevik creed. The Zionist socialist parties were of a moderate, non-Marxist Narodnik variety, linked both to the Mensheviks and to the Social Revolutionaries. Israeli socialism as it emerged between the wars, with its strong rural agrarian, anti-urban bias, its emphasis on the redemptive quality of physical labour, and its implicit belief in the virtue of 'the people', is the creed of the Narodnaya Volya[14], and the Social Revolutionaries come to life in an unexpected setting.

The programme of the Narodniks to create a specific Russian form of rural socialism, unsoiled by the corrupting ugliness of the city, and based on the village commune, the *obshchina,* found its fulfillment in the Israeli kibbutz. The great leaders and founders of the Mapai, Israel's ruling Labour party, were Russian Narodniks and Mensheviks in their intellectual formation, almost to a man. The general Zionists are descendants of the Kadets, and the manifold left-wing groups are linked to the traditions of the Mensheviks and the left Social Revolutionaries. *Hence the political life of Israel and the ideology of Zionism are an organic outgrowth of left*

---

[14] People's Will, or People's Freedom, a Russian terrorist group which opposed Czarist autocracy.

and left liberal movements which were the rivals of the Bolsheviks before and during the October Revolution, and which were defeated in the Civil War. In the sacred history of the Russian Revolution, which is being drilled into the heads of millions all over the Soviet bloc from the cradle to the grave, Kadets, Mensheviks, Social Revolutionaries and Bundists represent dark and satanic forces which were overcome by the children of light led by Lenin. And yet some of the demons escaped the avenging sword and set up a prosperous little state in the Middle East - a fact which is surely unbearable for the true believer. One might as well have asked of Catholic Spain at the height of the Inquisition that it establish normal relations with a small European community, led by Albigensian heretics, and to tolerate Albigensian sects on Spanish soil. It seems that as long as ideology and its demonological trappings retain some force among the determinants of Soviet conduct, normal relations with Israel and with the Jews will be very difficult. In the eyes of Soviet rulers, to have opposed the Bolsheviks in the Civil War is pretty much like having killed Christ in the eyes of a mediaeval Catholic; and there is no dearth of evidence to show that the secret police apparatchiks are quite willing to draw on the hatreds induced by the old legends to facilitate the spreading of new ones; on several occasions in the not so recent past, the infamous 'blood libel' was revived in parts of the Soviet Union, within a general context of propaganda against Zionism and Judaism.

The resistance of Jews to the process of totalitarian integration, their individualism, their international contacts, and their obvious affection for a 'foreign power', namely Israel, and Israel's links with American Jewry, supplied the theologically induced hatreds of the *apparatchiks* with a steady stream of fresh pseudo-evidence. It is to be hoped that as ideology loses its force among the springs of Soviet behaviour, demonology may cease to be a part of a living 'faith', it may become more and more a routinised recital of remote and meaningless 'history'. If that were to happen, the relations between the USSR and Israel would become normal. As long as the Soviet Union remains 'faithful to its Marxist-Leninist heritage', in any sociologically meaningful and operationally significant sense of the term, the relations will continue to be bad.

The responses to the Soviet debacle in non-Soviet centres of Communism bore the signs of tired non-inventiveness and confusion. Havana claimed that the Israeli army was led by Nazi officers. Hanoi celebrated a huge Arab victory. Peking accused Moscow of criminal collusion with the Zionist imperialists. Fedorenko-style cheating at the U.N. 'regressed' to the Moscow Trials style of 1938, though in the setting of the U.N. assembly it all sounded comic rather than ghoulish. Peking opened a second front against Israel's imperialism by dispatching a troupe of Red Guards to smash the spectacles of a British consul somewhere, thereby perhaps reducing future British subsidies to King Hussein by one pair of spectacles. All over the world, Peking-controlled mobs hurled lemonade bottles against symbols of American presence, such as it is. The overall impression of Communist behaviour was one of seedy phoniness and helplessness in the face of a nation whose leaders are made of sterner stuff than the average 'liberal' politician of the West.

The total collapse of the Nasserite military effort gives rise to a more general question. To what extent are the various nationalist-collectivist *risorgimenti* throughout the underdeveloped world powerful revolutionary mass movements, and how far are they synthetic rackets fabricated by demagogues and revolutionary intellectuals without effective roots among the masses? With Nkrumah and Soekarno deposed and Nasser voted out with the feet of his soldiers, is it not possible that the new emergent forces consist at least in part of fantasies projected into ex-colonial societies by guilt-ridden masochistic Western intellectuals? Yet whatever they may be, the Middle East crisis has demonstrated that they are not likely to form the basis of stable and peaceful governments. And yet we have been told again and again, on highest academic authority, that it ought to have been our policy in South East Asia to encourage 'Titoist' and quasi-Titoist solutions as an alternative to the present military involvements. It now appears that had this advice been followed, we would have still been driven into wars but under very much more difficult and precarious conditions, resembling perhaps those of Israel but without Israel's tradition of self-reliant toughness.

The spectacular success of Zionism as a movement is beset by paradoxes. Of all the 19th Century panaceas, Zionism was perhaps the tawdriest. Compared with the noble programmes of the Socialist Internationals or the fiery and intelligent dedication of revolutionary anarchists, and later of Bolsheviks, the Zionist movement seemed to hover somewhere between Christadelphians and Single Taxers. Almost all presuppositions of the movement could be viewed with contempt, and were in fact so viewed by many intellectuals, including, in particular, Jewish ones. That anti-Semitism is a relic of the past, tied to the dark forces of the Church and the feudal state, and that it would be dispatched to the rubbish heap of history with the onset of a socialist or a truly civilized society, was accepted as axiomatic by all knowledgeable men. The assimilation of the Jews, or their 'reformation' into an inoffensive and enlightened denomination was well on its way, particularly in that heartland of European culture in Hohenzollern Germany. The idea of solving the Jewish problem by shipping the Jews as settlers into a malaria-infested backwater of the Ottoman Empire was too comic for words. And yet the idea caught on, particularly in the ghettoes of the Czarist Empire. The movement which gradually emerged was most unappetizing. The ideology seemed a hodge-podge of bible bashing, racial pride, absurd historical claims, and hair-brained schemes of colonization. The organizations of the movement tended to attract the second-rate among Jewish leaders and ideologues. The founder, Theodore Herzl, was an un-brilliant Hungarian Jewish journalist with snobbish pretences and an 'interesting' private life. He fitted very well into the world of the *Neue Freie Presse*, the great pre-1914 centre of the sort of thing the Max Harrises of this world mistake for culture. Almost everything about Zionism appeared phony. The language of the movement, Hebrew, had been dead for over two thousand years (Christ, like other rabbis of his day, spoke and preached in Aramaic). And yet the Zionists spurned Yiddish, the true language of the Jewish masses.

The folk songs and dances of the movement were Russian or Romanian, with unwieldy Hebrew texts replacing the originals, and the anthem, the Hatikvah, was pinched from Smetana's symphonic poem 'Vltava'. And as the movement moved to the left, particularly after World War I, the tensions between its quasi-religious system of ultimate justifications (the land promised to Abraham, etc.), and the Marxist and Narodnik leadership, produced an aura of confusion and insincerity which gave considerable credibility to the official Comintern doctrine about Zionism - that it was a racket cooked up by rich Jews to protect British interests in the Middle East. And yet all the great social dreams and projects of the 19th Century turned into ashes, but the seamiest of them succeeded and it succeeded totally. The great era of perpetual progress and enlightenment terminated in the horrors of the First World War. The great centre of European culture, Germany, produced Hitler and the gas ovens. Lenin's bold and intelligent programme gave birth to the Soviet abortion and its ugly global effluvia. The dreams of the anarchists were extinguished in Catalonia. And yet in Jerusalem the Star of David flutters proudly in the wind, and Jewish labour made the Palestinian swamps and deserts bloom (labour issuing from the seemingly soft loins of the Jewish *bocher*, *pedlar* and *luftmensch*) and Israel's army is in *de facto* control of the Middle East. What was it that made the brilliant and the generous fail, and that turned the narrow, tawdry and commonplace into an impressive and lasting achievement of permanent value, not only to the Jews but to humanity? It seems that the success of Zionism lay in the political wisdom of its banality. Hannah Arendt's thesis that evil is banal must be supplemented by the notion that for the good to achieve a following and to succeed it must be banal too. The mixed-up goulash of official Zionist ideology merely articulated the sort of mish-mash the Jews felt about themselves anyhow but which they did not state. The *kitsch* of Zionism's bogus folklore was the *kitsch* of the very masses which it wanted to attract. The rebellious pride of the Jewish pariah which dissipated itself traditionally in millenarian movements was turned for once into the narrow channels of a fierce New Nationalism with an action programme of heroic pioneering, and Hitler did the rest.

The wisdom of Zionism can be stated in two simple propositions to which the movement clung quite tenaciously, and which it is fashionable to regard as somewhat ignoble. One is the simple assumption that only by self-help can an oppressed group be emancipated, the other is the proposition that the most effective device of such self-help is State power. It is quite obvious that these two basic propositions are profoundly anti-millenarian, anti-internationalist, 'anti-Jewish' in the traditional sense of the term, and that they imply a very skeptical assessment of the possibility that forces other than nationalism can provide an effective impetus to political action. It is also quite obvious that they are true.

It is interesting to compare Zionism with another eminently successful movement which is frequently accused of banality and tawdriness: the Catholic Church. There too, intellectuals in particular seem to be in a permanent stew about the stupidity of bishops, the authoritarianism of the clergy, the vulgarity of church art, the seedy spuriousness of moral theology, the hypocrisy of church politics, and the intellectual poverty of official pronouncements. Yet it is the very banality of Catholicism which makes it a religion of the masses rather than a sect for a few intellectuals, which it would become if the modernists had their way. It is only through banal, commonplace, and plebeian externals that 'the plebeians' can receive religious comfort and guidance. Jewish and Catholic organizations alike, if they were adjusted to the requirements of people like Hannah Arendt or Father Rahner, would not last for a week.

The emergence of Israel as a firmly established state, respected by her allies and feared by her enemies, has already begun to revolutionize attitudes and stereotypes among gentiles and Jews towards one another and towards the so-called 'Jewish problem'. In this respect too, Zionism as a programme has succeeded, since it was the intention of its founders not only to create a Jewish state, but to transform the character of the Jew and his relations to his gentile environment. The old anti-Semitic stereotypes of shifty, physically unattractive, cowardly and cosmopolitan Jews acted as a self-fulfilling prophecy in that they often forced the Jews into the very postures for which they were falsely blamed. The process was strengthened by Jewish 'identifications' with the hostile stereotypes of themselves. In sections of the Jewish ghetto community it became accepted that it is somehow 'un-Jewish' to be bold, strong, physically courageous, selfless and generous. The resulting Jewish 'pariah ethic', divorced of course from the official ossified ethic of the Talmud-Torah and maintained in unwritten hints, anecdotes, silent understandings, family traditions, and of course in the celebrated 'anti-Semitic' Jew jokes invented largely by the Jews themselves, led to violent outbreaks of Jewish self-hatred and anti-anti-Semitism among some of the best sons and daughters of Israel. Marx's famous essay on the Jewish question is a lasting monument to just this.

The vicious symbiosis of anti-Semite and ghetto Jew, locked in mutual self-projection and hate-filled identification, is now broken. The new representative of Jewry on the world stage is a cross between Beowulf, Bismarck and King Arthur. His military exploits leave Rommel for dead. His manner has the easy assurance of the successful military gentile, yet with just enough lilt in his voice and with that certain shrug in his shoulders to enable the Caulfield or the Bronx Jew to see him as 'one of us'. True, the Jewish real estate man and the Jewish intellectual remain in a way what they have been before; but they know that they could be different, that they have got it in them to be different, and their gentile neighbours know it too. In so far as assimilation meant the disappearance of the Jews as a unique and distinct sociological entity, Zionism has assimilated the Jews much more thoroughly than any other self-consciously anti-nationalist movement, such as early socialism. It has assimilated them by making the Jewish national 'us' just another one of 'them'. The shiftless *luftmensch*, the trader, the alienated intellectual, and the messianic revolutionary gave way to a new nation of workers, farmers and soldiers. With a dramatic shift in Jewish identity, a shift in standard political allegiances is likely to follow. On the whole, Jews tended to be on the left of the political spectrum, though there have always been important exceptions. The parties of the Left are perceived by the Jews as being opposed to hierarchical and social discrimination, religious establishment and lately, to 'fascism'.

Whether this is in fact so or not is beside the point. It is the way Jews see it to be, or have, at any rate, seen it to be until recently. The response of leftist sympathy was reciprocated. Leaders of left and left-liberal parties have always welcomed the Jews, if only because they brought with them talent, dedication, and, of course, money. Yet underlying these superficial reasons there are other more fundamental ones. The Jew was seen as the victim *par excellence* of the hostile system, of reactionary prejudices. The men of the establishment included among their values a distaste for 'Jewishness'; they discriminated against the Jew; they despised his pariah ethic. Hence the Jew had to be thrown into their face as victim. In so far as the non-Communist left fell into line with Communist fronts, the Jewish issue tended to split them whenever the Soviet government found it impossible to divert attention from its true attitude to Soviet Jews and to the Jewish state. Soviet persecutions of the Jews hurt the Western fellow travellers more than the shooting of strikers and slave labour. The worker has always been a rather notional figure in the mind of the Western dissident intellectual. His true essence has been corrupted by 'capitalism', and it did not really matter if a lot of lumpen proletariat was sacrificed on the altar of socialist reconstruction. The Jewish intellectual was real; he was a man one knew as a person; he was the man one knew and met as a personal friend and colleague; he was more or less a version of oneself. And yet the country of the revolution persecuted him!

A different form of philo-Semitism exists among the Manchester Liberals and the Liberal-Conservatives. These high-minded men found in Jews an ideal object for their high- mindedness. For them, Jews offer an occasion to be generous, fair minded, and unprejudiced. Jewish refugees became a suitable target for high-minded charity. Individual Jewish intellectuals could be shown off in a manner which made one feel a bit like Queen Victoria with Dizzy. Protecting Jews 'who fled to our shores' (a recurrent English description, whose romantic overtone hides the rather sordid details), one could even imagine oneself a little like Lord Palmerston dispatching a gunboat to protect a mere Maltese Jew, Don Pacifico, who could however proudly claim to be a British subject.

All this is over. It seems that the Jews have now ceased to be victims. For the 'gentlemen' of the Right there is nothing to despise among the farmers and soldiers of Israel. Military colleges all over the world would feel honoured if General Dayan and his brother-officers should agree to share with them the secrets of their martial vigour. There are no more Jewish refugees to be generous about, only Arab ones, for which the Jews cannot really be blamed. From the ashes of six million pariahs a pretty commonplace phoenix has arisen, one which looks very much like a tough Scottish, Yankee or French hawk.

The change in Jewish political alignments is inevitable. In losing their status as victims, as objects of patronizing generosity, the Jews will lose their status as pets of the left and of the liberals. In the eyes of the masochistic left they have, furthermore, also committed the most unpardonable of crimes: they have won, and they have sent the New Emergent Forces packing. It would be wrong to assume that the change in Jewish political alignments will be rapid, or that the process will be smooth, or that its consequences will be uniformly good or desirable. Yet it can be assumed that in all these changes Israel will be the pace-setter. There is nothing to be gained by Israel from the friendship of either the pro-Communist or the alienated left. The 'hero' of Berkeley and the 'hero' of the Sinai campaign are on different sides of the fence. No advantage accrues from the support of people who cruel Israel's pitch by their childish U.N. rhetoric, which if implemented as policy would condemn Israel to a permanent state of insecurity and rob her of the fruits of victory.

There is no doubt that the new situation has dangers of its own. Risks and incompatibilities of interest may well develop between the diaspora Jews, tied by habit and conditioning to their traditional friends, and the new *realpolitical* demands of an anti-Soviet European enclave of tough settlers in the Middle East. The old anti-Jewish stereotypes may be replaced by new ones. The old pariah cosmopolitan Jew may vanish from the stage only to give way to a highly suspect Jewish 'overseas-Chinese' or 'Sudeten-German'. The problem of dual loyalty is a real one and cannot be wished away by legalizing evasions or good public relations. Jewish loyalty to Israel represents, of course, no danger whatsoever to the countries of the West in which the Jews are living; but it may represent a danger to the Jews themselves, particularly in periods of international tension and panic. And yet the psychological benefits from the new situation, the birth of a new Jewish dignity, is one which seems to be worth the risks, since it is better for man to be respected than to be patronized, better to be feared than to be despised, and better to be admired than to be tolerated.

9

There Are No Youth Movements

(*Quadrant*, No. 54, July-August, 1968)

This article originated as a talk given at a seminar during the period of student riots around the Western world.

The first thing I want to say is that in my opinion, there is no student power movement in Australia which is comparable to anything in America, France or Germany. There is no radical movement among the students or staff of Melbourne University. Monash, which is supposed to be a centre of active student politics, is in my opinion dead. The university authorities have supported a caricature of a student power movement on the campus. So there is no point in discussing something which doesn't exist. There is nothing revolutionary about the idea of students participating in decision-making and having a bit more say in syllabuses.

What I want to discuss is the student movement abroad which is the only one which, sociologically speaking, exists. I haven't seen it myself, and it is possible the whole thing may be as phony as the Australian equivalent, but I am assuming there is a student movement in France, America and Germany. There have been a number of revolutionary happenings in the Sorbonne, at Columbia, at Berkeley, which seem to have a standard pattern. It usually starts with some kind of grievance about the university structure or administration. The student demands are usually granted very early in the piece by a hopeless administration, the demands are then escalated into general political demands, and they eventuate in such slogans as at Columbia university: 'Lenin won, Castro won, we shall win'. The movement is co-extensive of the New Left and it is not very highly verbalized. It is very emotional, very romantic, though there are some prophets, such as Marcuse, who make some sense - you can discuss their doctrines. One has to judge the movement by the symbols. One sees pictures of Ho Chi Minh, Mao Tse-Tung and Leon Trotsky. One doesn't see pictures of Kosygin or Brezhnev. The pictures one sees are all pictures of men whose activities and outlooks and methods are almost totally unrelated to the society in which the students are operating. Mao Tse-Tung and Trotsky were revolutionaries in agrarian societies; nothing they taught can be of any relevance in our industrial society. They were men who were nice chaps and who also were totalitarians. In this they differ from Stalin, who was not a nice chap but also a totalitarian.

So, the idols of the New Left seem to be all nice chaps, agrarians, revolutionaries, totalitarians, who set up totalitarian societies. Their slogans are 'restructuring of society' and 'participatory democracy'. One thing stands out. The revolutionaries refuse to discuss what they actually intend to do. They produce Ho Chi Minh when challenged. But, they say, we don't really accept his programme, he is a symbol of defiance. We have no programme for the future. This notion is an extremely respectable revolutionary attitude, it goes back to Marx, who said we are creatures of the past and we are confronted with the problems of the present; all we can do is overcome the present. The new so-called revolutionaries have lost the right to say this because the future has happened already in a number of places, e.g. in Bavaria, Catalonia, after the Russian revolution and in China. The future has happened and it is very difficult to get exit visas out of it. We know that an anarchist society cannot sustain itself for more than about four months, we know that it is followed by military dictatorship as in Bavaria, and we know what happened in Russia. Marcuse produces a list of revolutions which had beneficial results – the French revolution, the Cuban revolution, the Chinese revolution. I find there is an omission: the Russian revolution.

There is the problem of 'participatory democracy'. I was always puzzled by the time the Greeks spent debunking the notion; they said you just cannot run a society by an assembly of its citizens, that the masses are swayable by emotions, that government means continuity which means power in the hands of a small group of men. I always wondered why anybody could seriously think that participatory democracy is possible. Yet this is what is advocated by some of the current New Left activists; I am horrified that they obviously have not read the counter arguments of the Greek philosophers, where you cannot have participatory democracy in the strict sense of the word. Our whole philosophy of constitutional government is, inter alia, based on an attempt to synthesize the need for executive continuity and popular participation in government. The fact that these people talk as if all these polemics had never taken place is a frightening thing and it reflects on their teachers.

There are two views on participatory democracy – the romantic view and the Machiavellian view. The romantic view takes participatory democracy as coinage, but the more sophisticated chaps say participatory democracy is merely a device to make the system of totalitarian capitalistic pseudo-democracy unworkable. What they really want to do is to destroy the existing form of government, which is really dictatorship in disguise, and their gimmick serves this purpose. Once the existing institutions are destroyed, then the right historical perspective will take over.

The fact that the little there is of a student movement in Australia seems to be permeated by academic members of staff indicates to me that whilst the students provide the private soldiers, the actual intellectual planning and inspiration comes from members of staff, which is natural. There are no genuine youth movements. They are always devices manipulated by people who are not young, though they have never been as old as 70. Generally speaking, student movements don't differ in content very much. You have some which are Communist or Anarchist or Maoist. But the style is always similar. The actual movement is to be evaluated in terms of the political content, which in the case of the Western movements has to be inferred from pictures and the writings, perhaps, of Marcuse. In this respect, the student movement in the West is entirely different from the student movement in totalitarian countries. The usual slogan of students in Communist universities is that they want academic criteria to decide who is admitted.

I want now to discuss the ideas of Marcuse because it seems that if there is an ideal of the movement, it is Marcuse. He is a typical product of the Weimar Republic, a Weimar Republic bourbon - he has forgotten nothing and learned nothing since 1919 and he looks at the world through German spectacles. Marcuse's basic predicament is that he is a revolutionary intellectual who is marooned in a society without a revolutionary movement - there is none in America of any significance, or in France or England. The task is to explain why there is no revolutionary movement. His explanation is the following. He oscillates between Marxism and Hegelianism, and the problem he puts is: human development takes an Hegelian form. All social structures have to overcome forces negating it growing within its womb. Development is based on the negation of the negation. The working class has been absorbed. Since our society now has no major revolutionary force in it, it has become a stagnant society. He asserts that western democracy, America's in particular, is totalitarianism pursued by sophisticated means. The Soviet society is less totalitarian, it is Marxism gone wrong, but it has got internal, inbuilt means of improvement which Western society has not got. In his more recent work he maintains that despite the fact that there is no revolutionary class defined by social economic factors, there are people in spiritual revolt against our system of social oppression, an oppression of conceptual manipulation. They are the young intelligentsia. They are a minority and they are entitled by virtue of their historical mission to take power in order to abolish power.

He is opposed to pure tolerance. They are entitled to suppress alternative opinions, to dominate institutions, and to deprive other people of stating their views, if these people are historically doomed. What Marcuse is in fact propounding is a vision of society substantially not very different from the classical paranoid Stalinist picture of a few men in a dark room making decisions which benefit society as a whole. A representative from the Fascists, monopolists, security police and the Trotskyist organizations meet in a little room where they make decisions and impose them on the rest of society. Marcuse doesn't say this, he says that our way of arguing our internalization of values, and the way in which the mass media are run, in fact furthers the perpetuation of a self-co-opting oligarchy. The seemingly libertarian aspects of our society are tricks which consolidate the role of this oligarchy.

This then is Marcuse. It strikes me as fantastic that a man can claim these things, that men can convince themselves that they have the right historical perspective. How a man can say this after the last fifty years I find utterly fantastic. The uncharitable interpretation is that he is a racketeer. His appeal to the student is based partly upon the fact that he talks a lot about sex in the meadows and forests as against sex in cars. He talks a jargon which appeals to the bored Anglo-Saxon student who is driven up the wall with linguistic philosophy. I dismiss his analysis on conceptual grounds and his solution on empirical grounds. What would happen if the Marcuses got power is that they would grant self-government to everybody from the kindergartens and there would be a military dictatorship installed four weeks later, compared with which the previous regime would appear to be a tea party. This is what happened in Germany and in Indonesia. I personally prefer to be enslaved by concepts than to be liberated by men with the right historical perspective. I don't think the New Left is entirely Marcuse's but they usually have read Marcuse.

I just want to mention my views on the Australian situation. I would think that West is on the whole on the ball. Students tend to be bored because most of the teachers are incompetent and the courses are no good, the teachers are not interested in their students, they are afraid of them. Universities are ill administered monopolies. The structures under which they were set up were feasible at the time but now most staff members are neither gentleman nor scholars, and the students are just a mass. So you have a Marxist revolutionary situation. You have academic superstructures which have been outgrown by the social base. It is therefore necessary to change the universities. They will not be changed by students, because they come and go, and they don't understand the structure of universities, partly because of their age. It is necessary for you to have seen something before you can understand institutions, and on the whole you see more in forty years than twenty. It has to be done by people who understand universities. Nobody knows how universities function, their administration is completely opaque, the formal rules are vacuous rules and cannot serve as a basis for making decisions. We need competent establishment of the facts of how these institutions are being run. The *de facto* picture is of councils who are the employers who in turn hire servants - a fake hierarchy.

There is an argument that only academics in universities are capable of making decisions about what universities should do. This is like the factories who opposed factory inspections in the 19th Century saying - they are meddling in our business. I think there will be a running university crisis in Western countries. There will be student troubles, insurgencies, scandals – these institutions are collapsing. They function badly and the only way of changing the situation is by finding out how they really function and carrying out proper institutional reforms.

Dr Knopfelmacher followed up these arguments in his article on 'University Reform' (Quadrant, No. 62, Nov-Dec, 1969)

10

America The Bad Society

(*The Australian*, May 3-5, 1971)

A series of three articles describing a 1971 American visit which Dr Knopfelmacher said 'shocked me profoundly'.

1

I have been on a brief American visit once before, two years ago, and what I saw then struck me as depressing; but I half hoped that it may have been a mere aesthetic revulsion against New York rather than a rational, moral and political aversion. Now, after a longer, more searching, and geographically less-restricted visit, I can no longer dismiss my impressions lightly. From the moment of arrival in the United States, my faculties were bombarded daily, hourly, every minute, by loathsome signs and symptoms which a social scientist's mind cannot but decode almost automatically as evidence of social crisis and disorganization.

I sought at first to reassure myself that I was just being priggish, old worldly, personally prejudiced in a threefold way (as European, Australian, and assimilated-central European Jew versus east European Jew), exposed to accidentally biased samples, or perhaps just softened up by decades of living in the benign social climates of Britain and Australia. Yet, as time went by, my observations and inferences tended to be confirmed by other people. Also, following the advice of a student and friend of mine, now a London psychiatrist, I did not write at once, but allowed a time interval to elapse, a period of emotional 'recovery' from the trauma, letting the purely intellectual features of the experience assume clear contours and cool down. The conclusion seems to me now, unavoidable: contemporary America is a bad society, bad in terms of its own explicit values as stated by its political classics, and in terms of J. S. Mill's principle that societies must be judged by the type of person they produce.

How do I know? From watching people in the streets and elsewhere, from listening to what they say and how they say it, and from reading not so much 'social science' texts but the streams of unintended sociology in the inner pages of *The New York Times* – endless tales of complexly sordid frauds, scandals and violence, and the ultimate horror of their 'innocence' in total moral corruption. *They obviously don't know what they do.* Among their notorious 'cultural' publications, I found the less sensationally horrible stuff more revealing - for instance, a respectable *New York Times* article in celebration of Beethoven's bicentenary. In the article, it was gracefully conceded that Beethoven was superior to contemporary American pop musicians, but in many other ways was pretty much like them: he, too, was a 'revolutionary' and he, too, knew how to 'make out' (sic) good deals with publishers.' American 'cultural' writing has reached a level which makes it possible to reproduce long passages, which were written without satirical intent, as satire.

Words which are dead or inappropriate clichés in most non-American contexts come to life in America and acquire pressing actuality. Take 'the concrete jungle'. Following the breakdown of city government in America, walking the rubbish-littered streets after dark is like walking in the jungle at night. You move warily, with your senses on the alert, in the middle of the road, to avoid assault from the muggers lurking in the doorways. They need twenty five dollars a day to procure their 'fix' and they don't care how they get it. Walking up Broadway at night, with my wife at my side, I felt queasier even than on night patrols during the war. Then, I carried a Sten gun and a couple of hand grenades pinned to my belt. But New York's 'Sullivan law' makes it illegal to use any weapon, even under most desperate conditions, in self defence; and those who do may disappear into jail, sometimes for months, before coming up for trial. (The almost total breakdown in the administration of justice is closely linked with the general breakdown of city government).

Another cliché: the 'rat-race'. Americans live by the inversion of Kant's Categorical Imperative, in that the norm is to use people as means only. The term 'waste', for 'death', employed in Vietnam is no accident. For the opposite of death is life. The opposite of waste - use. A form of lethal acquisitive competitiveness permeates all spheres of life, even those which wither from it, such as the life of intellect. I watched a distinguished protagonist of non-worldly religious devotion negotiate with a religious youth group about his lecture fees: they offered $500, he demanded $750: two hundred and fifty bucks per mystical vision, plus travelling expenses. Needless to say, for some activities – cattle breeding, for one – financial acquisitiveness is an indispensable incentive, as the Soviets found out (or, rather, refused to find out) to their cost. Yet the very spirits of the hustler and the operator which have made America great economically are now turning it into a wasteland, by extension into spheres where they are, literally, death bringing.

Another two platitudes come to life: you cannot serve God and Mammon, and man does not live by bread alone. Which leads directly to the next platitude: the alienation of man in modern urban society. It is the loneliness and fear of the unprotected, continuously swindled and pathetically counter-swindling, stamped upon, helpless, ordinary men, human wretches on and off 'welfare', living in one of the innumerable 'apartment blocks' operated by professional slum lords who look and behave like incarnations of their own caricatures in Black Panther literature. With the de facto collapse of law enforcement, American cities approximate more and more Hobbes' 'state of nature'. Life in them is solitary, poor, nasty, brutish – and long. (Hobbes did not know of antibiotics, though Swift seems to have anticipated them: New York apartment blocks are full of wretched Struldbrugs.)

Before visiting America, there was one statement which tended to outrage me in particular: the assertion often made by new leftists that there was nothing to choose between America and the Soviet Union. I continue to hold, of course, that the statement is untenable, because it is empirically false, but I can no longer regard it as outrageously perverse. Not since I registered in myself, one evening, some emotional relief obtained from reiterating to myself that one is a mere visitor, and that soon one's plane to England will take off ... then I realized how horrible it would be to have to live in America. The pleasure of anticipating my departure was pretty much like the one I felt in Prague twenty-two years ago, *en route* to the airport with a beautiful exit visa in my pocket. Yes, I know, the emotion was an intellectually indefensible conditioned reflex; but then, can one blame others for having the same emotions and succumbing to them, if they lack the necessary political experience to control them?

The peculiar combination of near anarchy, violence, and total dishonesty which jointly permeate the life style of America make one feel exposed and helpless in the face of omnipresent threats of force and fraud, against which there seems no recourse or defence for the non-wealthy majority, which is the true silent majority of the American Republic. In Communist countries, the threat comes from the omnipresent totalitarian party state. In pluralist America, it comes from a plurality of little and big predators, unchecked and increasingly uncheckable, who swindle, exploit, rob, and physically violate the weak in innumerable and increasingly scientific ways, and among whom the police as well as the mushrooming private security agencies must be included.

It so happens that on the day of America's inverse My Lai, when the Lithuanian refugee Silas Kudirka, was beaten to pulp and kidnapped by Soviet goons aboard an American ship without help from anyone of the randomly assembled American officers and men, and with the lying connivance or complicity of at least two, if not three, Federal agencies, my wife saw a re-enactment of a similar situation in our neighbourhood supermarket. A frail and obviously ailing man of about 80 was dragged out of a queue and savagely beaten up for no reason whatever by one of the armed (and presumably drugged) shop guards. Nobody lifted a finger to help. One function, incidentally, of these guards (strapping young blacks) seems to be to 'manhandle', to insult and to toss about the masses of quarrelling and screaming old women who somehow seem to enjoy it. Concerning My Lai, it is a pity that the complementary nature of it with the Kudirka case is not appreciated. In My Lai, American soldiers turned on an SS performance when ordered to do so. In the Kudirka case, they did not turn off an SS performance because they were not ordered to do so. What sort of people are these American allies of ours?

Which brings me to Saul Bellow: it so happened that I read Bellow's story, *Mr Sammler's Planet*, on the very spot where this horrible little Sodom and Gomorrah story unfolded itself, on Broadway between 72nd and 106th Street. My wife remarked that it is only here one begins to understand what Bellow is about in this novel, that his story is about New York reality, and not the figments of a surrealistic imagination. And then I realized that for the past few days I had been 'doing a Herzog', writing long, involved and emotionally philosophical letters to friends and acquaintances in Australia which I invariably destroyed on rereading. And when I ran into a former student of mine, now at Columbia University, a hard-nosed little fellow, intelligent, tough, and seemingly cut out for life in New York, he also confessed, rather sheepishly, that he had been 'behaving like Herzog', writing away furiously and not sending the letters. One attempts to come to grips with a complexly horrible society which is at the same time very strange, and one finds one's powers of communication paralysed, by overloading with material which it is almost impossible to put into words both credibly and adequately at the same time. It seems that it is not only Stalinist Russia that can evoke 'strangled cries'.

2

When, after my American visit, I recovered my composure, the old habits of abstracting and theorizing took over. The mass of data was gradually losing its emotionally abrasive character and began to fall into shape as pointers of issues and hypotheses. Three questions began to loom large in my mind. First, was American society always like that, or had it deteriorated severely in recent years? Second, was America at all viable as a nation-state, and was it capable of an imperial role? Finally, in view of the character of America, which lacks or perverts most of the things I value both morally and esthetically, was it not grossly immoral that I and people like me have promoted, no matter how indirectly, U.S. political and military interests? All I can do in a brief article is to summarise my present attitude to the three issues dogmatically, leaving out most of the argument.

(1) There is a consensus among all three major ideological groups – the liberals, the radicals, and the conservatives – that America is deteriorating. Yet one does find many of the present ills described or anticipated in older authors through the ages from Tocqueville, via Henry James, to the radical authors of the 1920's and 1930's. One cannot, therefore entirely exclude the possibility that the present articulations of discontents are a mere restatement of complaints as old as the American republic, or almost as old, and that they are not much more than a contemporary variant of the venerable American tradition of muck-raking.

My own view is that there is more to it, and that America *is* deteriorating, for two principal reasons. The 'melting pot' did not melt down the constituents fed into the American dream-engine; and with the departure from the scene of the old WASP elites, there is nothing left to imprint a persona on the hotch-potch of a population which has no tradition-bound beliefs, customs, or foci of loyalty, and whose only implicit life doctrine is the sacredness of the fast buck. The attainment of super-power status and global influence and the development of the media, have merely made the American mess globally visible. They have also aggravated it by placing burdens on the American population and its State-apparatus which they cannot possibly bear. What we are hearing from America are the embarrassing squeals of protest of a pig which is being forced to assume the posture of a lion. The animal is not different from what it always was, but the demands made on it are new and entirely inappropriate. In America, the prevalence of capitalist values is totally unmitigated by remnants and customs of a pre-capitalist culture. It seems that a culture of this kind is not 'state-forming', as Schumpeter already foresaw, and may even lead to the kind of mass psychoses which are known to emerge when man is forced to live by bread alone.

(2) The notion that the American republic is 'disintegrating' is too obscure. Disintegrating into what, and how? Into successor states like the Hapsburg monarchy? Into bits to be gradually annexed or occupied by others? And if not what that? It seems, rather, that in view of its continental size, the military weakness of its neighbours, and the impossibility of launching trans-Atlantic invasions without a Britain type of bridgehead, the semi-polity of the American republic is most likely to continue to hang together somehow, though the underlying processes of solidifying the precarious togetherness will become increasingly sordid. Yet the belief that the US in its present state is capable of a sustained imperial policy or response anywhere strikes me as wholly nonsensical, belied by daily avalanches of counter-evidence.

(3) America is indeed a bad society, but the totalitarian systems of Russia and China are even worse. It is, therefore, not immoral to support at times, the lesser against the greater evil, though it may be prudentially unwise, if the lesser evil is politically non-viable as an ally and likely to destroy what it sets out to protect. Not to see that communist states are worse than America, from the left's own value standpoint, is simply an act of willful (and to me, now, understandable) blindness. The world would be so much nicer to live in if the most powerful non-totalitarian states in it were countries like the Scandinavian democracies, Switzerland,

contemporary Britain or, for that matter, contemporary Australia. Yet they are not and, perhaps, cannot be. It may very well be the sheer bulk of America, the monumental dimensions of everything in it, contribute to its repulsiveness and create many of its problems.

Now to the situation on American campuses...

Despite the deceptive quiet since the beginning of this year, the major campuses are firmly in the hands of the extreme left. Libraries are no longer burning, and direct violence seems no longer common on campus, but a generation of articulate Americans continues to show signs of total estrangement from its own polity, from parliamentary democracy, and it continues to engage in acts of fantasy identification with totalitarian despots. The SDS and similar organizations are badly split, permeated by FBI agents, and now wide open to orthodox Communist penetration and discipline, which is already making rapid headway. Towards all this, the American academic establishment combines an attitude of hysteria with an attitude of scuttle and cowardice. The influence of the 'revolutionaries' tends to be grossly overestimated; one is told they are everywhere, while at the same time, no effective action is undertaken to check or challenge defiance of legitimate authority. In this manner, capitulations in the face of one's own fantasies is the rule. And the authorities don't learn, repeating the same blunders over and over again. It is in relation to American campus unrest that I had to revise my own ideas most drastically. The American campus left and, generally, American campus unrest and rebellion, are totally different in cause and nature from their feeble Australian replicas, and quite different in texture from what I thought they were. This is the first thing any Australian observer must get straight. And more particularly, slogans and emotions which in an Australian context must be ludicrous, or simply fraudulent, are not so in America.

Many of the purely factual charges made by the radicals against American universities are warranted in a manner that is hard to imagine without having seen certain things with one's own eyes. Thus, for a long time now, leading American university departments and academics have been inextricably intertwined with Federal and State government agencies, with party and pressure-group bureaucracies – among which the mercenary and concupiscent lobbies of the three armed services must be included – and with a variety of corporate interests. This has happened to an extent which makes simple nonsense of any claim that American universities are 'free market places of ideas', or that their principal function is education. The American universities are market places, all right, but not of ideas; and their staffs – left, right, and centre – are, by and large, seekers after the fast buck, which they pursue quite shamelessly in the literal sense of the word. It took me some time to realize I wasn't even witnessing the doubtful virtues of frankness in corruption but, rather, the Sodom and Gomorrah syndrome: corruption as an unselfconscious, internalized way of life.

Many American academics offer themselves for sale, and like skilled courtesans they are usually willing to change their 'position' to satisfy the varying tastes of different customers, ranging from the CIA and the White House, with its variable occupants, to private corporations and revolutionary or communist governments and agencies. Large sections of the American professoriat, particularly in the social sciences, do not strive for achievement within the republic of letters, but they hunt for wealth and power quite frankly within the context of political and corporate patronage. This is true about liberals, radicals, and conservatives alike. The integration of academics, politicians, corporate and Federal bureaucrats, as well as military brass, into an interlacing power-elite is an indisputable and palpable reality in America. There is not much evidence that the proliferation of professors in corporate and political power-areas serves many useful purposes. This can actually be assessed, since in America 'classified' research is treated with almost total indiscretion. American officials and academics linked, say, with the CIA or the White House, do not have to sign anything resembling the British Official Secrets Act. Also, they tend to be vulgar and greedy men, without the British upper-class reticence born of a sense of public duty and a corporate pride in belonging to an elite of tight-lipped administrator-rulers. Too many of them are in it purely for the fast buck. As a result, Washington is a big sieve, with rival gangs of political professors and bureaucrats throwing at each other, publicly, secret and classified material with cynical disregard for the interests of the country, and with total disregard for the interests of allies.

Many of them actually seem to earn money, fame and academic promotion by breaking their trust and turning their country's secrets into best-sellers or well rewarded leaks. The radicals thus, frequently, get hold of such secrets (usually after everybody who cared could have known about them for years), and yet another 'expose' appears, say in the *New York Review of Books*. As usual, the left botches its case by misperceiving the manner in which its 'revelations' are truly damaging: What usually emerges is that a lot of professors or litterateurs have been taking a lot of public money – for instance, via the CIA or the military – for worthless pseudo-research on subjects such as insurgency, totally outside their competence (if any). The left presents the case as one of hireling professors whose hands are dripping with the blood of Asian peasants when in fact the 'operational research' couldn't harm a Viet Cong fly, though many hands are dripping with sauce from the academic gravy train, and the only peasants who suffer are the American taxpayers, mostly 'little people'. The moral impact of all this – and it has been going on for years – on morally sensitive young people is devastating. The fact that most of their professors are 'liberals' whose doctrines denigrate the very social system on which they built their personal affluence, merely aggravates the situation. Young radicals always detest men who, in the words of Heinrich Heine, 'publicly preach water, yet secretly drink wine'. Hence the paradox that the most permissive and liberal colleges were the most insurgency stricken.

It would be fruitless to deny that my US visit has shaken profoundly some of my views about the source of troubles in American universities. I can see now that the prime cause is not communist or anarchist conspiracy, but capitalist-bourgeois corruption of an estate – that of the learned – which requires for its authority and sustenance the adoption of an essentially non-capitalist life-style. Yet I remain adamant that campus disorder and insurgency, and the totalitarian ideologies sustaining them, must be defeated. This cannot be done by supporting a morally and politically bankrupt academic establishment. A university (and there are many such in America), split between students led by totalitarian revolutionaries and an administration which 'kept order' by employing gorilla-type goons as campus guards, is finished as an educational institution, beyond retrieve.

3

It does not take long to realize that the dominant name in Washington is that of Henry Kissinger. Kissinger himself is an intellectually quite mediocre politics professor, whose social background sheds more light on his present position than his theoretical ideas, such as they are. He is a refugee German Jew whose background however is not the common radical or ex-radical one but the much less frequent Teutonic liberal-conservative. His guru from an early age appears to have been a non-Jewish refugee German conservative called Kramer, a member of the 'intelligence community' now in the Pentagon. From the image which Kissinger is trying to project it appears that his ego-ideal is the conservative yet cynical upper-class political fixer and balancer. This may explain Kissinger's rumored fantasy identification with Metternich, and a liking for his policies and methods. If true, this would be a disaster, since Metternich was successful as a post-revolutionary statesman, not within a revolutionary situation, and his system failed, since it disintegrated.

My own initial (wrong) theory was that Kissinger had no real power and that he was a Nixon variant of a Kennedy type of 'dancing professor' whose main function was to keep the troublesome liberal professors happy by showing them that even under the presidency of the hated 'Hiss killer' one can 'make it'. True, this seems to be one of his functions; and the glowing feeling that any tin-pot professor may carry the special assistant's strings in his briefcase has helped to accelerate the 'rediscovery of America' and the 'conservative mood' now visibly in progress again among the professional chorus girls. Yet this is far from being Kissinger's main function. Despite his thorough intellectual mediocrity, he has emerged as one of the most creative administrative innovators in the history of the American chief executive bureaucracy. This, rather than his 'political vision' appears to be his forte. Presidential decision-making is no longer hamstrung as in the past by negotiations which once completed by presidential aides and secretaries of state, made it virtually impossible for a president to exercise his sovereignty by freely choosing an alternative option. Through Kissinger's celebrated 'option analysis' all issues are analyzed into action alternatives, with all competing and quarrelling pressure groups contributing to the pool of data. The material of the pool is then organized by Kissinger and his staff into 'options'. The set of options with some recommended by Kissinger goes to the President and he chooses.

Kissinger's formal power, apart from his unknown informal one, is thus two-fold; he determines what qualifies for 'an option' and he recommends some. The Kissinger method revolutionized the American presidency by turning it from an apex of a complex system of baronates into an absolute monarch's court with Kissinger as the principal courtier. The choice of Kissinger for the role was wise in that it revived the ancient tradition of the Hofjude – the 'court Jew' - Kissinger by virtue of being a foreign-born immigrant isolate. His Harvard reputation was that of a 'loner'; he has no power of his own, no 'native roots' unlike the powerful lords of labor, business, the armed forces, and the political machines. He owes whatever he has to the continuing grace of his sovereign. Out of the monarch's grace, he is nothing, and may even be expelled from the paradise of American university appointments. And if things were to go seriously and visibly wrong, he could fulfil another traditional function of the court Jew - that of a scapegoat.

Kissinger's most ruthless and probably most productive act was the liquidation of the State Department as a serious agency of government, perhaps the one and only development inside America in recent years from which her allies may derive some comfort. As for overall policy, particularly in South East Asia, two incompatible interpretations are abroad; fed, in an obviously intentional manner, by rumor mongers. One is that Kissinger's Weimar background has made him very apprehensive of a post defeat 'stab in the back' interpretation of the Vietnam fiasco, and the concomitant possibility of a right-wing backlash. He has therefore adopted a policy of 'bugging out elegantly' without injuring the sensibilities of the patriotic right - defeat in small painless stages. The second interpretation is that Nixon and Kissinger are, in fact, attempting a more sophisticated and economical reaffirmation of American global commitments, with less drama and by forcing more effort out of America's bludging allies.

For those who are a bit skeptical about a situation in which an administration known to leave nothing to chance in the PR field leaves the world guessing about the gravest aspects of its policy, there is a third 'version' Nixon has deliberately adopted: a policy of calculated unpredictability. Everybody is kept guessing what the giant will do, and since it is a giant who can strike terrible blows, the Russians and others will not dare to go too far. It is even asserted, that by becoming unpredictable America has restored its sovereignty and freedom of action as a great power. My own impression was that the interpretation most favored by competent and dispassionate observers is that of an 'elegant bug out' with the unpredictability thesis thrown in as a tranquilizer to abandoned and terrified allies.

My overall conclusion however is that America is incapable of defending effectively anybody, anywhere. Most Communists don't know it yet, since they are Marxists and cannot believe that a technologically advancing and expanding economic system may be politically decadent. As long as the Russians stick to their antiquated notion of 'no trouble in the superstructure without trouble in the base', we are relatively safe. But there are disturbing indications that the Soviet government has taken up 'Americanology' as a serious empirical study of the USA without Marxist bias. So far, the men in charge of the new venture seem to be suspected of 'cosmopolitanism' and don't get much hearing from the bosses. This happy situation may not continue much longer.

Taking the most conservative estimate of the consequences of the American crisis, one cannot seriously deny that 'unpredictability' is about the most optimistic rational prognosis possible. But since 'unpredictability' implies unpredictability in alliance-invoking as well as in alliance non-invoking situations, an unpredictable power cannot be relied upon to honor its commitments, though it may, on the other hand, undertake ventures to which it was not committed. A strictly logical consequence of unpredictability is that formal treaties and alliances with an unpredictable power are worthless: you have no guarantee that they will be around when treaty-bound, but, conversely, they may be around without a promise.

Among the current Australian views on our relations with America, there is only one which is wholly contemptible in its stupidity: the variant of the 'all the way etc.' position. On the other hand, the neutralist position of some ALP sections would be more defensible if it were honestly held and not propped up by a suppressed premise, namely, that the Communist powers are not really a threat to us. The third view, usually associated with the NCC-DLP complex, recommends that we should remain 'allies' of America but not count on them too much, treating their saving presence in an emergency as a bonus rather than a life insurance, though hoping that they will be around when needed. I find this last view closest to mine, though I can no longer accept it without two provisions: 'hope' about America should be 'pious hope'. And the following should be carefully weighed: to 'have an alliance' is not just to have something that is invoked in an emergency. It involves the allies in complex policy command planning and staffing entanglements all the time and not just in a crisis. When one power is very much bigger than the other, it means a unidirectional chain of command and flow of decisions in matters of foreign policy, military planning and intelligence, with a steadily shrinking area of independence for the client state. Now, if the major power is unpredictable, internally unstable or decadent, commanded by silly or irresponsible elites, the question has to be at least raised as to whether the advantages of alliance with a power whose protecting presence is unpredictable are not outweighed by liabilities flowing from the predictable and probably disabling internal difficulties of the protecting power.

Do we really wish to place Australian resources and Australian men, more or less unconditionally under the command of men and organizations whose characteristics would be merely comic if the consequences of their actions were not global and horrible? Shall we continue to desist from using military power in areas where we should (e.g. in what was once West New Guinea), and accept without query participation in military horror comics such as the Indo-Chinese operation? And what about the economic penetration by America of which the Canadians now complain so bitterly? For while America can at present defend nobody, it can still economically exploit and alienate resources of countries which it would not defend and whose capacity for self defence may be aggravated by the exploitation.

After the long chain of self-inflicted military political and moral disasters of the past six years, culminating in the Laos debacle and the My Lai catastrophe, not only the actual massacre – such occur in all wars – but the plurality of moral sewers exposed by the Calley trial and the public responses, both left and right, we should make co-operation with America in future military ventures strictly conditional on shared command control and intelligence, irrespective of the size of our contribution, or abstain from them altogether. We should also disentangle our military, political and other service structures from theirs as much as possible. There are voices coming from America that things are getting better, that all is well. Some are honest. Most are the voices of hired men. We must not forget that loyalty and disloyalty in America are just so many saleable commodities. And lying, as well as the species of lying known as 'image projecting', are just so many computerized techniques of keeping the suckers happy. The Nixon-Kissinger team is not short of technicians in this field.

But things are not getting better. Almost nothing is well.

Some of Dr Knopfelmacher's friends were surprised by these articles, which qualifies his previous admiration for the US and Australia's alliance with it.

11

The Parasite as Revolutionary: The Fleecing of America

(*Intercollegiate Review,* Summer, 1971)

A review of Charles Reich's The Greening of America (1970).

Serious political theory can be – very roughly – divided into three categories which I shall call respectively, the conservative, the liberal and the revolutionary. Their dominant themes run throughout the history of Western political thought, and while they sometimes overlap, it is by and large possible to fit any one thinker at any one time into one of the three. Not much needs to be said about liberalism, which possibly has dominated America since the establishment of the United States. The basis of this ideology is the belief that human secular destiny can be steadily improved by improving the environment, and that the human person is, by and large, the function of his natural and social conditions – and if you change the latter for the better you will improve the former. Not all liberals are starry-eyed optimists, and many are aware of the formidable obstacles to progress inherent in man's biological structure and ingrained belief systems. Also, the scope and width of possible improvements are disputed, ranging from claims that piecemeal, cumulative, gradualist solutions are the only feasible ones to the 'sweeping changes' schools of thought.

As against the liberals, the conservatives tend to believe that there are inbuilt, irremovable obstacles to human progress; that human nature is incapable of fundamental improvements; that it is irreversibly flawed. It is therefore not the task of the magistrates to strive towards human perfection, but rather to hold man on a leash, to tame his aggressive impulses by force and by conditioned fear responses, to circumscribe his anti-social aggressiveness by tradition-induced internalized prohibitions, and above all, not to tamper with institutions which have proved their mettle as instruments of human domestication.

The revolutionaries differ from both the liberals and the conservatives in that their 'ultimate' beliefs are closer to those of the liberals, yet the more immediately practical ones appear to be based on much the same assumptions as those of the conservatives. The revolutionaries share the liberal's trust that man can be perfected, or at least progressively improved, but unlike the liberals they don't believe that this can be achieved without a catastrophic restructuring of the world as it is and as it has been since the beginning of civilization. The revolutionaries, like the conservatives, believe that men, as we now find them, are flawed and as such are incapable of improvement. Yet the flaws have been built into them by psychologically crippling social organizations which have lasted for millennia and which still maintain their sway, thereby sustaining the flaws. Once the corrupting society is destroyed and its psychologically stunting effects removed, men can be redeemed.

The redemptive creed of the revolutionary differs from the liberal gradualism in that it presupposes the end of the 'old world' and the creation of a new one before any improvement in the quality of human life becomes at all possible. The revolutionary collapse of the old will be initiated by a crisis in pre-revolutionary relationships and by profound psychological shocks as the customary ceases to exist before a new consciousness replaces the old. The interim period justifies terror and perhaps even the genocidal sacrifice of the living, psychologically unredeemable human material as bridge-building matter and manure for the future. The chiliastic nature of revolutionary thought is now a commonplace among historians of ideas, and I shall not retell an old story.

The key concepts of the liberals, the conservatives and the revolutionaries are, respectively, freedom-progress, order-tradition, and crisis. Some revolutionaries and conservatives will be brought into psychological communion by their shared contempt for men as they are and for the liberals who expect to do anything worthwhile with *that*. Yet the revolutionary will at times join forces with the liberals to overcome the notion fairly deeply ingrained in Christian thought that by and large nothing can be done in this vale of tears, and it is better to tolerate established abuses which, as a by-product, maintain the social order, rather than to innovate by breaking the customary bonds of reverence and obedience - thereby risking the unleashing of a lawless 'state of nature' in Hobbes' sense, either between tyrant and a subjugated population or between members of a lawless human horde.

1

The New Left in America and elsewhere is revolutionary, insofar as it is made up of serious people who in some sense mean what they proclaim and who are not mere poseurs, TV entertainers, or promoters of exciting homoerotic fashions in the textile trade. Their prophets from Marx to Marcuse have made it abundantly clear that they reject our society in *toto*. By and large, also, the New Revolutionaries tend to display the classical specific differences in tactics, temperament, organizational methods and philosophy which have always emerged, in one way or another, within revolutionary movements; there are elitist Leninist or crypto-Leninist followers of Lukacs (whose work has been bowdlerized and popularized by Marcuse), the participatory democrat-anarchists who favour elective soviets, the advocates of more or less organizationally undirected individual action and nihilistic terror, and finally, the drop-outs, the hippie-freak element.

The drop-outs, which can be further sub classified according to costume, style of noise-making and manner of deviance, are, strictly speaking, not revolutionary. Their actions tend to be irreducibly apolitical and their life-style is far too erratic to lend itself to systematic political manipulation and direction by revolutionary technicians. Yet their actions tend to have unforeseen and unintended political consequences. The drop-outs are at the same time despised and courted by the revolutionary and counter-revolutionary alike, since both regard them as a hopeful sign. For the revolutionary, the drop-out represents a symptom of decadence in the target society, while for the counter-revolutionary, a sign of decay in the quality and morals of the revolutionary movement. Reich's book is essentially an apotheosis of the drop-out and his penumbra of attenuated imitators, and it represents an attempt to elevate him to the status of the revolutionary *par excellence.*

Visitors to America, like this author, are shocked by the extent to which 'the revolution' has become a lucrative industry, and they wonder whether the wealthy and powerful men who subsidize, exhibit and lionize the advocates of their own destruction are merely greedy and innocent, or perhaps symptomatic of the very insoluble internal contradictions which the revolutionaries claim to find all over America. It seems that the American revolutionary, and drop-out apostles of the 'counterculture' and the protagonists of the more traditional doctrines of the fast buck, have hit it off perfectly. The inhuman and shallow nature of most of the 'counterculture' seems if anything to heighten the lust of their adulterous embrace, which requires for its elicitation rather crude and excessively spiced fare. A thing which strikes a stranger in America is the blatancy with which the question '*cui bono?*' is relevant to the American culture industry and particularly to that part of it which may be called for want of a better name 'the academic racket' - not to be confused with the still sizeable islands of excellence and integrity which have managed to survive the 'educational' holocaust in America.

In this sordid world, in which not even the overwhelmingly ulterior motives of the culture-racketeers are the genuine ones, but a mere facade for yet more sordidly ulterior ones, the Kantian question, 'how is Reich's book possible?', must be asked. How is it possible that a badly written goulash of platitudes and clichés, betraying incompetence in many fields, destitute of even a shred of empirical evidence to back up hosts of sweeping and puerile utterances and without the redeeming qualities of genuine indignation and sardonic wit, was given the kind of promotion it received? Yet before one attempts an answer, the content should be stated and analyzed. Since Reich's thesis (I have avoided inverted commas because I could not decide whether to use them for 'Reich's' or 'thesis', and using them for both would give the article a distinctly Soviet flavor) is by now well known, I shall state it as charitably as I can, for it rests on the kind of now-fashionable pop-Hegelianism which cannot withstand even superficial philosophical analysis. Hence, if one wishes to discuss the stuff at all, one must improve on it in stating it.

2

Reich's basic concept seems to be the Marxist notion of the relation between material base and superstructure, or 'consciousness'. Thus, corresponding to three specific phases of American history, there are three types of consciousness, three families of ideological superstructure. Consciousness I is a function of pre-corporate classical capitalism or of America as a farmerist, free market democracy. Its principal values are thrift, industry, enterprise, faith in economic justification by cleverness and hard work, competitiveness, and a certain masculine robustness and ruthlessness to go with it. With the emergence of monopoly capitalism Consciousness I became dysfunctional. The race no longer went to the swift. With the crises of monopoly capitalism, Consciousness I simply could not cope: it became 'false consciousness'. The social and political actions of the New Deal which were undertaken to counter the effects of the Great Depression produced a new, managerial society, a network of hierarchically structured and interlocking politico-economic bureaucracies, a new power system, commanded by a scientifically trained, hierarchically-minded directorate.

The new social structure is sustained by command relations and programmed by a variety of conflicting managerial hierarchs who are, however, sufficiently coordinated (not by conspiracy or consciousness of interests, here Reich differs from Marcuse), but by an interlocking system of arbitration and conflict management, to warrant for itself the designation of Corporate State. Nobody *in particular* is really running this managerial society any more and the hierarchs of the military-industrial complex are themselves just so many cogs in the machine. The sustaining entity is not an apparatus or an elite, it is mental: Consciousness II. The old ideal-typical Protestant-ethic rooted entrepreneur has been replaced by the cool, sleazy or abrasive, ideologically aseptic organization man, who sets the pace, determines the fashions and dictates the trends. Consciousness II *has* improved America. Since the inception of the New Deal, the machine of managerial, statist, monopoly capitalism actually runs and is not bogged down in semi-permanent crisis. But it runs at the cost of dehumanizing its social actors. The trouble with Consciousness I was not that it was esthetically or morally bad. On the contrary, Reich indicates that it was quite fetching. It simply did not *work*. Consciousness II *does* work. The economy and the state apparatus function. But in working it destroys what is human in the social actors. There is waste, there are wars, there is private affluence and public squalor, there is alienation etc., etc.

The bearers of Consciousness II value advancement, the striving for power in orderly hierarchical bureaucracies by intrigue and merit, and they subordinate everything, even fun and games, to corporate ambition. Man becomes co-extensive with his officially accredited competences with a hierarchically stratified system of production and management. It is life without spontaneity, play and truly individual enterprise; just striving for power after power until death of the corporate salesman (Miller's [in *Death of a Salesman*] was really a Consciousness I bloke trapped in a Consciousness II world). The lifestyle of Consciousness II is psychologically deadening, yet man's spirit is immortal and resilient. It bucks the machine, cocks its nose at competence, hierarchies, and careers, and reasserts itself; Consciousness III is born. It is tantamount to a refusal of corporate discipline combined with an aggressive reassertion of non-corporate traits such as spontaneity, individual eccentricity, and the primacy of sensuousness over duty.

The central political thesis of the book is the proposition that the American corporate state will disintegrate purely as a result of a mental metamorphosis in its subjects and not as a result of political or revolutionary action. People's consciousness will simply change from II to III and the corporate state will wither away. The old corporate, anti-human *Gesellschaft* will give way to a free yet organic society of spontaneous sensualists and creative artistic producers. It is not quite clear whether Reich maintains (a) that the high level of automated technology makes significant societal repression redundant (Marcuse's doctrine of 'surplus repression') or (b) whether he holds that effort and labor will continue to be necessary but that they can be invested into production without the discipline of Consciousness II, i.e., without internalized notions of duty, levels of aspiration, and, socially, without hierarchy, authority, and division of labor. I feel that Reich oscillates between (a) and (b) being unaware that they constitute real alternatives.

What is one to make of all this? Some implications of the thesis are quite obviously incompatible with widely advertised alleged characteristics of Reich's *opus*. Thus Reich, or, if you will, the bearers of Consciousness III, are not, in any operationally meaningful sense of the word, revolutionaries. The minimum for being one is that one undertakes purposive political actions which, at least, do not exclude the use of violence and which are deliberately directed against the structures and personnel of the old order with a view to overthrowing them. The man who sits and waits for a spiritual rebirth and when it comes merely enjoys it may be all sorts of things: if he does nothing else, the use of the term revolutionary to describe him is a misuse of language. The Consciousness III chaps are not exhorted by Reich to do anything. As a matter of fact they are actually exhorted to do nothing *political* in the ordinary usage of the term. They are merely urged to drop out, to fall if possible on the soft cushion of sustaining corporate wealth and to enjoy themselves. They are in fact urged to become *idiots* in the original Greek sense of the word.

Reich qualifies in no intelligible sense of which I am aware for the label of Marxist, though he would obviously like to qualify. Should the pattern of intellectual and political fashions in America undergo one of its sudden and unpredictable changes, Reich will be able to state quite truthfully that he is not and never has been etc. without seeking the sanctuary of the Fifth Amendment. As a matter of fact, Reich seems to be that rare kind of man, an intellectual who amidst an unprecedented welter of Marx-debates and Marx-chatter has managed to misunderstand the principal political theorem of any kind of Marxism; namely, that it is not consciousness which determines social existence, but social existence which determines consciousness, and that the proper relation between advanced beliefs and backward reality is *political action*.

Reich is, actually, an almost paradigm case of a political 'idealist' in the half- technical and half pejorative sense in which the word is used by Marxists. For his central thesis is: do nothing and wait for the redemptive illumination to cleanse your soul. Let all those who are laboring in Consciousness II turn their minds to the things of the liberated flesh, to Consciousness III. Purity of mind is all, for the pure in Reich's rather fleshy spirit will by definition *be* the good society, the communion of saints. As a matter of fact, the movement which Reich's ideology approximates most closely is Moral Rearmament. The *practical effects* of accepting the proposition that personal purity must precede political action is, of course, political quietism. I would not be surprised if somebody, somewhere in the KGB or in some more creatively clinical, paranoid outfit of the New Left, were to rule that Reich is paid by the CIA to undermine the revolutionary potential of the American masses; but I shouldn't have said it, for, in the American culture racket, reality and the satire on it have by now become almost completely interchangeable. For all I know somebody may actually have already said it, or may get ideas by reading this article.

Reich fulminates continuously against 'false consciousness', another Marxist term which he has failed to comprehend. Yet, his own Consciousness III is a paradigm case of a false consciousness, a set of false yet comforting beliefs that you can have your cake and eat it. And this is true no matter whether one adopts a revolutionary or conservative philosophy of life. For there is one thing on which honest conservatives and revolutionaries can agree: the good life is not given to us. We must work hard at it, and hard work requires instinctual renunciation. Reich's chaps will not qualify as Marines or corporate executives. Yet neither will they qualify for death in the electric chair for acting on the (false but noble) belief that as long as somebody is in prison everybody is in prison, and that one should, therefore, do something drastic about a world in which there are so many jails.

3

We come now to the reason why. What has made Reich's book into a best seller? Why should it have sold so many more copies than other intellectually more competent books, which have appeared roughly at the same time, and which were written for a similar, fairly well-educated, middle to upper-middle-brow public? Why should men of affairs, and their wives, used to sound arguments in the pursuit of their corporate business and to good material texture in their private pleasures, prefer a discourse on the redemptive properties of Consciousness III on skis, in hip clothes, to sober and rationally argued treatises based on sound political knowledge and adequate empirical evidence? Perhaps somewhere underneath Reich's Consciousness III there lurks the old impish One and Two, an eye for the fast buck and a promoter's instinct for what the public *loves* (I am using the word in its currently obscene sense).

Everybody knows by now that 'radical' means 'chic'. Yet it is also common knowledge that 'radical' still carries with it *some* risks:

thus, even if law enforcement and discipline were to break down completely, there is always the danger of being mugged by a rival radical gang. And, there is, of course, the shadow of the backlash and what might happen to the kids if some law-and-order monster were to establish fascism in America by returning the safety of the streets to the old and the weak, and the college campuses to the pedagogues and scholars.

Even if one were to accept fully Professor Eugene Genovese's hypothesis that the American New Left is made up largely of economic parasites extruded from the loins, nurseries and schools of a liberal middle class which has by now mismanaged everything, including the socialization of their children, one may nevertheless concede that the enterprise of radically chic social parasitism is occasionally inconvenient, at times morally disturbing, and an object of sarcasm from both conservatives and from more seriously committed revolutionaries. The sense of one's own basic fraudulence – living in affluence and leisure, spouting a revolutionary rhetoric, and inducing in oneself counterfeit emotions of communion with the wretched of the earth – spoils at times one's delight with the game.

Reich's doctrine frees 'the kids' and their parents from all this. Reich, in fact, says that in being a social parasite one is being a revolutionary. There have been occasional parasitic playboys who were also revolutionaries – who, as it were, 'made it' in revolutionary politics, e,g. the younger Verkhovensky. Yet, according to Reich, the playboy no longer has to make it since he is *it*. No wonder the book should please so many. The law enforcement agencies and their allies will naturally opt for revolution in the minds, rather than by bombs, violence and political subversion. The media will welcome a revolutionary who does not question the legitimacy of property, but the most delighted will surely be the liberal academics and the college presidents, for here at last is a radical whose message does not increase the insurance rates of academic real-estate. The replacement of arsonists and bullies by bums and deviates will relieve many an administrative headache.

The people who should be disturbed by the prominence of Reich's book are those, American and non-American alike, whose personal freedom and survival is linked with the fortunes of the American republic. For it is obvious that the real revolutionary, as against the psycho-revolutionary of Reich's Consciousness III, represents no serious danger in America. Like all modern state machines in developed countries, the American state apparatus is effectively unchallengeable from within. Foreigners like myself, and even some natives, are deceived into believing that a violent revolution is possible in America by the degree of tolerated violence and dissent, and by the remarkable extent to which Americans tend to *doubt* the stability of their social order. The amount of slippage in the American law enforcement apparatus is, perhaps, greater than in any other highly industrialized society, and certainly greater than in other 'English-speaking' cultures, but there is no evidence that a head-on challenge against the social order would not be swiftly and successfully crushed.

The 'anti-Vietnam movement' is actually the best evidence for this thesis. The 'movement' operated with no holds barred, and it included men and organizations who would stop at nothing and whose hostility and rage against America's social structure was implacable and absolute. And yet, there was no significant interference with the military effort in the field. By and large the conscripts joined their units, obeyed orders, and handled their weapons as well as they usually do. There was no interference with troop movement, no mutinies, and no sabotage of transport and logistic support. The revolutionaries did not even begin to accomplish the task of 'turning the imperialist war into a civil war'. As a matter of fact, as far as the war effort *per se* went, they were not even in the game and that, characteristically and humiliatingly, despite the high proportion of blacks among the American soldiers.

Yet the new left is divided into two groups, of which by far the greater part would opt for the role of comfortable social parasitism celebrated in Reich's book. The values of that group have now permeated American society down to the women's magazines and comic books. The situation is reinforced by the fact that the belief in the basic dispensability of government in the pursuit of individual happiness is one of the most cherished American myths. In no other developed country is the need for sovereignty and government viewed with greater suspicion than in America. Indeed, the lurking feeling that governments are dispensable after all, or, if not, that they should be reduced to the barest minimum, provides an occasional link between the thinking of the left and the conservative Right in their joint nostalgia for a vanished past. It is a part of American *tradition* and, hence, even conservatives are highly vulnerable to it.

And yet, American society – both in the conduct of imperial policies and in her management of internal affairs – will require more and not less discipline, more and not fewer controls by experts, bigger and not smaller doses of guidance by the military-industrial complex in the coming technetronic age. Whether the elites will be nominally Federal bureaucrats or corporate managers with massive links to the state apparatus has been shown to be irrelevant in Burnham's *Managerial Revolution* in 1939 and remains irrelevant today. The serious problem is, surely, how to work safeguards of individual liberty into the interstices of the managerial-corporate state, which cannot be abolished because with it our technetronic culture would also go, and with it our civilization. For whenever a Reichian Consciousness-III switches on the light on his desk to write an essay against Consciousness I and II on his electric typewriter, he votes against his essay with his typewriter keys.

At the present time the still open societies of America and her allies are challenged by totalitarian despotisms of various kinds, of which the USSR remains the most formidable. They can withstand the challenge only if they consolidate and extend their institutions of conflict management to prevent disruption of the minimum of continuity and coherence which are a prerequisite for the successful conduct of world affairs, and if they can confront the system of terror and propaganda which threatens us from without by a force based on an internalized sense of civic responsibility. There is only one libertarian counter to terror and totalitarianism: determined resistance based on a civic consensus rooted in loyalty to the Republic, and supported by a variety of virtues, shrewdly tamed vices, and skills which together constitute the functioning human person within the context of his culture-bearing polis. The polis, any polis other than a tyranny, requires consciousness II. Consciousness III is for those who wish to like, like animals, men whom the ancients called *cynics* – the *dog-like*. If the Reich ideology were to prevail in the U.S., and if Americans in large numbers were to follow the pied pipers of social irresponsibility, we might yet see the 'greening' of America, since the grass might grow where the machines of civilization once stood. And life would again become solitary, poor, nasty, brutish and short, though admittedly with lots of unpolluted fresh air.

Yet, more likely, we would witness the internal disintegration and eventual conquest of a sensate, demoralized, and self-hating mass of crazed consumers by other tyrannical societies based on order, myth, hierarchy, and unrestrained violence. And their regime would be oppressive in the palpably real sense rather than in the contrived-pickwickian sense propagated by Marcuse and aped by Reich as a sophist's weapon against the legitimacy of the social order of the American Republic.

A member of the US Congress, impressed by this article, had it read into the Congressional Record.

12

What Makes Australia Tick?

(*NewsWeekly,* November 17, 1971)

A review of Ronald Conway's The Great Australian Stupor *(1971)*

'Poor dear psychology...spins out the correlation of trivialities into endless refinements.' And Professor C.D. Broad, who wrote this scathing indictment some 40 years ago, added that the rest of psychology was largely waffle. Since then, the situation in the subject has improved, and contemporary psychology is a loose federation of disciplines, some fruitful and some barren, and most of them linked more closely to 'non-psychological' subjects (e.g. sociology or neurology) than to sister members of the federation. Mr Ronald Conway is a leading clinical psychologist. Clinical psychologists are people who concern themselves with research, diagnosis and therapy in the field of abnormal behaviour. They tend to work alongside psychiatrists, who differ from them in that their basic training is medical. Clinical psychologists receive their basic training in Arts or Science faculties of our universities.

Conway's book shows a number of things. One is a wide critical intelligence, ranging far outside the narrow confines of what he calls 'nervous hypotheses', of a strictly 'scientific' nature. Conway's is a cultured, urban mind, with profound historical and sociological insights into his own society, a rare feat. Social critics benefit from a little alienation, a little 'foreignness', since it gives detachment, and supplies them with that lack of tact without which serious social critique is impossible. Yet Conway, while managing to be as tactful as is humanly possible and compatible with integrity, is remarkably detached.

Another thing to which Conway's book, and its rapid sale, bears witness, is the fact that politics, in the original Greek sense of the word (as the discipline pertaining to matters of the community) is now concerned, at least in Western societies, with matters which are largely 'in the mind', rather than with the traditional hard stuff of class, property, empire and civic rights. It has become, in the jargon of American sociologists, symbolic. After all, what is a man like Langer really doing? Entre nous, this intelligent young upper-class mathematician of European origin cannot 'believe' in the ordinary sense of the word that he is establishing a Maoist (i.e. peasant-autocratic) dictatorship in our computerized society, by turning the life of a benign Quaker-technologist-daddy-Vice-Chancellor into a perpetual nightmare.[15]

What symbols are being exploited, and by whom, behind the façade of this kind of pseudo-politics? Examples of symbolic politics abound, and they justify the growing claim, of which the present book is an implicit example, that the study of politics, or at least much of it, has moved into the pigeonhole of the social psychologist, and psychopathologist. Evidence for this is also the growing unpredictability of Western societies, the growing lack of correlation between the old, rational, solid stuff bound to the struggle for material and power interests, and the actual behavior of leaders of followers. The glory that was Charles de Gaulle, broken by pseudo-revolution triggered and promoted by a refugee adolescent with a Cherub-like face![16] The chief executive of the biggest and most powerful heap of men and hardware on earth

---

[15] Albert Langer was a Maoist leader of student riots at Monash University at the time.
[16] A leader of the French student riots, Daniel Cohn-Bendit.

– President Johnson – chased out of office by a set of academic scribblers and ordinary pornographers.

What's going on? And where – in which compartment of the human personality? Conway's book devotes itself to the relation between Australian institutions and what he sees as the 'Australian personality', of which he distinguishes four sub-varieties. The classification is based on the Freudian notion of an identification with parents. The patrist-autocratic products of harsh, cruel, father-centered families, are tough, legalistic, with fascist leanings. The patrist-conservatives – and Conway sees himself as one – are the Burkean traditionalists, flexible yet firm guardians of a legitimate social order. The matrist-indulgent are the modern permissive liberals, and the fraternalist-anarchic variety are the larrikin trade union types of Australian legend, with anarcho-communist leanings.

Among the wealth of Conway's insights I found the following the most interesting. Australian families tend to be mother-dominated, the fathers bludging, or hanging on, in the process of child socialization. This supports the trend towards a permissive liberal society. Australian males are repressed, i.e. unable to verbalise about their intimate problems. Also, they tend to be, by and large, non-spiritual, utilitarian, hedonistic and intellectually indifferent. Universities are factory-like training agencies, processing for diplomas.

Since it is impossible, in a review article, to do justice to all of Conway's observations, I shall end by restricting myself to a summary of critical comments. By far the best passages are those which are obviously based on Conway's clinical observations at St Vincent's Hospital, Melbourne, and on his private practice. Yet I suspect that they would be based on a statistically somewhat biased sample, in that Catholics would predominate in them. This may account for some of the discrepancies between Conway's conclusions (e.g. on Australian family climates) and those of others. Like all psychologists, he tends to under-rate the fact that human attitudes and motives have unintended consequences, and that, for this reason alone, a purely psychological assessment of society is impossible. Thus, a gentle pacifist like Lansbury may have helped to hand over Europe to the Nazis, to be liberated by patrist-autocrat generals like Patton and Montgomery. Conway actually recognizes this limitation implicitly, but his failure to make it explicit lays him open to serious, undeserved criticism.

And finally, Conway has not entirely convinced me that his book is about specifically Australian characteristics. Thus, his charge of spiritual laziness and hedonism is one which can be levelled against all ordinary people everywhere, under conditions of relative affluence, and it is perhaps an unfair charge. In times of political normalcy the masses are quiescent everywhere, thank God. I have seen them – twice – in a state of political enthusiasm, and I wouldn't like to repeat the experience. It is quite possible that the Great Australian Stupor is merely another term for law, order and peace, uninterrupted by wars and civil commotions and invasions. I hope it will be with us for a long time.

Conway, a patrist-conservative, is a Tory, who longs for an aristocratic heritage in an irreducibly plebian society. Many of us Europeans share his nostalgia, but I, for one, do not believe that it can be established here. And, having lived the reality (as against the dream), I wouldn't be particularly keen on having it around. Space and fraternal interest in increasing the author's royalties forbid me to say more. Those who wish to find out more should read the book. It is excellent in style and content, and eminently readable, as well as easily intelligible to non-psychologists.

And it is, very intimately, about the readers.

13

Wilhelm Reich, the Founder of Porno Politics

(*NewsWeekly,* February 14, 1973)

Wilhelm Reich, whose original contribution was to combine Marxist and Freudian analysis, wrote among other works 'The Mass Psychology of Fascism', 'Listen Little Man', and 'The Sexual Revolution'.

'The more things change the more they remain the same' is a saying applicable to the affairs of the Left with particular force. The sight of student newspapers and other leftist magazines, combining 'advanced' ideas in sex with revolutionary politics, are now a boringly common feature of our cultural landscape. Pornography, sexual deviance and revolutionary cultism (or, should one say occultism?) are now a syndrome in Western countries: pinpoint any one and you can anticipate the others. Commercialized pandering has merged everywhere with pseudo-revolutionary 'politics', to such an extent that it is usually impossible to be certain about publicists like, say, Germaine Greer, whether their prime object is to change the world, or to improve their bank balance.

The beginning of it all was born in the brain of an extraordinary and tragic man: Wilhelm Reich, the true founder of porno politics.

His career started, needless to say, in Vienna, a place described by the great Viennese satirist Karl Kraus in 1914, rather prophetically, as the research station for the end of the world. Reich himself was born in Romania, and moved, like most brainy young people of those days who came from the Hapsburg province and adjacent areas, into the Austrian capital to seek fortune and fame. Vienna was then both the gateway to culture from the Balkans, and one of the major cultural centres of the world.

At the outbreak of the First World War, Reich obtained a commission in the Austro-Hungarian Army, and acquitted himself well in the field. After the war, he completed his medical studies in Vienna, and joined the elite circle around Sigmund Freud, devoted to the propagation of psychoanalysis. He also joined the Communist Party. Such dual conversions had been typical of the period, and resulted in rather odd consequences. The two basic prophets of the 'radical' point of view were, and still are, Marx and Freud. The two had one thing in common, and one thing only: their doctrines were profoundly subversive of established religious and political authority.

Otherwise, they differed totally. Marx believed in the perfectibility of man, whereas Freud was a pessimist. Marx believed that the key to progress lay in change of the social milieu. Freud adhered strongly to the view that men everywhere were motivated by basic instincts which were intrinsically anti-social, have to be curbed by force and custom, at the cost of psychological health, and that this state will most likely last forever, irrespective of changes in social organization. In fact, Marx was a typical product of the enlightenment, cheerful, robustly optimistic and full of fight, whereas Freud was a deeply skeptical Manichean, resembling in many ways the great thinkers of the Right, such as Thomas Hobbes or Joseph de Maistre. Yet both men were anti-establishmentarian atheists of great persuasive force, they became the culture heroes of bohemian and revolutionary intellectuals in Central Europe at the beginning of this century, who, in buying them, did not yet realize that their ideological poke contained a cat and a dog.

After some time Reich left Vienna, and set himself up in Berlin, where the real action was. The German Communist Party fell, gradually, into the hands of uneducated apparatchiks, hand-picked by Stalin, with the left-wing intelligentsia of the Weimar Republic existing precariously on the fringes, tolerated rather than leading, and always a source of heresy. The intellectuals asked uncomfortable questions. The key question in the Weimar Republic was to explain why so many lower-middle-class Germans, and, indeed, German workers, followed the parties of the Right, and the rising Nazi movement, rather than 'their own' parties. Why were workers who 'had no fatherland' so intensely proud of their war decorations? Why did their wives, both Lutheran and Catholic, still go to church? And why, in the words of George Orwell, do the children of pacifists play with tin soldiers rather than with tin pacifists? More generally, what was it that enabled the ruling class to maintain its ideological grip over the proletariat throughout the Great Depression?

It is at this point that Reich has his one flash of genius, in producing the most brilliantly conceived, though false, theory of lower-class deference, by a synthesis of the doctrines of Marx and Freud. Marxism, Reich argued, is based on the assumption that the workers are capable of comprehending their interests, that they are capable of thinking rationally. This is, however, not the case. Their intellectual and cognitive processes are fog-bound - the reason for it is neurotic irrationality: hang-ups, induced by sexual repression. They are, therefore, incapable of seeing the world without phantasy distortion. Church, school, official morality – but particularly the fetters of the Judeo-Christian monogamous family – are holding human sexuality in chains, serving thereby as neurosis-inducing agencies perpetuating the psychological hegemony of the ruling class over the masses. Thus, the socialist revolution must be preceded by sexual emancipation, because the former is psychologically impossible without the latter.

Reich and his disciples expounded their theses in floods of articles, books and organizations, and they set up propaganda institutes throughout Germany. Reich's major work, *The Mass Psychology of Fascism*, is, perhaps the most widely and unscrupulously plagiarized work in modern Left-wing history, and the only original book of lasting and obvious merit in this particular field of social psychology. For Reich broke with the Communist Party shortly after 1933, reached America at the eve of the war and became, gradually, violently anti-communist. Eventually, for reasons connected with an early family tragedy in his childhood, he succumbed to insanity. In a manner resembling Nietzsche's decline, his writings became more and more phantastic and magic-ridden, discovering cosmic physical energies underlying the healing power of the orgasm, etc.

He died in 1957 in prison, having been sentenced to a two-year prison term for contempt of court by an embarrassed and charitable American judge, who did everything to help him. The U.S. Food and Drug Administration took out an injunction against the distribution of Reich's magic product, which he ignored, and in court he refused to plead. There is some conjectural evidence hinted at by Reich's widow, that his former communist comrades may have acted as finger-men for the authorities. America is notoriously quack-ridden and Reich, in his insane phase, was quite harmless. Why pick on him? The authorities were being sooled on by somebody. Also, the first public attack on Reich's magical activities seems to have come from fellow-travelling sources.

What is one to do with the work of a man such as Wilhelm Reich? As the de facto patriarch of porno-politics he is, undoubtedly, one of the most important influences at the present time. As a man who, in his sane phase, attempted an ingenious synthesis of two major social theorists, Marx and Freud, and who created a major school while still in good standing with official Marxism - and a host of quite unscrupulous plagiarists following his ex-communication (e.g. the whole Frankfurt School, Marcuse, Adorno, etc. and most of what passes as 'advanced' on contemporary American campuses) – he cannot be dismissed lightly. His subsequent insanity is, of course, no argument against his ideas whilst he was sane, and neither are the possibly harmful social consequences of his ideas.

The only legitimate question is simple: is Reich's theory true? For, bereft of auxiliary hypotheses, fancy jargon, and the politics of the period, Reich's sociology of culture rests on two serious propositions which must be examined: (1) the institution of the Judeo-Christian family, and the sexual prohibitions which help to sustain it, are a major source of human irrationality and a barrier to human progress, and (2) the family, as an institution, is dispensable. It seems that at the present time, the answer must be a firm 'no' to both propositions.

Paraphrasing, slightly, Aristotle's famous argument against the feasibility of Plato's 'Republic', one must insist that there exists at present no known society without some form of family structure, that no such society has ever existed, and, therefore, it cannot exist. The conscious attempt by Israeli socialists to replace the family by elective communes has failed. The old family system has fully reasserted itself throughout the kibbutz movement, which would have otherwise disintegrated. And as for the Communists, they no longer even pretend that they would do away with the family, and they don't when they get into power. And family instability throughout the Western world, easy divorce, sexual promiscuity, etc. do not seem to make people more rational. The argument against Reich's basic premises, like so much else in Aristotelian thinking, may seem logically loose. Yet it is sensible, for it rests on the suppressed premise that an institution which is both historically and culturally invariant up to a point, has a *prima facie* claim to indispensability. What always was and is, and what permeates our thought, language, emotions, and life so totally – the family – is something we are unlikely to be able to do without.

14

Modern Australia British to the Core

(*Nation Review*, March 8-14, 1974)

A piece written by Dr Knopfelmacher before he coined the word 'Anglomorph', those positively influenced by being raised in a culture shaped by Britain. Two decades later he published 'The Crown in a Culturally Diverse Australia' (1993), the last article in this book, which updates the themes of this piece.

It is, of course, impossible to be 'objective' about the Mother Country, for pretty much the same reasons that one cannot be objective about one's mother. As one who has his own idiosyncratic and alien prejudices about British affairs, it is perhaps possible for me to introduce a slightly 'un-Australian' perspective. I am an Anglophile or, perhaps, an Anglophiliac. I love England. My affection started early, at the age of ten, when most of the heroes and places in the detective stories I was then reading in Czech had English names. My family was of the Czech-German-Jewish bourgeoisie, whose Anglophilia was a sort of escape dream generated by the autocratic and anti-Semitic milieu of central Europe.

England represented style, masterfulness, enormous economic and political might, sobriety in thought and action, and above all, gentleness combined with resolute strength and absence of Jew-baiting. Much of all that was fantasy, of course, of an essentially Germanic kind, dialectically related to the hostile fantasies of the German Anglophobes, whose paranoid preoccupations with 'perfidious Albion' and *einkreisungspolitik*[17] contributed to the two world wars (Kaiser Bill, and all that).

For those who did not experience it, it is hard to imagine the trauma of Munich. For people of my origin and orientation it meant not only personal and physical ruin, but the collapse of a world picture, in which 'England', with her civilizing mission, played a significant part. From September 1938, in my fantasy life an England of a different kind emerged: corrupt and decadent lords and their hirelings trying to save their slave empire by throwing humanity to the wolves. Since the incidental by-product of the Munich trauma meant, for me as for countless others, a conversion to revolutionary Marxism, the dissolution of the noble Albion chimera coincided with the beginning of analytical thought on politics. Between November 1939, the month I left home, and August 1943, when our troopship reached England from the Middle East, my life had been solitary, poor, brutish and nasty: it was the life of an unwilling Jewish pioneer in Palestine and later of an inept soldier in the Middle East forces.

I fell in love with England on the first day of our arrival. The reasons? The English landscape, its beauty magnified by the absence of the Middle East landscape. An English major used the word 'please' when directing us from the ship into the troop train. As against European troop trains consisting then of cattle trucks with notices saying 'eight horses or 40 men', we were seated in an upholstered compartment with an English NCO serving tea. And then the freedom - the unprecedented, undreamed of freedom in the middle of a total war: conscientious objectors, anarchist newspapers attacking the government, Labor Party meetings at which nobody agreed with the chairman and everybody attacked the Lord Privy Seal, Mr Attlee.

---

[17] Encirclement (of Germany)

Politeness and good manners: the grotesque English of a twenty year old Central European verbalizer; I remember pronouncing the word youth as 'yath', and nobody so much as chuckled. Also, the girls and the women, both very friendly and very available in a non-whorish sort of way, particularly the older women. Books, newspapers, debates, *and* total mobilization combined with an indomitable resolution to fight. I experienced what Max Weber meant when he told Germans that the English were the true herrenvolk, for every Englishman is a *Herr* in the sense that cringing and servility towards statutory *obrigkeit*[18] are not part of the system, whereas liberties of the subject are, in fact as well as in the letter of the law. Yet what impressed me most was the quiet, tough, total and utterly *civilian* manner in which the war effort was being pursued. I thought that if there ever was a free people in arms, with unity based on consensus rather than coercion, this was it. Naturally, with increasing age and familiarity, the infatuations dissolved, but the love of England remained.

What do we owe England? As Koestler pointed out ten years ago, about everything. For had it not been for the courage of the British nation in 1940, Hitler would have occupied Britain, and the Eurasian continent would have been indefinitely at the mercy of Hitler and Stalin or, more likely, of Hitler alone. Civilized life as we know it would have come to an end, since there would have been no liberation, for the Americans could not have landed in Europe without the British launching platform. What is wrong with England? Again, taking my cue from Koestler and finding it amply confirmed by my own observations, above all it is the class system.

Britain is the only civilized country in which 90 percent of the population is condemned to live in a state of mild social inferiority. It is the only fully industrialized country with two languages, one for the people, the other for the elite. After nineteen years of teaching at an Australian university I still cannot tell which of my

---

[18] Authorities

students went to state and which to private schools. In England, it took me about three seconds to identify the social status of almost any person. Life for a non-Oxbridge Briton continues with snubbing, petty annoyances, one-upmanship and exposure to ceaseless social sniffing and the humiliation of false pretences. The archaic system of castes and classes contributes to counter-meritocracy on top, and to lazy indifferentism among the workers. There will, of course, be no revolution. Vanessa Redgrave and Mr McGarvie won't form a counter-government. There can be no Gaullism in a country where glory and political power are strictly separated and where the majority still loves the monarchy and the trappings that go with it and regards all politicians with mild contempt.

The celebrated resilience of British institutions will prevail. Yet it is now, perhaps for the first time, that this very resilience may prove fatal, for the country is in a bad social state which Aristotle called *stasis*: a social and industrial stalemate. It is quite possible that in order to solve its problems, the low work output, the chaos produced by a maze of 400 or so trade unions, the inefficient management, the incapacity to translate brilliant achievements in science and basic technology into industrial application, the British may have to jettison some of their habits rooted in the past. Even the British past can become an incubus. Not being a prophet, I don't know what will happen in the end. Probably something quite undramatic, unexpected, and gradual, as it always does in England. As for Australians, they will continue to be British-Irish or nothing. If anything, the conditions created by the modern media and cheap jet transport will increase the organic link between Australia and the Mother Country.

For there is no such thing as a specific *Australian* culture. The animosities between Poms and Ozs are of a bantering kind akin to those between Yorkshiremen and Lancastrians, rather than similar to the abiding and fundamental hatreds of, say, Poles for the Russians. British sex scandals in high places are headlines in Australia; Italian or French scandals are 'foreign news', barely rating a mention. And if a Roman cardinal were found to run a brothel, it would be headlines here only because it relates, however indirectly, to Irish-Catholic-Labor politics and the Irish question – two quintessentially British-Australian issues.

The Australian institutional network is British to the core, colonial-British, but British nevertheless. Not a single continental of note occupies a position of importance in Australian life except in music. Those continentals who have achieved some status have done so by way of 'assimilation', to *British* ways, that is. The number of influential immigrants from the UK in Australia is legion. And they do not have to assimilate. They are, more often than not, *invited to strengthen and to consolidate what there is,* and what is seen to be also theirs. Since I cannot see any reason for 'exploring alternatives', such as encouraging a form of Australian populism, an amalgam of lower middle class folksiness and excessive addiction to alcoholic beverages, I can see no reason why we should attempt to cut ourselves from the fount and origin of the greatest of modern cultures, to which we in fact belong. Contemporary Australian 'nationalism' is a 'British' affectation.

In the third last paragraph Dr Knopfelmacher describes the malaise Mrs Thatcher set out to overcome a few years later, in a more dramatic way than he predicted.

15

The Case Against Détente

(*Nation Review*, July 19-25, 1974)

Argues against the policy of appeasement of towards the Soviet Union, with the looming failure of US policy in Vietnam in mind.

The policy of détente between the USA and the Soviet Union is neither new nor the invention of Dr Kissinger. It is, in fact, the continuation by other means of the policy of containment fathered by George Kennan after World War Two, in contraposition to the policy of liberation, whose principal spokesman was James Burnham.

The 'liberation' school argued that the United States should use its technological superiority to impose a peaceful world order on the planet, sustained by American imperial hegemony, and should bring the Stalin regime to its knees by force. The most articulate English spokesman of this policy was Bertrand Russell. The containment people, whose doctrines have formed the implicit base of US foreign policy ever since the Berlin blockade, and its explicit ideology since the ascendancy of John F Kennedy, are a sophisticated lot who have won out in fact as well as in debate. Their policy is now in ruins since it has turned out to be based on wrong premises; it has become the sad lot of Kissinger to be the principal PR man and failure manager of a bankrupt undertaking. Kissinger's policy of détente is an attempt to disguise and to contain the consequences of failed containment. Simplifying enormously, one could summarize the premises of the policy of containment as follows.

The Stalin type of communism is not liveable-with, but must change since it is incompatible with the process of modernization. The western developed countries are safe against internal communist takeovers and are adequately protected by American nuclear power. The Communist power system is split between rival centres and thereby weakened. Internal changes within the USSR as well as communist polycentrism will lead to a gradual relaxation of the Soviet grip over its East European empire and its gradual peaceful dissolution. The emergence of managers in the place of *apparatchiks* as the dominant section of the Soviet ruling class, as well as their thirst for consumer goods and stability, will transform Russia from a totalitarian dictatorship into a normally autocratic conservative power, internally liberalizing, and increasingly resembling the United States 'convergence theory'. Yet one unstable zone remains, and it is there that US power ought to be fully deployed: the underdeveloped countries. They are in real danger of communist takeovers and must be shielded by a combined policy of counter-insurgency and economic assistance (for example, Vietnam). The process will be facilitated by polycentrism, since quarrelling communists will be easier to knock over one by one. (For a more extensive discussion readers are referred to a symposium contained in *Quadrant,* Sept-Dec 1973.)

It is almost gratuitous to dwell on the extent to which the containment assumptions failed to pass the tests of recent history. The invasion of Czechoslovakia followed by the explicit Soviet policy 'to hold what we have' has put an end to the empire dissolution bit. The return of a cultural freeze since Khrushchev's downfall has extinguished illusions about internal changes. The Soviet managers turned out to be a politically castrated lot, resembling in an aggravated manner the nationalist liberal bourgeoisie of imperial Germany. The western world, whilst not showing signs of an impending proletarian revolution on classical Leninist lines, exhibits other ominous pre-revolutionary symptoms, such as a general breakdown of legitimate authority, and a consequent inability to fight wars for the preservation of vital economic resources such as oil. The notion that 'our democratic way of life' may have to be replaced by harsher regimes is becoming conventional wisdom in Italy, a respectable prediction in England and a matter of consensus between such diverse types as Enoch Powell, Willy Brandt and Dr Kissinger. The American counter-insurgency program in the Third World, if not in ruins, is severely mauled by the Indochinese debacle. And, finally, the world imbalance of military power continues to shift in favour of the USSR.

In the light of all these facts, freely and commonly discussed in the high-quality press of Europe and North America, it is truly frightening to behold the terms in which the situation is debated in Australia. And there is no doubt that the vacuous rhetoric of the Whitlam government has contributed massively to the de-education of the public. The vast bribing operations conducted by the present Australian government among journalists and intellectuals are rapidly drying out the last resources of intelligent comment. Paradoxically, it is the extreme left which helps to maintain a residual bit of public debate, for their utterances, by their crazy perversity, disturb the somnolescence of a fraudulently induced consensus and provoke spirited responses and, hence, political thought. An example is the recent Brown scandal. Opposed as one may be to everything Senator Brown and his mates stand for, how can one seriously dispute that, stripped of its paranoid paraphernalia, the Brown version of Australian-American relations is substantially nearer to the truth than the Whitlam version? The fact that Marshall Green is one of the most resourceful, tough and brilliant American diplomats is common knowledge.[19] What is it then that induced the US administration to dispatch a heavyweight into a colonial backwater, hitherto manned by sinecure-holding nonentities? What have the Americans (and, hence, we) to fear from the new (Whitlam) government in Canberra?

There are three ways in which détente is discussed in Australia. The first is wholly idiotic and does not deserve serious consideration. It consists of the simple trendy affirmation that détente is chic, the thing to wear. It goes with bell-shaped pants, long hair, grass, etc. The second is based on the old Australian belief that foreign policy is a symbolic gimmick in the tribal war between the fundamentalist Mick-Hick segments and the rest. Anticommunism, along with anti-abortion, sexual hang-ups, state aid, censorship, corporal punishment, Anzac Day, etc. are the marks of the troglodyte. To be against détente is just another way of saying that homosexuals ought to be drowned, atheists persecuted, and Portnoy's complaints dealt with by the vice squad. Yet there is a third way, the one around which intelligent arguments can be constructed. It is based on the counter-position of alleged realism, represented by Kissinger et al., and moral idealism represented by Solzhenitsyn, Sakharov, and all those who maintain that one ought not to have dealings with an unrepentant genocidal system. If it were indeed true that the only, or even the principal, argument against détente is of the 'idealistic' kind, I for one would side with Kissinger against Sakharov, for I believe, with the Pope, that man lives in a vale of tears, and, with Max Weber, that to engage in politics effectively presupposes, inevitably, to compromise with evil forces.

Yet this is not the issue, and this is not the way in which Sakharov, Solzhenitsyn, and the rest of us reffo paranoiacs present our case.

---

[19] The left-wing Victorian Senator Bill Brown, an outspoken opponent of US and Australian intervention in Vietnam, in mid 1974 called the United States Ambassador to Australia, Marshall Green, 'the top U.S. hatchet-man', whom he alleged was in Australia mainly to protect US business and military assets. Prime Minister Whitlam was forced to publicly rebuke Brown.

What we argue is *not* to steer clear of the Soviets and keep our powder dry because communists are *evil*; what we argue is that the particular form of evil characteristic of the Soviet regime constitutes evidence that their system has not undergone the minimum changes which are necessary for a policy of détente to succeed. *We are against dütente not because it is immoral but because it does not work.* We are against it because they are arming whilst we are disarming. They are sending their lethal hardware and advisers into the old British bases evacuated by 'imperialist' England. Their youth is militarized and infused with a mindless jingo militarism from the age of three whilst our young ones smoke pot, burn flags and refuse to enlist. Their dissidents are in concentration camps and mental homes and their traitors face the firing squads. Our dissidents run our cultural life and our traitors are national TV celebrities. We are subsidizing their ramshackle industry and agriculture, whilst they are hell-bent on controlling our industrial life by keeping a stranglehold on our oil and on our trade unions.

One could continue the tirade by adducing a long string of other examples. The upshot of it all is simple: the assumptions on which the policy of containment were based did not materialize. Détente now, therefore, means piecemeal capitulation. It might be argued, with Irving Kristol, that there are no alternatives. Yet clearly there are; with the China problem unsolved and festering the Soviets need us more than we need them. We should, therefore, stop subsidizing their economy, thereby helping them to arm. We should no longer maintain our self-denying ordinance of not answering their lies about them and us with the truth (a state of affairs commonly referred to as 'the end of the Cold War'). And we should make their conflict with China insoluble by making it clear beyond reasonable doubt that if attacked China will receive the full measure of American technological assistance, including, if necessary, supplies of nuclear weapons. And we should be ready to soften, as soon as it becomes reasonably evident that the necessary internal changes in the Soviet system, which alone can make détente meaningful, are in fact taking place. And of those internal changes a Dubcek-like policy of granting civil liberties inside the USSR is by far the most important one, not for 'moral' but for purely *realpolitical* reasons.

16

Manhattan Versus the Vatican

(*Nation Review*, August 29-September 4, 1975)

How we try to cope with the disappearance of family stability.

A friend of mine recently remarked that ideas don't grow in Australia. They are made elsewhere, and sweep this country like locusts, leaving behind a bit of reversible damage. The debate on the family is presumably of this kind. Yet, as in the rest of the world, in Australia too the traditional 'Judeo-Christian' family is in trouble. It is becoming increasingly unstable, the taboos consolidating it are weakening; and its general weakening is likely to alter the culture of the country significantly. Naturally, there are already ideological camps taking up opposing views: the 'permissives', who welcome the process and whose thinking is almost entirely derivative, and the conservatives, whose lack of originality is even more striking. It looks like a war fought by the colonial troops, between Manhattan and the Vatican.

The sociological causes of the disappearance of family stability are well known, and already have been closely studied and understood by the classics of modern social theory from Durkheim to Tonnies, at the turn of the century. The Industrial Revolution and the concomitant political revolutions, of which the most significant one was the French, undermined the sociological props of the conjugal family unit. It is no longer, entirely or at all, a unit of production, education, social welfare, religious indoctrination and defence, in that alternative associations have now become available to perform these functions.

The clear-cut distinctions between male and female roles have lost their groundings in the social structure with the growing emancipation of women, and the consequent confusion of sex roles. And the growth of science and the proliferation of scientific attitudes have led to a demystification of the world, which tends to be incompatible with religiosity as a mass-attitude yielding tangible social consequences, such as obedience to ecclesiastic authority - as obedience induces severe personal hardships, such as large families, within a modern urban setting. The stability of the family has now become dependent on two rather weak reeds; emotional ties, and the enforcing agencies of an otherwise thoroughly secular state, the latter being operated, incidentally, by a majority of unbelievers.

The trouble with the anti-familists is due to the fact that, whilst they acknowledge the decline of the family, they refuse to face the serious nature of the consequences for general social integration, and for the moulding of the young human person. The traditionalists, on the other hand, have at least understood that the subject of family disorganization is not to be treated frivolously or lightly, yet they are unable or unwilling to grasp why it has happened. This applies particularly to Catholic conservatives. Their arguments are reminiscent of the husband who, having caught his wife in adultery decided, there and then, to preempt any such future occurrences by throwing out the sofa on which the event had occurred.

In a recent interview with Archbishop Little of Melbourne (*The Age*, August 23, 1975) the interviewer Mr Mark Baker finally brought the archbishop to the crunch. Non-committal and soft-shoeing on everything else, Dr Little finally identified the central political evil of contemporary Australia with almost brutal bluntness: the Family Law Bill. In the view of this columnist, the only good thing the present abominable government has done. One of the two issues (the other being abortion) on which the Archbishop found it 'worthwhile' to speak, he condemned it as a 'most insidious piece of legislation'. Not being one 'to cry wolf too often', he reserved the weight of his authority for just this.

I find it hard to understand how a mystical view of marriage can be reimposed on a demystified population by hired squads of private eyes, agnostic cops, atheist and agnostic judges and magistrates who are very much a part of that population, participating by omission in the multiple perjuries, indignities and publicly enacted obscenities which have hitherto formed the terminal stages of eroded Strindbergian 'marriages'. And all this under the benevolent eye of the Royal representative, a former state chief justice, himself married to a divorced woman.

It is, I believe, no accident that the soft underbelly of Europe, the part of it most acutely threatened by totalitarianism from within, is its Catholic part. Readers taking their cues, say, from *News Weekly*, and expecting social collapse and ensuing communist takeovers in the hated Scandinavian democracies, are entitled to some explanation. Some of them may even wonder why it is that the only intact political organization to emerge in Portugal after 45 years of firm guidance by such wise Christian statesman as Salazar and Caetano should be the Communist party. Why are Christian secret policemen so good at destroying liberal alternatives to themselves and so absolutely lousy when it comes to the Communists? I do not know whether the guardian spirit of the visible church is supposed to have wings, like a guardian angel. If he has, one knows already that the left-wing is no good. The right one is not much better.

17

The Murky Origins of the Russian Revolution

(*National Times,* August 9-14, 1976)

A review of Solzhenitsyn's Lenin in Zurich *(1975). Solzhenitsyn's Lenin is 'an opportunist uncontaminated by humanity or patriotism'.*

It is becoming gradually obvious where the principal difficulty in evaluating the current work of Alexander Solzhenitsyn lies: he addresses himself to two entirely different publics at the same time, the Soviet and the Western. And it would be bootless to pretend that the problem of communication and effectiveness is not one weighing heavily on the mind and pen of a man with Solzhenitsyn's daemonic sense of moral and political mission. The morally grounded sense of an urgent political apostolate is overwhelmingly there, overshadowing everything else, whatever other excellencies Solzhenitsyn may possess as an artist. Hence, to judge Solzhenitsyn's work in terms of conventional 'lit crit' gimmickry is tantamount to refusal to evaluate him at all. His business is far too serious to be left to the prissy fingers of literary critics, and far too complex for the paws of conventional political analysts.

The two publics which Solzhenitsyn addresses at the same time are, by now, separated by an almost impenetrable conceptual and attitudinal barrier. Not, of course, in the idiotically conventional, 'official' sense of 'Soviet man' and 'Western man' being respectively motivated by socialist and capitalist *Weltanschauung*. The problem is, if anything, obverse. While there are large and diverse sections of the Western publics for which official Soviet doctrines have retained some credibility, or at least some coherence, there are no such publics within the Soviet Empire itself. This does not mean, of course, that the inhabitants of the Soviet bloc are in a permanent stew about the system which they bear. Far from it. Some actually do very well out of it, or, at least have no feel for any other way of life, and thus in so far as they hope to do well, they hope within the political constraints of the system and its indispensable and magnificently ingenious pattern of *blat* (honest graft) growing out of the very bowels of the *nomenklatura* (the Soviet privileged class).

It is, however, only in the West that the hierocratic creed of the early Bolsheviks is still regarded as a co-motivator of Soviet behaviour. Within the USSR itself the sacred history of the Revolution does not really differ that much from sacred histories in other Caesaro-papist societies except that the lies and fakes tend to be 'un-Burkean', machine-produced by professionally qualified bureaucratically organized fakers, rather than left to slowly growing folk-tales and gently fostered legitimizing prejudice. You cannot plant durable oak trees and engage in landscape gardening in Gulag country on permafrost land. Solzhenitsyn's *Lenin in Zurich* is a political novel. There is not much in it which serious students of Lenin in the West did not know. Thus one of his publics – the less important one – will not be surprised to hear once more, that Lenin, far from 'hating' the war, welcomed it as an unexpected boon and desired its prolongation in 1916 along with the rest of the Zimmerwald Left.[20] In a lecture given in Munich in 1919 (sic) Max Weber mentioned this fact casually to an audience of

---

[20] A minority faction headed by Lenin during the first world war, a forerunner of the later Comintern.

students, in a tone which implied that everyone knew of course, using it merely as an example of Machiavellianism within a group generally misunderstood as being motivated solely by 'absolute ideals'.

The well-known fact that Lenin foresaw very little about concrete political events and that his mastery consisted in putting ex-post-facto theoretical interpretations on unforeseen contingencies (e.g, the February revolution) is reaffirmed once more. His phony 'scholarship' is described with unrivalled mastery as a futile day in the Zurich library, filled by lame attempts to collect debating points about a subject of which he knew, obviously, next to nothing – Persian agriculture – and which bored him to distraction. Until, finally, a fit of hypochondria centered on an attack of migraine drove him back to his long suffering and loyal wife Nadezhda Krupskaya. His emotionally parasitic and inconsiderate love affair with Inessa Armand is described with Solzhenitsyn's now notorious irony, yet in a manner which keeps it well within the bounds of authentic Christian compassion and impeccably good taste.

Lenin's total incapacity for personal or political friendship is brought out both in relation to fellow Bolsheviks and to the hands that fed him in exile: the good-natured and trusting Swiss and Austrian Labour leaders, whom he despised more than anyone else. Lenin's virtuosity in splitting other people's organizations is brilliantly re-described and woven with great skill into his unpleasant character-structure. For Lenin scholars the most interesting section of the book is one dealing with the relation between Lenin and Helphand-Parvus. Parvus, a Germanised Russian Jew, an outstanding social theoretician, played a leading role in selling the idea of breaking Russia from within, by fostering internal turmoil, to the German authorities.

Parvus, a close associate of Trotsky, was by all accounts a formidable personality. Yet Solzhenitsyn turned him into a truly Faustian figure, the only man Lenin respected and feared. And he hints that it was due to Helphand alone, or, nearly alone, that Lenin accepted the German financial and logistic connection. The train that took Lenin and his entourage back to Russia and the financial support by the German government made the success of the Bolshevik October coup possible, in a country where the only free election produced an overwhelmingly Social Revolutionary parliament. Solzhenitsyn's Helphand is not a socialist (much too bright for that), he knows and understands infinitely more about power and the world than the 'student politician' Lenin. He hates Russia and loves Germany, and regards German hegemony in the East as a culture-bearing and liberating force. Lenin on the other hand, hates Russia, but he hates Germany equally and loves only The Revolution, an entity which Parvus seems to be willing to use, but to use it as a lolly to coax a wayward child back to school; a tough and orderly German school, the school of civilization.

The Lenin-Parvus confrontation is quite obviously the punch-line of the novel, and its most masterful as well as controversial part. For the Soviet public, it drives home the point Solzhenitsyn is intent on making again and again; namely, that the old Bolsheviks were a bundle of alien riffraff (Lenin's non-Russian Kalmyk-German antecedents are, perhaps a bit gratuitously, played up), non-Russians and motivated by pure *ressentiment*, and lust for power. The few 'good' Bolsheviks were those within Russia not the émigré intelligentsia; people like Shliapnikov[21], and – yes - you know who. But Solzhenitsyn can afford not to mention young Stalin, for at that time the future Generalissimo was, indeed, a nobody. It is an interesting inversion of the Western-liberal thesis, popularized in Koestler's *Darkness at Noon*. According to the latter the Russian revolution was ruined when the émigré-cosmopolitan Old Guard was driven out by the domestic proletarian 'bandit' element led by Stalin, whose 'Tartar' political formation was never adulterated by contacts with Western civilization.

---

[21] Alexander Shliapnikov was a Russian post-revolutionary Communist trade unionist who led an opposition movement in the 1920s.

The conversations between Parvus and Lenin, are, of course, fiction, the Faustian dimensions of Parvus are probably overdone, but the Parvus type is both historically documented and authentic. The financial and political links between Lenin and the German General Staff have been well established and documented for the past 20 years. To a generation which grew up after Auschwitz it seems incredible that only two generations ago, East and Central European liberals and progressives, Jewish and non-Jewish alike - men like Helphand and August Bebel - looked with favour at Germany's *mission civilsatrice* among the lazy, vodka sodden, pogrom prone, barbarous Slavs. Yet so it was.

For the Soviet public Solzhenitsyn's book is the foundation stone of a counter-mausoleum. It makes it clear beyond doubt that the stuffed carcass on display in the Mausoleum on Red Square is of a man who never was.

18

A Quiet Scholar Dies Hard:

Jan Patocka

(*Nation Review*, April 6, 1977)

When I saw a brief notice on page 11 of the Melbourne *Herald* on Labor day, under the heading '*Quiz – Then Rebel Dies*' I skipped the article assuming that it was about some trendy freak who dropped dead on TV. On turning the page, the name Patocka caught my eye and I read again. 'Quiz – Then Rebel Dies' turned out to be the way in which ockerdom was introduced to the news item that Professor Jan Patocka of Prague, the official spokesman for Charter 77 (a manifesto for civil liberties, issued by the leaders of Czechoslovak thought, letters and politics in support of the Helsinki agreement at the beginning of this year) died of brain hemorrhage which set in upon conclusion of a police interrogation lasting for eleven hours. It took Patocka nine days to die at 69 years of age after months of harassment and a day of torture. Not a mean achievement for the world's leading Husserl scholar.

When I enrolled at Charles University Prague in September 1945 at the age of 22, my British battledress and campaign medals commanded respect. The general atmosphere of the country was already appalling, not the least inside the university. The valley of the shadow of death has a murky stench about it, which those who know it only from Gustav Mahler's final period cannot fully appreciate. For in addition to the thick stench of Auschwitz, and the sight of its cadaver-like survivors there was a cauldron of barely repressed hatred, bloody- mindedness, suspicion and fear. As an officially certified 'member of the resistance', I with a few others who served in allied armies were exempt from most of the common tribulations to which ordinary Czechs and Slovaks were subjected by the new authorities. Thus, one was not at the mercy of one's old personal or political enemies, who could turn informers, finger you to the 'purification authorities' and thereby dispatch you, after a mock trial and bogus appeal, to the gallows, all within one morning. (I did watch a few of the hangings which in the first weeks were performed in public, on medieval gallows - acting on the assumption that a budding young social theorist should do a bit of fieldwork.)

Neither did I require a 'certificate of national reliability', a document needed for purchasing or keeping the necessities of physical survival such as food, shelter, or medical attention. This document issued by the communist-dominated national committees was subject to renewal every three months. Thus I enjoyed a measure of freedom and could take liberties. Like my German predecessors I carefully avoided the new Belsens, in which dying Sudeten-Germans – babies and the old – were caged waiting for deportation into starvation-ridden Germany; though I can plead in my defence, that I smuggled out letters about the scandal to the British weekly *Tribune*, and thus may have contributed in a minuscule way to the stink generated about it by a group of Labour MPs in the House of Commons - and, I am proud to say, by the Jewish publicist Victor Gollancz. And, together with a few other uniformed friends, I broke the national consensus by attacking on campus, openly, the deportation policies of the new regime.

But then, for the reasons indicated above, I could afford it without much risk. I, and people like me had, however, their own problems. We were isolated survivors of huge, exterminated and affluent Jewish families and our physical survival impeded the smooth working of the communist-controlled office for the redistribution of German property, whose discriminating largesse formed the economic base for Communist party penetration into the greedy Czech and Slovak lower middle classes. Jews were never particularly loved in Czechoslovakia and, except among the intelligentsia, thinned out by Nazi terror, the population by and large wished that we had all gone 'up the chimney' in the idiom of the Auschwitz days.

The Philosophy Department of Charles University Prague in which I enrolled was dominated by three men: Josef Kral, a Czech historian of philosophy - cunning, peasant-like, boring and erudite. JB Kozak, a former Protestant theologian, one of the most brilliant lecturers I have ever had, was fresh from exile in the USA. I still use my notes of his lectures on St Augustine in my adult education courses. Personally he was a swine, collaborating with the Communists. And then there was Arnost Kolman, imported from Moscow, our resident NKVD dialectician, sizing us all up for the gulag. He has now, I understand, become a dissident, at the age of 80 and lives in Sweden. Jan Patocka was at the time a mere lecturer and held classes on his specialty which was phenomenology. When I enrolled in his seminar, he gave me a friendly, non-exploitative and non-frightened look and said with a smile 'Welcome *pane kolego* [honourable colleague], they don't read phenomenology in England, or do they?' For the first time, I felt what I had come to Charles to become, a pupil eager to learn from a master. No politics. No 'topical' comments. Just phenomenology in the first few sessions read from galley proofs, and monologue-discussions, with Patocka pacing up and down. I understood next to nothing. At the time I was a totally hidebound positivist, beholden body and soul to the Vienna circle, to Russell and to Popper. My favourite hobby was to bait (remember I could, for I was in uniform!) the communists by urging them to define such marxist-leninist nonsense terms as 'negation of the negation'.

By 1947 the university was a national storm-centre, and we all knew that a showdown was imminent. People took up positions, construed alibis, ran for cover, or organized. Yet Patocka would have none of it. His class was like a windowless monad, long strings of concepts without percepts, walking up and down peripatetic. The world of *praxis* was not there. Though we were poles apart intellectually Patocka and I did develop a mild friendship. Seeing that he was (unlike Kozak) neither a traitor, nor (unlike Kral) a mere professional peasant-survivor, I sought friendship and guidance as the young do. Yet any attempt to raise political issues just dissolved, didn't get off the ground. That he liked me I knew indirectly from little unsolicited acts of kindness, such as helping me to get private tuition, one of my pupils being his brother, a leading biologist whom I coached in English. Yet in his vocation, philosophy, he viewed me as a hopelessly Anglified 'under-laborer' in Locke's sense, a 'mere positivist'.

The communist putsch of February 1948 took him completely by surprise, and like some others who lived in a political dreamland he was utterly shattered. He was not expelled at once, but tolerated for a while. And our personal relations deepened. The extent of his political helplessness and inability to comprehend was moving. I felt embarrassed, for our roles were about to become reversed. I lectured down to him – on communism, Stalinism, the gulag, offered him a copy of Koestler – and he listened. I doubt that he took much of it in. It wasn't his world. For the only remark he ever made was: 'But I can't understand. Stalin is supposed to be interested only in socialism in one country!' After this I gave up and I never talked politics to him again, for I felt that his kingdom was not of this world and I would be importuning a trapped and anguished man.

I left the country, pretending to go to Israel (*plus a change*...) for England in August 1948 with a generous testimonial from Jan Patocka, among others. He survived the years 1948-68 as a school teacher, producing about 130 unpublished technical and historical papers, and what is to me a major new work on Aristotle. During the Prague Spring of 1968 he got a chair in philosophy at Charles which he promptly lost again a few months later after the Soviet invasion. I very much hoped to visit him in the course of a free trip to Europe offered to me by the German government in order to attend a Marx conference in Trier in April 1968. Yet I never got to Prague - for reasons known to those Australian criminologists specializing in the Australian tertiary underworld.

An unexamined life is not worth living. Whatever Patocka may have ignored, he could not have ignored the Socratic maxim. I find it near impossible to comprehend fully a man of his kind. It requires persons like Solzhenitsyn to describe the calvary of their lives, and for me, some kind of music of which I yet know nothing, to make it intuitively comprehensible. The reason why he consented to become the official spokesman of what a child must have known would be a most dangerous act of defiance, Charter 77, one can only guess. Very likely he had to, because he could not do otherwise, in the sense of Martin Luther.

Yet the awful suspicion cannot be entirely dismissed that the man who could say about Stalin in February 1948: 'but he wants to build socialism in one country only' may have accepted the Helsinki fraud as good coinage. Which would make him yet another central European victim of what used to be called anglo-saxon perfidy, and what should be called the anglo-saxon death wish.

Dr Knopfelmacher kept among his papers the reference Patocka had written for him.

19

Terrorism and Reason

(*Nation Review*, October 22, 1977)

Paul Johnson is a man with his heart in the right place, a matter of interest only to his God and to his cardiologist. For he, more than any other Western publicist is responsible for the dissemination of one of the most misleading fallacies, the proposition that terrorists are 'dangerous madmen', unlike, say, the Kremlin junta, who are, at least, rational. Some of Johnson's practical recommendations, particularly his advocacy of the use of the death penalty for terrorists, are sound for the wrong reasons. Yet most of his general policy recommendations, such as seeking a global consensus against all types of terrorism are, therefore, just childish.

Morally, contemporary terrorism is not better or worse than other forms of war and lethal political violence. It is, actually, just a variant of guerilla warfare, a method of combat, literally as old as the (inhabited) hills. From this simple insight it does, of course, not follow that we should or should not 'loathe' terrorists. (I personally quite admire them: I would never have the guts to do what they are doing, physically I mean). Such self-indulgent psychologisms are out of place – along with moralizing tripe - in a political analysis. What we have to do, if we wish to protect our social order against them, are three things: understand them, kill them (without hate), and prevent their recruitment from our student populations, the stratum from which the large majority of them come.

The principal difference between the modern terrorist and his pre-modern ancestors, e.g. among the Spanish guerilla fighters against Napoleon, is the chiliastic-cosmopolitan nature of their ideology, their technical potential in a highly 'organic', interdependent, and therefore, very vulnerable technological society, and the military scope made available to them, at least potentially, by nuclear and biochemical weapons-technology. The modern terrorist, no matter whether belonging to the Baader-Meinhof gang, the radical PLO or the Japanese Red Army, adopts a Sodom-and-Gomorrah model of our society. [He believes] modern capitalist societies are historically, actually, or both, parasitic upon the subjugation of the Third World and its ruthless exploitation. The bodies of *all* our people, are, literally graveyards of billions of subjugated, violated, starved, and murdered colonial coolies. The modern 'small l' liberal lot who pleads for the survival of ten just men in Sodom has no case. By the very act of participating in the benefits of the modern industrial society we batten on the life-blood of millions whose dark, short and martyred lives are crying for vengeance. No matter what we do, we exploit, whether we 'intend' to do so or not. Even the seemingly bright features of our societies are crypto-diabolic: our metropolitan redistributivists, from liberals to radicals, are merely clamouring for a greater slice of the colonial booty for the working classes. The survivors of Auschwitz are now among the most rapacious of all the colonial ghouls.

The system has to be smashed by total war. Our industries must be disorganized, our military power smashed, our access to raw materials interdicted, and the authority of our public agencies such as the state, destroyed by mockery, disobedience and terror. And, with about one half of the world outside the capitalist politico-military reach already, it can be done for the first time since the industrial revolution. The modern revolutionary terrorist is no madman or dreamer; he is one of the principal political realists of our age, bold but entirely rational. And whilst basically misunderstanding the nature of our society he sees accurately, with the acute perceptiveness of hate, our growing weaknesses; guilt, self-doubt, and the disintegration of effective sovereignty among the representative governments of Western industrial societies. Wherever terrorists gain power, as in Russia in 1917 or in Cambodia in 1975, they apply the methods of total social surgery against 'their own' populations. The dreaded Cambodian Angkor is led largely by former Indochinese students whose minds were formed twenty years ago, not in the jungles and rice-paddies of South East Asia, but in the Latin Quarter of Paris and at the Sorbonne. Conquest of power transforms terrorists into Chekists. Like the guerilla who cannot live unless he can swim in a sea of peasants, the modern terrorist owes his survival to the surrounding sea of 'small l' liberals.

Their universities generate and hatch him, their mass media propagate and advertise him, their courts and lawyers shield him, and he himself is a self-hating member of the bourgeois clerisy. His enemy is above all, the ordinary blue-collar worker, particularly the one who dons the military and police uniform. I am still not convinced that Max Weber's assessment of trade unions as the principal pillars of social order in modern industrial societies is out of date. It is in places such as La Trobe University, rather than in the La Trobe Valley, that our guardians should erect their main watchtowers. The hi-jacking of the Lufthansa liner, the execution of its captain, the reconquest of the liner by a German military unit, the death of a socially prominent hostage, and the death of Andreas Baader and his two principal accomplices were followed by a wave of retaliatory bombings - and by a barely disguised shift of liberal sympathy from Dr Schleyer[22] to the Baader three. High-ranking police officials in Australia have indicated that there exists evidence of a terrorist infrastructure in this country. What can be done in Australia? Since we are still in the initial stages prevention

---

[22] The German business executive Hanns Martin Schleyer, the 'socially prominent hostage' who was kidnapped in September 1977 by Red Army Faction terrorists and later murdered.

can be successful. One wonders what our 'secret' bodies are doing and how well equipped they are to deal with terrorists and pre-terrorists. A few proposals:

(1) Since terrorism is merely one aspect of a general assault on our society it is pointless to discuss it in terms, say, of 'airport security' as if this were an isolated problem. Attention has to be focused on the talent spotting and recruiting areas, which here as elsewhere in industrial society must be the population of tertiary institutions, universities more so than colleges. So far, the conservative press has chosen to discuss items clearly connected with terrorism and its infrastructure in terms of 'student politics' and has left decisions about the future of Australia's main terrorist propaganda agency in the hands of the Minister of Education and Vice-Chancellors, and resistance to their conniving incompetencies in the hands of near-adolescent student-politicians who, however brave and intelligent, haven't been around long enough and lack experience.

(2) An 'orthodox' police force is not equipped to deal with the modern terrorist. A special force, with its own intelligence (collating and evaluative) and operational sections ought to be created, trained and deployed as quickly as possible. In the meantime, existing state-power should be deployed to enforce the law wherever it is broken and particularly on the territory of university campuses, if necessary without the permission of university administration. The emergence of extra-legal and extraterritorial campuses is a notorious preamble to guerilla and terror operations, formerly restricted to Latin America but nowadays near-universal.

(3) Efforts at an intelligent evaluation of the modern terrorist problem should be actively fostered by all sections of the population interested in the maintenance of the social order, a very wide spectrum ranging nowadays from conservatives to some members of the CPA (in a latent sort of way). A bipartisan approach should be sought, wherever possible, and in no circumstances should the terrorism issue enter the party-political arena. If it is, unwisely,

thus introduced, say, by a Labor MP, the greatest degree of self-denying ordinance in not using it against the ALP as a whole must be exercised by the government. Any Conservative politician who uses terrorism for ALP or union bashing is helping the terrorists.

(4) The relation between terrorist groups and Communist state agencies, particularly the KGB, should be discussed and intelligently publicized. Many terrorist leaders obtained their basic training in Soviet-bloc countries, and terrorist training and indoctrination centres flourish in Soviet controlled or influenced Arab areas and also within the Soviet bloc. The attitude of the KGB to terrorists is ambivalent: it supports them uneasily, for Bolsheviks loathe anything they do not totally control. The tendency of distrust towards 'petty-bourgeois adventurists' combined with contempt for all revolutionary groups was a salient feature of the Stalin era, wholly reversed by Khrushchev; the crunch being Soviet support for Castro, including the betrayal of their Cuban agent Anibal Escalante in his confrontation with Raoul Castro. The post-Khrushchevian, highly bureaucratized Brezhnev policy is marked by a somewhat more cautious approach towards terrorist groups not directly generated and totally controlled by the KGB. One reason is, presumably, the growing bureaucratization of the KGB, a sort of creeping 'due process' mentality even among Chekists.

(5) The death penalty should be reintroduced for acts of terrorism. The reason for it is neither the desire for vengeance nor bloody-mindedness but dire necessity. One of the principal features of the terrorist creed is their disbelief in the long-term stability of the target society and her institutions, including its jails. An imprisoned terrorist does not feel stigmatized and does not feel crushed, for he believes that very soon either the collapse or decadence of the society or a bold act of his comrades will get him out of jail. His punishment lacks credibility to him and is, therefore, no deterrent. Yet even he must believe that death is permanent and irreversible by structural change or revolutionary solidarity. The most effective post-war safety poster on British roads said: 'Drive slowly, death is so permanent'.

20

Among the Flesh Pots: Solzhenitsyn and the West

(*Quadrant,* October, 1978)

'Woe to him who seeks to pour oil upon the waters when God has brewed them into a gale!' Herman Melville, Moby Dick

Since the trickle of Soviet dissidents to the West started ten years or so ago, a certain pattern has emerged. To understand that pattern, the cultural political significance of the dissidents to various western publics has to be understood. For there is a sense in which those dissidents are nowadays no longer messengers from the other side of the moon, but occasions for assessing and recontesting specifically Western culture-political power struggles. This was not the case in the good old days of Uncle Joe. When you came out you were automatically classified as a criminal by the Stalinists, and as a (perhaps) tragically uncomprehending, warped freak, driven into paranoia, by the Kingsley Martin, Brian Fitzpatrick types of fellow-travellers.

The social democrats of the Attlee-Chifley-Gaitskell variety accepted you as an honest Menshevik comrade exiled by the Bolshevik traitors to true, moderate socialism within the bounds of the law and loyalty to King and Country. The Conservatives saw you as yet another victim of socialism. There was no *ambiguity* about you anywhere. For people more or less pro-Soviet you were a criminal or a lunatic. The anti-Soviet public treated you as a legitimate victim. Since then, the situation has become much more complex: communist polycentrism, the emergence of the New Left, détente as an ideology, the growth, for the first time in history, of a more than microscopic Trotskyist movement, the leap to the left of the Catholic intelligentsia and the simultaneous leap to the Right of the Jewish one, and now an American administration which treats (quite properly and legitimately) the Soviet human rights issue in part as a strategic factor in relation to America's principal military adversary.

The result of all this is that a newly 'exit-permitted' intellectually articulate refugee from Sovietistan finds himself surrounded by more or less transparent representatives of different culture-political agencies – all offering guidance, shelter, contacts, and jobs for the price of political identification. Putting it crudely: *they* are telling *you* what you witnessed, how you saw it, how to explain it on TV (e.g. by understating it for tactical reasons) and, mainly, why you came. Unless you have at least near perfect knowledge of your host country's language, or some promptly marketable skill, such as virtuosity on flute, piano or cello or an established reputation as a scholar or writer in a non-political subject, you will be forced to accept one or more offers. If that happens you may sooner or later find yourself in the position of a performing monkey for street artists (a self-description actually used to me by a Soviet dissident), whose purposes may range from the most noble – such as to secure the release of, say, yet another victim of Soviet polit-psychiatry – to sinister disinformative circus acts; such as a performance, the object of which is to produce the well-known global fake scenario which equates the unparalleled monstrosities of Communist regimes past and present with the thoroughly repugnant, but infinitely less numerous and irremovable, transgressions of Western democracies or some of their autocratic client-states.

The Soviet dissident is claimed as a symbolic martyr by a vast variety of agencies and sects. Many of these agencies, for example, Amnesty International, do not act in the interest of the captive nations under Soviet rule. Some have unduly close ties with Western governments which come and go, and whose attitudes to the Soviet regime vary with economic and strategic contingencies. And there are groups who, objectively or by design, consolidate the very Gulag whose actual and or potential victims they pretend to patronize. It is a messy situation. Fortunately for Russia and the rest of us Solzhenitsyn could escape it. He is nobody's performer. Nobody can tell him what he ought to say or not, or with whom he ought to associate for one very simple reason: his financial independence. He is, in fact, the only independent spokesman of the Soviet opposition in the West. Sakharov is nearly another, with a plainly different basic social philosophy from Solzhenitsyn's, though in agreement with him on political issues. But for tactical reasons of obligation to his friends and allies (Sakharov is totally unconcerned with his own personal safety) [he] is in need of Western press-goodwill and the goodwill of Western academic brass.

In his Harvard Address Alexander Solzhenitsyn declared that he did not regard Western liberal societies as suitable models for Russia. Western leaders were cowardly, the legal system did not work and was largely for the rich, the press was shallow and much too influential and the population was spoilt by affluence. He spelled out the symptoms; selective indignation in humanitarian concerns, all hell breaking loose when a banana republic dictator commits an atrocity, and silence in the face of massive crimes by powerful governments. Like his great Austro-Jewish predecessor of two generations ago, Karl Kraus, he identified the press as being among the principal agents of social dissolution.

There is, in my view, little doubt that what Solzhenitsyn says about the West is largely true, and that his views are shared, with the odd reservation here and there, by the overwhelming majority of Soviet-bloc exiles. Yet there is one point, a major one, on which skepticism is advisable: Solzhenitsyn is a cultural pessimist *about the contemporary West*. He thinks we are a pretty poor lot and that we are getting worse. Yet he also thinks that there were times when the West was nobler, bolder, better. I personally tend to doubt this. Taking, say, Britain as an example I find no evidence that it is, today, a less acceptable society than in the past. For most people who live there the opposite seems to be true. True, the British Empire, a product of Britain's monopoly of industrial power, was a civilizing enterprise of major significance (as even Marx freely conceded) and it was more humanely administered than any other Empire known or remembered. Yet it was, like other empires, based on the sword and on an ultimately degrading class structure, and the side effects of massive human misery both psychological and material, which would have outraged Solzhenitsyn. The press is pretty bad, yet it has at least not deteriorated since the days when jingo hate sheets were accusing Oscar Wilde of 'hunnish erotomania', to cover up the imbecilities of British military leadership in the Great War. The electronic media have reproduced the evils of the press in an immensely aggravated form, a fact not due to moral decay but to technological progress.

Democracy may be by its very nature 'unheroic', its citizens selfish hedonists as Tocqueville already observed, without Solzhenitsyn's anger; yet commerce, industry, science and culture flourish better than under any alternative systems of government known to men. It is also probable that it is a system dependent on the hegemony, within it, of Anglo-Saxon institutions. It is very likely true that the West has lost much of its war-making capacity. Yet that was true already in the 1939-45 war, for had it not been for our alliance with Stalin's hated USSR, the land-war against Germany could not have been won. We defeated the Nazis by burying them under a gigantic heap of military men and hardware outnumbering tenfold their own, and in alliance with the most lethal totalitarian dictatorship in history. The military leadership of the allies was of remarkable incompetence, highlighted by the black humour of the situation in the hegemonial country of the enemy camp, where a grotesque psychopath had, as we now know with final certainty, total personal control of the war effort. All is not lost yet, for our developing links with China may replace the Stalin muscle of 1941-45, a scheme repudiated by the Russian patriot Solzhenitsyn.

One wonders how much of the currently fashionable cultural pessimism on the Right, among native citizens of the West, is not just biological pessimism induced by the painful biological processes of ageing. For they lack Solzhenitsyn's daemonic indignation and his passionate will to action. And also his ultimate hope for the future. Let us beware of what Karl Kraus called *Die Untergangster des Abendlandes*.[23] Solzhenitsyn is right in claiming that the American social and political structure is not suitable for Russia. Let us be grateful for having in our midst a man of genius and great eloquence 'from the other shore' whose total personal independence allows him to speak freely and widely and whose message is therefore unpolluted by 'tactics'.

---

[23] *The Decline of the West*, the title of a book by Oswald Spengler.

21

No Breaking Ranks If You Weren't in the March

(*The Age,* January 12, 1981)

A review of Norman Podhoretz's Breaking Ranks: A Political Memoir (1980)

In a world increasingly dominated by the Middle East crisis, the influence of Jews on American politics and culture is becoming a major topic in any intelligent discussion of future contingencies. That influence is based on three major factors of American Jewish existence: the concentration of Jews in a few key urban electorates, the political activism of American Jews and, in particular, their truly gigantic contributions to party campaign funds, mainly to those of the Democratic Party, and finally, the very high proportion of Jews in the verbalizing and ideology-producing professions within the media, the universities, publishing houses and in the entertainment industry. The above-average wealth of the American Jews ('money power') is not crucially important per se, for it was present in countries such as pre- war Poland, Hungary, Romania and indeed in pre-1917 Russia, where the

Jews had the status of pariahs despite their wealth.

A striking feature of Jewish political behaviour in America and to some extent elsewhere in the free world, is an anomalous correlation between their political behaviour and their socio-economic status. It is summed up in the well-known crack that American Jews live like WASPS and vote like Puerto Ricans. American Jews are largely Democratic voters (even the egregious McGovern collared 65% of the Jewish vote). In the mass they tend to be 'small l' liberals and they have, until the early 'seventies, supplied much of the manpower and brainpower for American left radical organizations. The anomalous socio-political profile of American Jewry has its historical roots in the cradle of American Jewry, which is Eastern Europe, including Russia. It stems from a socio-political tradition moulded by threats to Jewish existence which were seen to be located almost entirely on the Right. Conversely, promises on liberation and emancipation came from the liberal Centre and, most energetically, from the Left, including sections of the revolutionary Left.

After the transplantation of the East European Jewish *shtetl* to the 'New World', the 'red shift' in the American Jewish political spectrum received a tremendous boost by the rise of Hitlerism, and by the sympathies which the Fascists seemed to enjoy among conservatives, and on the Right, in most industrial democracies including the United States. It was at the height of Hitlerism that the minuscule American Communist Party reached a Jewish membership of 95% (a microscopic fragment of the Jewish American population, then about five million). Jewish political behaviour in America is, in fact, a striking example of a cultural lag, in that ideologies and attitudes formed under conditions of extreme deprivation in the iniquitous slums of Eastern Europe were retained, developed and cherished most inappropriately within the context of a free and meritocratic republic.

At least since the Six Day War and increasingly so since the Yom Kippur War, there has been a Jewish move to the Right in American politics. One can discern at least three principal reasons for this: (1) The survival of Israel is now plainly and totally dependent on American power. (2) The Soviet Union has finally emerged, in a manner impossible to ignore, as the principal threat to Jewish existence everywhere. A superpower, it is the only major force still promoting, often in a clandestine manner, the otherwise discredited doctrines of anti-Semitism, and it is the *de facto* fount and origin of the effective physical threat to the existence of the State of Israel. (3) Finally, the urban turbulence associated with the accelerated emancipation of the American blacks has given rise to a populist form of black anti-Semitism, directed in particular against liberal Jews with a long record in the American Civil Rights Movement in the US. What we are witnessing in America at the present time is a new Exodus of the Jews, this time from the Left towards the strange territories of the Right. And, at least among the verbalisers of this great trek, Mr Norman Podhoretz has emerged as the principal *vertrekker*, a Cicerone, a guide of newcomers in unpromised and often unpromising old lands, a powerbroker mediating between the newcomers and the somewhat baffled old settlers.

Norman Podhoretz is the editor of the American Jewish magazine *Commentary*, a post which he has occupied since 1960, when he assumed it at the age of 30. *Commentary* is published by the American Jewish Committee, a conservative Jewish organization. The magazine is now one of the most influential journals of opinion in the Western world. The founder of *Commentary*, the late Elliot Cohen, was a pioneering figure in American Jewry in that he initiated a process in American Jewish life which has now become irrelevant, namely the emancipation of the then predominantly still semi-alien East European Jewish community of the US from the myths (by no means largely or even predominantly Bolshevik) of the Russian Revolution.

At a time when it was still very unfashionable to do so, Elliot Cohen along with a few other Jewish activists launched a campaign of implacable public exposure of the Soviet system and its propounders in Jewish America. It was not an easy or life-enhancing task, as Elliot Cohen's suicide in 1957 tragically testified. After an interregnum described by Norman Podhoretz somewhat opaquely in his autobiographical masterpiece *Making It,* Podhoretz assumed control of Cohen's heritage. He introduced initially three major changes: he turned the magazine away from Cohen's uncompromising, and morally based, anti-Communist line towards a more conciliatory attitude; he tarted up the publication by scanning the market for chic authors; and, finally, he transformed a rather musty, crusading and purely Jewish entity into a bright and sophisticated forum for cultural and political celebrities of all kinds.

Since Podhoretz's early zig away from anti-communism, which coincided devastatingly with the Vietnam War, a zag to the old position took place gradually around 1970 and Elliot Cohen's spirit may again rest in peace, though the overwhelmingly moral orientation of that spirit may perhaps be a little uneasy about the motives of the recent zag. How much good a crusading anti-Soviet publication of barely disguised Jewish identity can do in the world of today remains to be seen. That *Commentary* wreaked havoc in America in the years of the Vietnam War and contributed appreciably to the disorientation of the intellectual home front and to America's defeat - with its establishmentarian solidity, much more so than the bizarre and offputting 'kids' from the radical sects - is beyond reasonable doubt.

Most English reviewers have read the above book as New York-centered cultural gossip and it can indeed be so read. It is a tale of 'who did whom when and how' in the New York political and literary world. Thus the bad taste and unappetizing personality of one totally uninteresting Jason Epstein is lovingly described (he is a friend). We read that he sends his shoes for resoling to London; and the time he used his first obscene expression in public (thereby capitulating to the counterculture) is solemnly recorded. We are told about a little indignity committed by Hannah Arendt in private conversation with the author after the attacks on her following the publication of her masterpiece *Eichmann in Jerusalem*. One reviewer has described Podhoretz's book as a 'mafia hit job', and there is some truth in that allegation though the nature of the mafia is not entirely clear.

A long list of OK figures from the Kennedys to Susan Sontag and Noam Chomsky are given the low down. Conversely, hate figures of Podhoretz's former mates such as Lyndon Johnson, are posthumously rehabilitated. What makes the overall character of the book so unpleasant is the fact, that it is first and foremost a bean-spilling operation, directed against a large number of public figures and ideology-makers whose personal friendship and confidence Podhoretz had assiduously sought and cultivated, or at least not rebuffed when they were proffered. This is forgivable as an incidental feature in the works of grand apostasy, such as the books of Koestler or Whittaker Chambers, yet it is not quite permissible in the journalism of a man who could not really 'break ranks', because he never marched. He just hung about on the sidewalks, vaguely cheering or booing as the fashion of the day indicated. Podhoretz claims, without credentials, the status of a heretic. That claim must be denied for there was no creed he ever embraced. In his book he betrays no doctrine, for he never committed himself to any. He merely supplies many useful people with damaging data, thereby becoming himself a useful person. Podhoretz is a culture-political gossip columnist; no more, no less.

In claiming that Podhoretz's book is one of the most important to come from the US since the Vietnam War this reviewer is consciously making a somewhat Stalinoid assessment, for he judges a book by its political utility rather than by its literary or intellectual worth, which is virtually nil. The fact that the book is a hatchet-job is not at issue, for the literature of character destruction contains some of the great masterpieces of contemporary English prose. Thus Muggeridge's disposal of Anthony Eden ('Boring for England') is a comic masterpiece which permits of no resurrection of the victim. Yet quite apart from the immense disparity in the quality of the writing between say, Muggeridge on Eden and Podhoretz on Kennedy, Podhoretz's vastly inferior products are less implacable. There is always some escape door, some allowance on which to hang a future revaluation. For Podhoretz is an operator who also moralizes when it is expedient to do so, and who may have to praise tomorrow what he had to condemn today. Whereas, Muggeridge is a moralist first and foremost who may sometimes operate in a private sort of way just a little. His basic commitments are not movable by 'reasons of state' of any kind.

The great French reactionary philosopher Joseph de Maistre has become notorious for his celebrated essay in praise of the executioner, whom he describes as the main pillar of the social order, unjustly shunned by polite society. De Maistre's witty and perverse arguments, restated in plain English, amount to this: somebody's got to do the rope and trap door job professionally and he is unlikely to be the sort of fellow we would like to have as a guest for dinner. It is in this sober and pragmatic spirit that one can write in praise of Norman Podhoretz, for the price of replacing politics by aesthetics is too high just now.

22

Arthur Koestler: The Mole of God

(*Quadrant*, October, 1982)

Koestler's work can be analyzed, very roughly, into three major components which are not entirely sequential. They are (1) his communism-centered phase (2) his contribution to the history and philosophy of science, and particularly his critique of behaviourism, and, finally (3) his preoccupation with Zionism. Unlike the first two components, which can be 'dated' (the dividing line between Koestler the political writer and Koestler the philosopher of science being, roughly, 1954), Koestler's preoccupation with Zionism (that is, with his Jewishness) spans his entire life and is the key to his entire oeuvre. How does one know? Hermeneutically, by way of *Verstehen*, as a result of one's shared ethnic and cultural background, and from the simple truth that, if an issue bugs you all your life and interpenetrates everything you do, it is the dominant impulse of your existence.

Ian Hamilton's *Koestler: A Biography*, (1982), is unsatisfactory, but it has a number of incidental major virtues. Hamilton concentrates far too much on Koestler's not very interesting private life after his arrival in England during the Blitz of 1940. He is obviously not equipped to deal with Koestler's philosophical work, and the parts on Koestler's involvements with communism tend to be a mere simplified restatement of Koestler's own masterly autobiography. Nevertheless, the publication of Hamilton's book is a good thing for a number of possibly unintended reasons. The author's very intellectual weaknesses make him a faithful chronicler, for he cannot tell Koestler's toy-bombs from his real ones, and not having any axe to grind, he does not 'discriminate' (a double-edged word, if ever there was one!). The book is wholly about Koestler and not at all about Hamilton. Also, it presents the lot, it lets all cats out the bag, including the very old ones, which everybody, including, one suspects, Koestler himself, would rather not see again. Among those almost forgotten ones are the data about the dominant role of Koestler's Jewishness.

Koestler and Communism

It would be pointless to restate Koestler's significance as witness and analyst of *sovietica*. Its principal features are now common knowledge. Inside the Soviet bloc Koestler, the anti-Communist, still retains his impact as a permanent and handy source on the origins and nature of the regime's incurable criminality. It is an entirely different impact from the one he once had on a previous generation in the West, whom Hitler drove to the altars of the God that Failed. That Moscow is ruled by implacably malevolent men has not been news to anybody since 1956, and it has certainly no news value whatever for the contemporaries of Aleksander Solzhenitsyn and Lech Walesa. *Darkness at Noon* remains the definitive and unrivalled literary masterpiece of this aspect of Koestler's work, the rest being essentially supportive, very high-class journalism of a didactic kind, probably the best Sovietology that will ever be produced.

The interesting thing about Koestler's anti-communist work, today, is its now established ineffectiveness, despite its general dissemination and impact, which it shares with all other truthful and hence 'hostile' analyses of communism. For it cannot be denied that since 1940 when *Darkness at Noon* was published, or for that matter, since 1954, the year Koestler bade farewell to anti-communist politics, the global balance of power has shifted drastically in favour of the Soviet Union, and that Western policy towards Moscow in 1982 is much more confused and unprincipled than that of the Attlee and Truman era.

It is quite likely that Koestler's immensely sensitive antennae ('all antennae' was Muggeridge's first impression of Koestler), gave him foreknowledge about the practical futility of the Witness testifying in the wilderness. For what was the point of it all, if as late as 1973 virtually the whole Western intellectual establishment on both sides of the Atlantic could more or less actively promote the cause of Ho Chi Minh. True, there were conflicts of disloyalties among the *literati* but the unity in infamy was solid. The war in Indo-China was lost in Western universities by treason of the clerks, if anything more massive and far less excusable than that of the 'thirties and 'forties. The reason why? Veteran participants in public debates on ideological issues in Western societies soon learn, or else they learn the hard way, that Western politics is about the internal structures of status and wealth. The rest is supportive rhetoric. The 'supportive rhetoric' includes of course 'defence and foreign policy' which the more intelligently constructed bits of the supportive rhetoric invoke as ostensible grounds for preoccupation with communism.

Seemingly ideological debates (e.g. on Vietnam, Poland, Israel, to give a few recent examples) are coded language-games, hiding the real games which are complex manoeuvres in the pursuit of class and status, including ethnic status. A lot of it is coded class and status defamation (e.g. union bashing or raids on 'Croat terrorists'). Thus much, though by no means all, of the Australian Vietnam controversy was a continuation of the Mannix v. Protestant ascendancy (now deemed 'effete') struggle conducted by other means. The recent Australian debate about 'Lebanon' was motivated (though not instigated) by interest in the socio-economic role of Australian Jews. The debate bored most people outside the Jewish community except the four or five key participants, which provides evidence for the almost complete lack of a general interest in Australian Jews, and the consequent absence of any present danger of anti-Semitism in this country. A corresponding example is the impossibility of getting an IRA (or anti-IRA) lobby off the ground in Australia; the traditional rivals for the soul of Australia, the 'Proddies' and the 'Micks', have finally made it up and merged into one nation. Their respective socio-economic profiles are becoming indistinguishable.

The cryptographic nature of ideological politics is particularly evident in colonial societies such as the USA and Australia, which are rich, and perceived by universal consensus as safe, i.e. sheltered against invasion. For the only way in which a public can be sensitized for the message of the likes of Koestler is by personal experience, either actual, or imminently, clearly and presently threatening. It is bootless to inveigh against this state of affairs, and call people names (consumerists, materialists, hedonists, etc.) for human action and human experience are related to each other in a manner which, simply, precludes certain impulses and responses. Political sensibilities are generated by basically personal social experience, within a given social milieu. The KGB was very clever when it expelled Solzhenitsyn, a religious fundamentalist who does not understand the West, and kept Sakharov, a skeptical scientist who does, at home. The upshot of all this is that the message of *Darkness at Noon* can only be understood when it is too late. How is it then, that we are still around unconquered? The internal contradictions of communism and above all, the Sino-Soviet conflict are doing the trick for us.

Koestler and Behaviourism

In 1955 Koestler announced: 'Cassandra has gone hoarse and is due for a vocational change'. The new vocation, history and philosophy of science was, in part, a return to his early, pre-communist interest in scientific journalism. Yet it was much more than that. His *Sleepwalkers*, of abiding value mainly for the outstanding portrait of Kepler, is now a standard text in every respectable university department concerned with the history of scientific discovery. The most important effort was, however, reserved for a sustained assault on behaviourism in modern psychology (*The Act of Creation, The Ghost in the Machine*). Many would share Koestler's disdain for behaviourism but they may disagree with his reasons. For Koestler's opposition to behaviourism is metaphysical rather than practical and epistemological.

Koestler rejects behaviourism because he finds a universe in which behaviourism could be an appropriate methodology of studying the human person, intolerable. There is an alternative, and probably sounder reason for rejecting it - namely its substantive barrenness, which is due to its intellectual fraudulence or conceptual confusion. Koestler's attack on modern behaviourist psychology is a part of his general rejection of philosophical mechanism. He does not believe that complex aggregates could be exclusive and exhaustive functions of their constituent parts. Nor does he believe that emergent properties of complex aggregates should be viewed, programmatically, as functions of hitherto undiscovered properties of their constituents or as effects of interactions with hitherto unsuspected or unnoticed aggregates. From this there follows a disdain for philosophical mechanism in biology, an attitude of barely disguised unease with modern genetics and neo-darwinism based on random mutations of genes combined with chance-environmental selection.

The same metaphysical sources nourish Koestler's 'thirst' for some sort of cosmic purposiveness, a nit-picking attitude towards the soundness of the probability calculus, an interest in parapsychology and the fury of his assault on psychological 'behaviour theory' of the kind produced in the 'forties by Hull, Spence, Skinner and popularized in the 'sixties and 'seventies by Eysenck. And finally, Koestler uses some recent findings in brain research to construct a neuropharmacological model of original sin and redemption (*The Ghost in the Machine*). Koestler sees all components of the body, of society, and of the universe as 'Janus-faced' - self-contained structures *as well as* components of higher-level self-contained structures (he coined for them the term 'holon'), which are, in turn, components of yet higher-level structures, etc; and all of them 'Janus-faced' in what is presumably a rather Aristotelian, teleological universe including hidden purposes in a mysterious, empirically not really accessible, domain which occasionally pops out in parapsychological ways and which we generally intuit.

Koestler is, in fact, a crypto-mystic among the illuminati, a sort of mole of God among the heathens of the Enlightenment, though he is himself Janus-faced in a different sense: a double agent working for occidental mystics among rationalists as well as for occidental rationalists among mystics. One is relieved to know that he rejected quite unambiguously oriental mystical quackeries which became fashionable during the Pandit Nehru days (*The Lotus and the Robot*). Believers in psychobiography may be able to perceive in all this a restatement in post-enlightenment terms of the traditional Catholic world picture which Koestler, like other products of the Holy Roman (Habsburg) Empire may have imbibed in his early milieu, perhaps even from some of his inevitably Christian domestics and nannies.

Unlike Koestler, contemporary opponents of behaviourism within the profession of psychology and related social sciences reject it on pragmatic grounds, for its sterility. One might even argue that by treating behaviourism as a threat, Koestler pays it an undeserved compliment by taking it too seriously. Views on the reason why behaviourism is useless tend to differ. The one adopted here has been stated with devastating brevity by Wittgenstein:

> The confusion and barrenness of psychology is not to be explained by calling it a 'young science': its state is not comparable with that of physics, for instance, in its beginnings (rather with that of certain branches of mathematics, Set theory.) For in psychology there are experimental methods and

conceptual confusion. (As in the other case conceptual confusion and methods of proof.) The existence of experimental methods makes us think we have the means of solving the problems which trouble us; though problem and methods pass one another by. Wittgenstein: *Philosophical Investigations,* XIV.

The concepts of psychology outside its very few, neuropsychological sub-branches – as, indeed, those of all other modes of discourse centering on persons, cultures, and human society – and the experimental methodology kidnapped by philosophers from the physical sciences are *unrelated*. Attempts to relate them were the category-mistake which has turned psychology, for quarter of a century, into a useless bore.

Modern 'behaviour theory' is an unviable compound of a misunderstood 'philosophy of science' based mainly on an application of Russellian logic to the structure and methods of physics and on a misunderstanding or misuse of Pavlov's work. Last but not least, it is a *tour de force* induced by social embarrassment with the obviously hopeless attempts to turn introspection into an 'exact' scientific instrument. Putting it brutally one can describe behaviourism as an attempt by status hungry psychologists to 'create' scientific psychology with the aid of a philosophical brew, extracted by logicians from their analysis of theoretical physics and presented in a recipe on how to cook 'science' in general.

The irony of behaviourism lies in the fact that it is a paradigm case of the most serious of all sins a positivist can be accused of, namely restricting his research by taboos derived from loyalty to a philosophical deity - in this case the restrictive tenets of logical positivism and its Oxonian successor ideologies. More than the much abused 'armchair psychologists', the ratomorphs (as Koestler calls them) of behaviourism have replaced empirical enquiry by dogma induced acts of 'satisfaction' offered to a philosophical conception. A philosopher's stone replaced meaningful enquiry by what Sigmund Koch, the leading historian of and subsequent defector from 'behaviour theory', calls 'meaningful' research. Historically, 'behaviour theory' is the stillborn child of a marriage between philosophically raw American behaviourists and logical positivists, men such as Neurath, Carnap, Frank, Feigl, et al., honourable and decent people who emigrated to America from central Europe to escape Hitler. Together they transformed psychology from simplistic but intelligible humbug into a desert landscape of unutterable barrenness, the horror of which only those who had to teach the stuff, year in year out, can fully appreciate.

For thirty long years, the white albino rat of impeccable Wistar stock, together with the forefinger, the eyelid, and the movements of the American sophomore reigned supreme in North American psychology departments. Now fully computerized, they are still boring for science, less confident of themselves, made tolerant by fear of the student movement, and spurned by the psycholinguistics who blew them. Chomsky's demolition of Skinner's behavior-theoretical analysis of language in 1957 is the only ground on which I would commute Chomsky's long overdue death-sentence, which he so richly deserves.

The one movement which blocked behaviourism from becoming a bogus psychological paradigm was psychoanalytic theory. After a serious of futile attempts by the behaviourists to 'operationise' Freud, i.e. to 'explicate' his theory in terms of the prick twitch (stimulus-response) ideology of official behaviourism, the project was passed on for behaviourist-futurist treatment, a favourite last resort. The standard operating procedure of the futurists in 'behaviour theory' proceeds, roughly, in the following manner: at present, in its primitive, pre-scientific state, psychoanalytic theory (or any other interesting psycho-social theory) must be indulged and permitted anthropomorphism introspection and the free use of mentalistic concepts. In future, when many more data of a physicalist kind will be available, it too will be 'reduced'. Behaviourists too hungry for instant scientific status (e.g. Eysenck) refused to go along with the futurists and simply rejected psychoanalysis as humbug, using crude medical validation procedures to make their point. It is, of course, true that psychoanalysis is not a science. It is a philosophy of culture, expressed for contingent historico-personal reasons in medical metaphors. Unlike 'behaviour theory' it does, however, address itself to actual social problems, and has now become, like other influential social philosophies before, a part of 'ordinary language'.

It is strange that of all of this Koestler's attacks on behaviourism say nothing. There is polemical abuse, 'knowing' scientisms, but barely any conceptual analysis. In part this may be due to Koestler's general lack of interest in philosophical analysis apparent from a dismissive little piece he once wrote about Wittgenstein. Yet another, more direct reason may be Koestler's unfamiliarity with the routinisation of the psychological research business, i.e. his lack of true professionalism. For a professional is not one who *knows* more about an academic subject than an amateur, but one who is familiar with the daily chores, swindles, arm-twistings and gimmicks on the low and middle levels of an academic workplace. Koestler is a member of high-prestige learned societies, personally acquainted with the top-brass of the British scientific establishment and on intimate terms with Nobel Prize winners. Yet he never worked in the ranks or on the middle levels of an actual academic or research department in psychology for a living. Thus, what he knew about the Comintern, where he did just that, he does not know about universities: the seedy features of their bureaucratic institutionalization, on the low and middle [level], where the actual trickeries and false pretences are cooked up to be handed for sale and advertisment to the *chefs* whose time is entirely devoted to fund raising and the higher levels of office-politics.

Koestler's critique of psychology is like the war-reporting of a correspondent who converses with staff-officers and generals, and never gathers primary data of his own at the front line. To press the Comintern analogy further: Koestler's knowledge of modern psychology is like the Soviet expertise of men who knew and read Lenin, Stalin, Bukharin, and such likes, but who never even heard of Munzenberg, Katz, Kisch, or, for that matter of young Koestler, and who, unlike young Koestler (or Muggeridge) never actually lived and worked for their living in the Soviet Union. Scientific dogma is not sustained by intellectual endeavours but protected as an ideology bestowing legitimacy on academic bureaucracies of various kinds. And, as in the Comintern, which Koestler knew from participant observation, the techniques of conflict are not struggles of ideas but contests for power pursued by administrative methods, i.e. by bureaucratic strategies. This is particularly true in the humanities and in the social sciences, where the powerful market forces emanating from successful technologies generated by Research and Development related to the physical sciences do not compel a modicum of intellectual integrity on the struggle of interest-constellations.

Psychology, sociology, and – the most bizarre of them all – political 'science' departments (at their best cosy sheltered workshops for journalists who cannot write) are not arenas of titanic struggles between rival *Weltanschauungen*, but strange bazaars without real trade, in which incessant haggling for carpets, secretaries, gadgets, trips, leaves and a large variety of funny monies is taking place. They call it 'research' and it is supposed to be impeded by 'teaching'. The low-down supplement to Kuhn's classic *The Structure of Scientific Revolutions,* a sort of tactical manual to guide the practitioners, still remains to be written.

Koestler's biologised restatement of the doctrine of original sin and redemption (*The Ghost in the Machine*) has been reviewed in some detail by this author in publication (*The Bulletin,* January, 1968). It can be outlined as follows: The enormous cerebral cortex of the human brain is activated by messages from a borderline (limbic) projection system with close neural links to the old brain, which mediates impulses from the viscera. The limbic projection system is tied to the old brain by powerful and ample neuroanatomical links, thereby forming a functioning unit, called the limbic system. Yet its links with the cerebral cortex are slender and devoid of feed-back loops. Interspecies comparisons will furthermore reveal that, whilst the limbic systems of, say, man and crocodile are not greatly different, the ratio of neo-cortex to the rest of the brain varies enormously, with the human neo-cortex being overwhelmingly predominant in comparison with other vertebrates. Thus, whilst man has an emotive apparatus not very distinct from low species, his cognitive computer is both immensely more powerful and anatomically isolated from the 'seat of the passions'. The upshot is a confused centaur with the appetite of predators and the intellect of a god.

Since the computer lacks monitoring devices feeding back into the organ of passions it will be unable to control the motivating forces, whilst being available for the construction of the most ingeniously fiendish technological devices to gratify them. Thus, man is a self- destructive freak, doomed to extinction, unless the computer constructs a bio-chemical device which will compensate for the missing control-links from the neo-cortex to the limbic system. The hope for redemption thus lies in the availability, in time, of a meta-ataraxic drug which will correct a biologically defective nervous system.

Shorn of neurological trappings the message is this: Man is a vicious but clever freak doomed to self-destruction, unless corrected from without. It is a doctrine with which St Augustine and his successors would agree. Yet they would frown on the notion that man can redeem himself pulling himself up by his own bootstraps, as it were, and replace the operation of divine grace by a bio-chemical device. Koestler's *Ghost in the Machine* brings out his intellectual double agency more clearly than anything else he wrote. For he is trying to subvert Christian belief by demonstrating that the living Christ can be replaced by a Gnostic prescription of manipulative self-help through biochemistry? Or else, conversely, is he not attempting to embarrass the optimistic temper of the heirs of the Enlightenment by demonstrating, in a language which they cannot reject, how hopelessly dark the light of reason must be, at noon and at any other time?

Koestler and the 'Jewish Question'

Koestler's preoccupation with the 'Jewish question' is the one issue he has never wholly abandoned. It cannot be otherwise in a Jew born in Central Europe within a time span of twenty-five years or so, before or after the turn of the century. For to be thus born amounted to a congenital catastrophe without parallel in European history. Unlike Polish and Russian Jews, Central European Jews born within the cultural orbits of Prague, Vienna, Berlin, and Budapest were assimilated, and unprotected by the walls of a separate ethnicity. They were good, and often, outstanding, Germans, Magyars, and, less frequently (for Czechoslovak Jewry was Germanised or Magyarised) Czechs and Slovaks. Unprotected by the walls of the *shtetl*, they suffered and died together but alone. Those who survived have to live with internal injuries which, like all chronic diseases, get worse with age.

Koestler's father was a Hungarian Jewish businessman, and his mother a member of the Prague German-Jewish patriciate. When Koestler was nine years old, in the first year of the great war, the family shifted to Vienna, the intellectual laboratory which produced both Theodor Herzl and Adolf Hitler and a lot of other things, which made Karl Kraus call the city, in an obituary written about the Archduke Franz Ferdinand, in July 1914, 'the research station for the end of the world' - a truly prophetic aphorism. On entering the University of Vienna, Koestler joined the Jewish dueling fraternity *Unitas* (of which my father was by then an old boy) whose most illustrious honorary member was Vladimir Jabotinsky, Begin's mentor, and founder of revisionist Zionism, then a strongly anglophile, non-socialist branch of an otherwise predominantly social democratic movement. In 1926 he left Vienna for Palestine to join the kibbutz Hevtsibah as a labourer.

It so happens that thirteen years later, I found myself in a kibbutz about a mile from Hevtsibah at the age of sixteen, and

Hevtsibah was the place I occasionally visited to chat with my father's friends there (some of them also Old Unitas boys) to alleviate my unhappiness. Moving from Vienna to Hevtsibah in the then malaria-infested swamps of the Emek[24] was no joke, but a sacrificial act of great moral seriousness. For the year was 1926 and Vienna a paradise for young men of Koestler's ilk. Koestler the hedonist did not meet the criteria of eligibility, then based on a socialist ethic which made Calvinism appear a doctrine for rakes, and had to leave Hevtsibah. He stuck it out in the Holy Land more or less down and out for three years and by 1929 he was in Paris as correspondent for the liberal German Ullstein newspaper chain. By 1931 he had joined the Communist Party in Berlin, driven into it by the impact of Hitlerism. Within the party he did chores for the global network of Soviet disinformation agencies, then headed by Willy Munzenberg, and marginally, for Soviet intelligence.

As Thomas Mann pointed out, the Nazi period was a morally happy one. For the forces of evil then appeared to be defined with a clarity which is quite untypical of our rather *blasü*, sophisticated civilization. Whatever one may otherwise have suffered, there could have been no doubts or ambiguities where one's duty lay. There was plenty of scope for heroism but none for *anomie*. For once, the enemy was, indubitably, The Enemy. They were also happy days for communist greenhorns, as Koestler then was, because for a short time the Soviet disinformation agencies could actually do their job best by telling a part of the truth. The Hitler regime needed no embellishments to make the capitalist world which bred and supported it stink. About events outside the USSR, in the years 1936-1939, the London *Times* actually lied more and more dangerously than *Pravda*.

Almost all major jobs which Koestler did for the party carried great personal risks - and entailed torture and violent death if

---

[24] The Jezreel Valley (also known as *Emek* Yisrael) is a flat area of the Galilee in northern *Israel*.

bungled. He was certainly not one of those Left intellectuals, who, in Orwell's withering aside 'happen to be always somewhere else when the trigger is being pulled'. In Spain, he escaped a fascist firing squad by a hair's breadth and the trauma of imminent execution appears to have altered a 'cool' Bolshevik attitude to 'liquidations'. The Great Terror and Munzenberg's name on a KGB hit-list were the last straws and he left the party. Shortly after his illegal landing in England, the first news of the mobile gas-vans disposing of Jews began to filter through. It seems that from then on his Jewishness overwhelmed him and towards the end of the war and shortly after, and again under physically dangerous conditions, Koestler worked furiously and quite obsessively for the creation of Israel.

There is fairly conclusive evidence that his writing and pamphleteering contributed significantly to the swaying of the relevant committees and commissions which are normally repelled by the wailing *schmalz* of official Zionist propaganda and by the general style of Jewish pleading. Koestler's pen was a major force in getting the numbers for the formation of a Jewish state. Shortly after the founding of Israel Koestler wrote his own peculiar 'Zionist' testament, which appalled the British Zionist establishment. It was followed by attacks and counter attacks in the Jewish press. The final and definitive statement is contained in the essay 'Judah at the Crossroads' (in *The Trail of the Dinosaur*) published in 1955. It constitutes what one may call the Koestler Thesis, and it is next to *Darkness at Noon* his most important contribution to politics. It is, in fact his answer to the problems posed by the Holocaust. It corresponds closely to my own views and I shall restate it in my own way. The Koestler Thesis is in fact far less shocking than it sounded to the Anglo-Jewish communities of thirty years ago, for it summarises views not very different from those stated at the turn of the century by the unsentimental founders of the movement hardened by virulent anti-Semitism such as Theodor Herzl and Ber Borokhov, a marxist-Zionist, and the most sophisticated of the Founding Fathers.

The Thesis is based on the originally Weberian proposition that the Jews are a self-segregating entity of pariahs. They are now neither a race nor a nationality, and the vast majority have no religious beliefs, though once most of them adhered to a religious doctrine of redemption with highly nationalist and vindictive overtones. Their socio-economic distribution is lopsided, i.e. virtually no blue collar and all white collar, with higher average wealth than the host-nations, yet without corresponding status (Borokhov's famous 'inverted pyramid'). The so called 'Jewish characteristics' are stigmata acquired, predominantly, by millennia of social learning under conditions of disprivilege, yet also by selective breeding of certain characteristics to the exclusion of others (e.g. brain rather than brawn) and by genetic drift ('inbreeding') in small geographically segregated communities.

The central doctrine of the religious Jew in the diaspora was the Promise of Return to the Land of Israel, and the principal devices of self-segregation were strict sexual and dietary taboos excluding commensuality and Gentiles and exogamy, and a complex general chain of rituals which made ordinary social intercourse with persons other than Jews virtually impossible. The self-imposed stigmata were, of course, immensely aggravated by the hostile external pressures, which they did not cause but which they facilitated. There is no evidence that the separatism of the Jews ever imperiled any host nation, but the evidence is overwhelming, that it imperiled for millennia, and since 1870 in the most acute manner, the Jews themselves.

The 'Jewish problem' can thus be stated as one of Jewish self-destruction. It is *only* a problem for the Jews, for the Jews of the diaspora have never threatened anybody but themselves. Any attempt to derive aid and comfort for anti-semites from the Koestler Thesis can be done only by turning the thesis into its political opposite. The only viable solution to the 'Jewish problem' is assimilation. Yet assimilation cannot be achieved without psycho-social normalization which is precluded by the 'inverted pyramid' of the Jewish economic profile and by greatly over-learned techniques of mutual separation between Jew and Gentile consolidated by old cultural traditions. The solution, therefore, entails the creation of a Jewish State, which will provide a milieu of psychosocial normality for those who wish to remain Jews. Those who wish and can assimilate to whatever host nation they are living with will be free to do so, without the burden of renegacy[25]: for the promise has been fulfilled. The Land is now available for the cost of a single air fare to Israel.

The Holocaust has demonstrated that the enlightenment does not protect the Jews of the diaspora from destruction, and that the weakening of Christian orthodoxy, the traditional source of the fateful Christ-killer myth and, hence, traditional anti-Semitism, far from helping, actually aggravates the danger; for the post Christian varieties of anti-Semitism are much more deadly, since they cannot be evaded by conversion; as, for example, in fifteenth century Spain. Koestler's advice, therefore is to emigrate to Israel or else to assimilate without reservation and residue. After a brief period of diaspora support for Israel (say five years) the links must be severed. The Israelis have already lost most of the traditional 'Jewish' characteristics by auto-emancipation within a nation state, and the diaspora Jews will lose them by assimilation. For a Holocaust survivor, it would be both impossible as well as grossly dishonourable to pretend not to be a Jew and to forget Israel. Yet he has no right to pass the burden on to his children.

The specifically Jewish contributions to our culture and morality are organically integrated with Christianity and its secular *sequelae*, a part of our general cultural heritage. They have not been a specific Jewish preserve for about two thousand years. Hence the disappearance of the Jews will be no *moral* resource loss. And as for other Jewish excellences (the Einstein-Freud-Marx syndrome) they are not *Jewish* excellences but simply contributions to European culture by Europeans who happen to be Jews. And even if there were specific 'ethnic' Jewish components in the

---

[25] Going back on a promise or commitment.

above-average contributions of secularized Jews to culture, the price for it is too high on both sides. The risk of inflicting on future generations the equally appalling fates of innocent victims and dehumanized killers is excessive and fear of it is amply warranted by historical experience. To those who still waffle on about a non-specific 'Jewish mission' in more or less schmaltzy tones, Koestler gave the following devastating reply:

> Apparently the official organ of British Jewry still regards 'the ideal of righteousness and brotherhood' as a Jewish monopoly; it actually drove its message home with the somewhat dated quotation: 'and ye shall be unto Me a kingdom of priests and holy nation'. If the paper's claim were to be taken seriously, it would mean that Messrs Ben Gurion and Mendes-France, Comrade Kaganovich and Henry Morgenthau, Albert Einstein and Louis B Mayer of Metro Goldwyn-Mayer, are all commonly engaged in carrying out a specifically Jewish mission. It is precisely this kind of turgid bombast which gave rise to the legend of the Elders of Zion and keeps suspicions of a Jewish world conspiracy alive...The fallacy of postulating a special Jewish 'mission' and 'tradition' becomes evident if we consider that in these terms Disraeli was part of the mission, Gladstone was not, Trotsky was part of it, Lenin was not; Freud was, Jung is not; and that the Jewish readers ought to prefer Proust to Joyce, Kafka to Poe, because the first in each pair is part of the tradition, the second is not.
>
> '*Judah at the Crossroads*', pp126-127, 132-133

The practical implications of the Koestler Thesis can be summarized thus: (1) Jewishness has become a pointless self-destructive burden for those who carry it. (2) Its resolution is possible by the interacting effects of a Jewish nation state, and by assimilation of the Jewish diaspora. (3) After a brief period of protective tutelage the State and the diaspora must part company.

A quarter of a century has elapsed since the Thesis was formulated and it is now evident that it does not work. In a curious book published fairly recently, *The Thirteenth Tribe* (1976), fifty years after his kibbutz days the old man Koestler returns to his Jewish preoccupation in a manner which demonstrates again the paramountcy of it in his life. The principal theme of the book, namely, that contemporary Jews are predominantly descendants of the Khazars, a Turkic tribe from Russia converted to Judaism in the ninth century AD, is unimportant, and may very well be true. It is certainly more probable than the official story of orthodox Judaism and Christianity, namely, that Jews are semites descended from the 12 tribes of ancient Israel. For all practical purposes the bulk of European Jewry seems to be traceable to medieval Poland. How they got there is of interest only to fundamentalist theologians, historians, and cranks. Yet towards the end of the book, Koestler revisits, briefly, the Koestler Thesis and shows no signs of unease. The old precept 'emigrate to Israel or assimilate' is firmly restated. Yet what are the facts?

True, there is some assimilation. In the free world, particularly in its anglomorph heartlands, Jews do intermarry with non-Jews quite frequently, yet even in the USA at least two-thirds of all Jewish marriages are still endogamous. Anti-Semitism is being promoted throughout the USSR and the Soviet bloc by Moscow, and directed against fully assimilated Jewish communities. For the tragedy of Soviet Jewry is not that they are prevented from living as Jews, but that they are being forcibly derussified and rejudaised, in the early Nazi manner by a totalitarian anti-semitic government. Anyone who has actually *met* recent Jewish emigrants from the Soviet Union will be struck by the fact how totally *Russian* these people are, quite unlike their Yiddish speaking forebears. Yet Koestler was convinced in 1955 that Moscow will actually assimilate Soviet Jews with its customary brutality. It is, in fact, *disassimilating* them with its customary brutality. For most of them, permission to go to Israel is merely a way of getting an exit permit. Once out, most of them go elsewhere. And as for Israel, it finds itself on one of the world's major powder kegs, and depends for its existence totally on the protection of the USA.

As Vietnam, Iran, and many other examples in recent years have shown, American protection cannot be taken for granted, even if major American interests are sacrificed by not exercising protection. It is by way of the Jewish lobby alone, which in turn depends on the political influence of a *distinctively Jewish* and hence *unassimilated* American Jewish population, that US protection is secured. Thus the assimilation of Jews in North America, the largest and by far the most influential centre of the Jewish diaspora, and the survival of Israel have become incompatible. And what applies to American Jewry applies *mutatis mutandis*, though to a small degree, to other free world Jewries. For quite apart from strategic considerations, the standard of living of the Israelis is culturally tolerable only because of diaspora subsidies. *Israel is a powerful European Western society only because Diaspora Jewry keeps it that way.* If this linkage were to remain, the Koestler Thesis would fall to the ground, and the old horrors would return. The situation has become more acute with the passing of the generations, for the living memory of Auschwitz kept diaspora Jews on their toes, even if they were not formally Zionist. No normal Jew, with the fumes of Auschwitz in his nostrils could contemplate as possibly acceptable 'the liquidation of the Zionist entity', the key item on the PLO agenda. For too many know that terms like 'liquidation' are not used metaphorically East of the Channel.

The new generation of Jews has no *real* knowledge of the horror, only a *notional* one which, as Cardinal Newman observed in another context, does not suffice. It is, therefore, not surprising that the Israeli government should be worried about the future. For some time now a process, which one may call the Beginisation of the Diaspora, has been taking place. It can be described as the transformation of Jewish communities and organizations throughout the free world, into professionally organized machines for the exercise of Israeli influence and propaganda. The old free and easy relationship is being replaced by a bureaucratic one managed in an opaque manner. The process may be inevitable (which I fear) and necessary (which I doubt) but its implications must be faced without attempts at self-deception, which, unlike ordinary deception, is always worse than a crime: it is always a mistake. What are those implications?

Whatever sociological theories of anti-Semitism one subscribes to, they have one thing in common: they presuppose the existence of Jews as a recognizable separate entity within host communities, or, at least (as in contemporary Poland) living memories of such entities. In colonial societies with populations of mixed ethnic origins such as the USA or Australia, it is important not to confuse Jews with ethnics, for Jews are truly multicultural: they come to New Worlds from diverse countries with diverse cultural formations - ranging from British to Ethiopian. Unlike ethnics, Jews are not defined by one country of origin or one culture. Moreover, New World ethnics assimilate in two or three generations. In the last war Australians and Americans of Italian and German ancestry fought loyally against their ancestral countries of origin. In America, and to a lesser extent in Australia, many anglomorph Jews indistinguishable from WASPs disassimilated, by becoming Zionist, i.e. attached to what is now a very real state, with a very real economy and an extremely real armed force. And the process of disassimilation was in the direction of a state and culture from which they did not come.

For a Jew, Israel is not his country of origin but his country of the mind, a bit like Russia for an older generation of fellow-travellers. The absorption of ethnics entails toleration of a certain amount of cultural and possibly political separateness which disappears in a couple of generations. It sheds no light on how the new form of Jewish separateness generated by Israel will be ultimately received. The usual sequence of successful Jewish assimilation in X was from pariah in X via *parvenu* in X to plain X in two or three generations. The transition status of *parvenu* created resentment in older aristocratic societies, e.g. in America or Germany. In anglomorph colonial societies and to a lesser extent in Britain, new wealth is welcome and ostentation tolerated. Yet what will happen if the pariah is replaced by a separatist? Anglomorph societies are very tolerant of diversities, but perhaps because of it they become very edgy when their organs of sovereignty are being tampered with directly or by implication, particularly in Britain.

What will the future be like, given the following scenario: a powerful State in a strategic key area, subsidized by free world countries, maintains itself by manipulating in its interest a global network of pseudo-ethnics operating within powerful societies very sensitive about sovereignty? Moreover, the groups in question happen to be traditional targets of social opprobrium and suspicion. It would be pointless to spell out the obvious dire forecast.

There are less daunting alternatives. First, the spectre of a sort of Zionintern directed by the Israeli government is misleading because Israel is an open society. Without a totalitarian dictator – and neither Begin nor anyone else in Israeli politics even remotely resembles one – there would have been no Comintern as we knew it. Second, the peculiar sensitivity to Jews which led to the Holocaust was a specific, East-Central European characteristic under-girded by Teutonic thought styles. There is little of it in anglomorph countries, though one would perhaps not particularly enjoy living in the UK with four million unemployed, as a suspected separatist Jew. Yet, granting all this, it is essential to develop alternatives which would unite Israel from the diaspora and restore the plausibility of the Koestler Thesis, which is the only variety of Zionism an assimilated Jew can accept. A number of practical suggestions come to mind.

(1) The Likud leaders must be firmly told by as many Jews as possible that support for Israel does not entail support for them. For it is extremely unlikely that the Labour alternative would contemplate an analogue of the Beginisation program.

(2) Israel must strive harder for economic independence from the '*schnorr*' (a contemptuous Yiddish word used in Israel for the subsidized part of the Israeli national income, originally meaning

'beggary'). For Israel is not entirely immune from the ill-effects of 'foreign aid' on third world countries, analyzed e.g. by Peter Bauer. Guaranteed, ideologically extracted aid breeds political recklessness and adventurism.

(3) Jews must be reminded by other Jews that the ultimate test of allegiance is the gift of life. Persons in lucrative jobs in the diaspora who show symptoms of having internally emigrated to Israel, particularly men of military age, that is, roughly under forty-five, ought to be reminded that Israeli defence forces have an urgent need for manpower, particularly for its infantry units - not really replaceable by airpower in street fighting against guerrillas, as the campaign in Beirut has clearly shown. As tests of seriousness, the finger on the trigger, and the manifest readiness to shed one's blood are totally irreplaceable. It is, one regrets to say, a case of putting up or shutting up. This is how it was for my generation, of which Mr Begin is one of the most outstanding and heroic personal examples.

(4) Jews and other people must be free to criticize any act of any Israeli government without fear of being bullied, manipulated, or instructed about the errors of their ways in a certain characteristically hectoring manner by a growing number of peculiar people.

Old Holocaust invalids are Jewry's Old Diggers. They deserve the respect which is granted, in non-decadent societies, to ex-servicemen who saw action in battle. No more and no less. Claim to special respect does not entail personal achievement, for there is none. They are what they are as a result of a ghastly piece of bad luck in time and place of birth. Yet among them there are a few who have the gift, in C. Wright-Mills' words, to translate private problems into public issues. Of those latter ones Koestler is the greatest. Yet it would be unfair to ignore that Menachem Begin is not only another one, but he happens to be the only chief of state who on top of it also graduated from the GULAG, the only Old Archipelagonian among a lot of Wets in the free world's chancelleries. We ought to listen to their parting words, even if we must disagree with one of them.

In his book *Warrant for Genocide*, Norman Cohn, the British historian, gives an account of how The Protocols of the Elders of Zion were fabricated and how they included acceptance of the Final Solution. A powerful Jewish state, boosting its strength and influence through a bureaucratically managed Jewish diaspora which it controls is bound to generate those very impulses naturally, which the fakers of the protocols had to induce by falsification. Recent incidents, even in remote Australia, indicate that something like this may already be happening. There is no closer friend of Israel and the Jewish people among the world leaders than Malcolm Fraser. Yet after a recent entirely legitimate (though in my private opinion factually mistaken)* criticism of Israel's action in the Lebanon, he found it necessary to address himself directly to Australian Jews (about one half per cent of the total Australian population) and invite what he termed their 'leaders' for some sort of 'negotiations'. (This article was written before the Beirut massacres (September 1982) to which this comment does not refer.) Perhaps unbeknownst to himself, and with the best possible intentions, a political leader whose sympathy for Jewish and Israeli causes cannot be bettered has found it necessary to treat the minuscule Jewish fraction of his voters as representatives of a totally friendly, but nevertheless very influential *foreign* power.

The very fact that Fraser is a close friend, actually highlights the dangers inherent in the Beginisation of the diaspora. For once a dangerous image of you is shared by your close friends you are in real trouble. The concluding words of Koestler's essay, 'Judah at the Crossroads', though expressed with a pathos which sounds inappropriate thirty years later, are still worth repeating despite the style blemished by the passage of time. For the warning contained in them is, if anything, more topical today than it was in 1954, when the taboo on anti-Semitism was still functioning:

The mission of the Wandering Jew is completed; he must discard the knapsack and cease to be an accomplice in his own destruction. The fumes of the death chambers still linger over Europe; there must be an end to every calvary.

This essay won the George Watson Prize.

23

In (Mild) Defence of Karl Marx

(Quadrant, July, 1983)

Written to mark the 100th anniversary of the death of Karl Marx by an anti-Communist whose cast of mind was deeply influenced by Marx.

The year 1983 makes one appreciate one other beneficial consequence (there are not many) of Germany's defeat in the First World War. For had the Schlieffen plan succeeded in 1914 and had the Wilhelmine Empire established its hegemony over Europe, we might have witnessed, in 1983, the outbreak of a new malignant brain disease induced by an unprecedented epidemic of boredom: the two Great Centenaries of what had to be the top culture-patriarchs of our hypothetical Wilhelmine Europe, Richard Wagner and Karl Marx, would have coincided.

Can one imagine what one might have to endure from the German *Bildungsbuergertum*[26] and its ethnic clones – half Marxian and half Wagnerian, and some of them mixed – in terms of celebration, musical noise, seminars, cultural events, and Congresses for

---

[26] The German educated and intellectual bourgeoisie

Cultural Boredom? For long operas breed long Congresses and long speeches. The style of Marxism would have been, of course, totally unrelated to the contemporary Marxism-Leninism-Cannibalism of Pol Pot, Mugabe and their likes. Marx's true vocation of a German philosopher would have dominated the field. The word *Gulag* would not have existed, yet many a journalist would have had to come to grips with Concrete Universals. Alas, it was not to be: the Cossacks invaded Prussia ahead of schedule, von Kluck blundered on the left, Galieni's taxis got to the Marne whilst the Army corps which would have smashed them were bogged down somewhere in Germany en route to the East[27], and the world was made safe for democracy first, and for our present sunny uplands (Churchill's term coined in 1940) later.

Marxism is now an exhausted intellectual enterprise. There is nothing new to be discovered about it, yet what 'Marxist studies' actually are has to be restated from time to time, since the word is used almost exclusively for the misleading language games of cops employed by one or more of the most vexatious Caesaropapisms in history. The term 'Marxism' as used by better academic professionals stands for at least five logically independent bodies of studies: (a) the theories, ideologies and opinions generated strictly and only by the man now buried in London's Highgate Cemetery; (b) the above as well as the products of his serious contemporaries and successor disciples such as e.g. Engels, Stalin and Trotsky; (c) the study of Marxist political parties; (d) the study of modern sociology (and, perhaps economics), the former virtually unthinkable without the inspiration or irritation of Marx's thought; and, finally (e) Marxism as a branch of political criminology; that is, its function in contemporary communist societies.

The central weakness of counter-celebrants such as Conor Cruise O'Brien, Kenneth Minogue and locally Anthony McAdam, is that they are trying too hard, to deduce (e) from (a). For it is not

---

[27] Military manoeuvres during the first world war

entirely true, though of course largely true, that the doctrines have always led, when applied, to intolerable regimes. Not in Austria before February 1934, and not in the Marxist section of the Israeli Kibbutz movement. There are grounds for insisting, still, that the way from (a) to (e) was strictly contingent. Philosophers of science will know that anomalies in a paradigm, however *prima facie* minute, are ignored at one's peril. And, for that matter many sensible people still do prefer Kuron to Cardinal Glemp, and Sidney Hook to Robert Nozick.

Psychopolitics is a most dangerous enterprise, particularly if combined with psychobiography. The fact that Marx was a cantankerous autocrat means nothing. So is the most influential and persuasive philosopher of freedom of the post-war world, Sir Karl Popper. This really is just gossip in the ordinary usage of the word and shouldn't be used. The fact that Marx did not take bribes and tempting offers (e.g. from Bismarck) and that a hundred years of diligent muck-racking did not rake out a single instance of political corruption or manifest intellectual dishonesty is decisive. Micropolitical faction fights are poisonous everywhere, among the émigrés of post-1848 London no less than among the various self-appointed Apostolates of, say, Cambridge or Melbourne. Let us admit it: Marx was a great man, one to whom I for one would have deferred unconditionally in my youth had he been my teacher, and whose displeasure would have reduced me to moral insecurity and anguish.

What are his abiding achievements? He turned the question '*cui bono?*' into a near scientific discipline. The study of ideas and doctrines as *interests* in the manner of Weber and others would have been unthinkable without him. Without Marx, the sociologico-materialist theory of ideas – how do ideologies grow out of social class stratification, and bitchiness out of social pique, and all of them out of technological change – would not have commanded the deserved attention it does now. The squalid word 'principle' (also loathed, so I am told, by the late Dr Mannix) would not have been expelled from the vocabularies of intellectually hygienic men without Marx. On the negative side we all do know the worst for Marx: Capitalism flourishes. Classes in the industrial democracies did not polarize but proliferated. Revolutions did occur - at the wrong time and in the wrong places and never in an industrialized society. Patriotic sons of rednecks hunt the traitorous sons of millionaires in capitalist security agencies. Not only does the proletariat have fatherlands, but it seems to be the social class most appreciative of them.

The crossbreeding between Marxist and Narodovolist conceptions in Russia, and Lenin's *ex post facto* Marxification of political opportunities unanticipated by Marx, produced the monster which is at the bottom of our most pressing concerns. Marx's chiliastic features just may be to blame for Marxism-Leninism, but so may be the imbecility of German imperial bureaucrats who financed Lenin. And, for that matter, genocide was pioneered at Verdun and the Somme where praxis definitely preceded nontheory. There is a sense in which the toleration of the *Gulag* (or for that matter Auschwitz) would have been unthinkable without those nice elderly gentlemen in khaki who planned the 1916-18 offensives on the Western Front. They were none of them Marxists, not even the only intelligent one among them, who did less harm, a colonial Jew of Prussian descent called Monash, who therefore never made it, and who at least understood the industrial character of modern warfare.

As a living faith, Marxism, any form of Marxism, is dead in Transcurtania.[28] Kissinger's development of the silly image of the Soviet Union from that of a murky variant of Imperial Germany to that of a malign giant ruled by ideologues is a slight improvement, but only a slight one. Soviet motivation – the birds are singing it all over Transcurtania – is an entirely negative one. They know that they are no good. And the only way they can keep themselves going is by destroying or undermining all alternatives to themselves. Marx no longer comes into this, nor

---

[28] Beyond the iron curtain, i.e. Communist countries of the Eastern bloc.

for that matter, the man and thinker Uljanov-Lenin. Yet some intelligent sociology, strongly influenced as it must be by the work of the man buried in Highgate, may help us to defend ourselves.

24

Nineteen Eighty-Four

(*Quadrant,* January, 1984)

> '*If there is hope, wrote Winston, it lies in the proles.*'
> (*George Orwell Nineteen Eighty-Four, Part 1, Ch vii.*)

At the time when the first advance notices about *1984* appeared in the newspapers of 1949, I was an undergraduate at Bristol University, in my middle twenties, about six months out of Prague. The sheer delight of having escaped the Horror for a second time within a decade is hard to recapture thirty-five years later. It kept me in a state of bliss throughout my two years in Bristol, the happiest days of my life. It was also a period, when I lived in near-absolute harmony with my environment, and loved and respected not only my peers, but my 'betters', that is, my teachers – all of them. And I loved the country, England, in all its social, political, and aesthetic manifestations. Since my working day was still that of a pre-war Continental swot – from twelve to eighteen hours a day, with shop talk as my principal recreation – time for politics was severely restricted to bare elementary duties of a survivor from 'communazism', speaking up at the occasional meeting when Soviet affairs were touched and 'patiently explaining' to my comrades in the Labour Club, the official Labour Party society at the University of which I was a member, the need to resist Stalin.

I read my copy of *1984* on the day the first consignment reached Bristol. I still possess it — vintage Secker and Warburg 1949, purchased at George's opposite Wills Tower, the citadel of Bristol University which dominates the city's skyline. I understood the book at once – I had known Orwell's writing since 1943, the year my unit arrived in England from the Middle East – and I have never changed my mind about it. It was the most persuasive and brilliant attempt to explain to an English public what it was like to live in the Soviet Union, and what sort of society the Soviet Union actually was. Since I was barely six months out of Prague, there was for me no excitement of discovery in the reading: merely the fascination of reliving the recently experienced and the narrowly avoided, and heightened admiration for Orwell who put it so well to a yet unknowing world.

The early reviews and comments from my fellow-students convinced me that Orwell must fail, for the only people who will understand his message will be those who don't need it, and those who don't know will misunderstand. The first person I lent my copy to was the secretary of the Conservative Club, whose idiotic comment is scribbled in his own hand on the margin of page 208 [reproduced in the original article]. It reads: 'Labour Policy leading straight to communism'. Presumably by Attlee, Bevin, Morrison, and Cripps. The marginal entry above, reading 'Stalinism', is my own.

The best way of explaining *1984* today is by recapitulating what it is not:

(1) It is not an agonized cry of the dying Orwell. In so far as the book contains glimpses of warfare, they are no more than authentic reproductions of what any combatant, or for that matter any witness of the Blitz or of an average Atlantic crossing around

1940-1941 might easily have seen in the then not so distant past. As for the nature of life in Oceania's Airstrip One, it is simply *Another Day in the Life of Ivan Denisovich – before* being dispatched to the gulag, and throughout his interrogation. The terms, technical devices, and the jargon are anglifications of Soviet reality to fit English imagery, devices to strip the exotic and replace it by the potentially familiar. Ingsoc is Marxism-Leninism-Stalinism, doublethink (explained with unsurpassed brilliance) is 'thinking dialectically', newspeak is the party jargon used by higher and middle-rank apparatchiks, and duckspeak is the political language of the masses on the rare occasions when they speak official politics, as well as the sloganeering of low-level Party agitators.

(2) The book is not in any way whatever a manifesto against socialism, as the term was understood by Orwell himself and by his friends, from Michael Foot to Tosco Fyvel. It is not anti-Labour in any sense whatever. Current attempts to recruit *1984* for monetarism and related econometric models stemming from von Hayek, Friedman *et al* are absurd. Since monetarism is widely misunderstood in Australia as an ideological superstructure for tax evasion and graft, it is a violation of Orwell's personality as a moralist, which he undoubtedly was, to link him with it. The famous quote from *1984* 'it had long been realized that the only secure basis for oligarchy is collectivism' has indeed been long realized. For it was the distinguished austro-marxist ex-mentor of Lenin, Rudolf Hilferding, who spelt it out explicitly in relation to the Soviet Union in 1940, and one might add, not for the first time on the Left.

(3) The book is not a historical prophecy about the world in general and the West in particular, though extrapolations are among its pedagogic devices (e.g. the elimination of major wars and their replacement by warlets for bits of a huge Third World slumland, the scientific, and technomanagerial decay under totalitarianism, and the division of the world into three super power zones). It is, therefore, inappropriate to measure *1984* against 1984 and score pluses and minuses.

(4) The book is not a utopia, that is, a book about nowhere, for it is about somewhere, namely the Soviet Union as it then was.

What then is *1984* if we disregard the litcrit idiocy of treating it as a novel worthy of the full boredom of litcrit obfuscation analysis? The nearest definition is that of a Weberian Ideal Type of totalitarianism, based on the only fully available historical experience of Bolshevik Russia; an ideal type defined without sociological jargon, by one of the great masters of the English language, with brilliant neologisms serving to name entirely new and unprecedented experiences and assisted by a fictitious, yet entirely plausible case-history (the story of Winston and Julia) again constructed from ideal-typical individuals.

Much of the book consists of extracts from a mock treatise about Oceania by Emmanuel Goldstein – an undisguised replica of Trotsky in his terminal and frankly pessimistic phase – merging with the then new 'development' of Trotskyism by James Burnham, whose bleak views on the future of socialism Orwell condemned a few years before *1984* ('Second thoughts on James Burnham'). Thus in an intellectual sense Orwell did become more pessimistic, he gave up, 'officially' as it were, his disagreement with Burnham (a mock disagreement I felt on reading Orwell on Burnham, one of Orwell's rare, though not unique bouts of wishful thinking). For *1984* is a variant of Burnham's managerial society. Between 1940 and 1960 Burnham was the best American political analyst I knew, despite his many mistaken factual predictions and his unclear variant of conservatism. If Orwell conceded the argument to Burnham, it is no matter for shame.

As for the substantive content of *1984*, it is simply about life blighted by totalitarianism. A self-co-opting elite rules, totally, the whole of society, by systematic and total terror and propaganda. The function of propaganda is not to persuade, but to destroy the human capacity for assessing facts about anything. Memory holes destroy the trust in the usefulness of memory, they don't just suppress factual evidence. The cognitive part of personality becomes a source of thought-crime, whenever it reverts to 'conventional' empiricism, coherence, and thereby deviates from doublethink, newspeak or duckspeak. Empirical assessment and non-dialectical reasoning are redefined by doublethink as delict-punishable by vapourisation-liquidation. It's all a redescription of what already existed in Orwell's days: the drive against 'bourgeois' logic and positivism - their replacement by *diamat*, the physical liquidation of scientists and philosophers suspected of 'reactionary' trends, the arbitrary decision-making by Big Brother-Stalin in areas ranging from biology to linguistics, etc.

Only six months before reading *1984*, I was still diverting myself by lampooning Diamat in the Aula of Charles University, my helpless, and, fortunately uncomprehending listeners being newly brainwashed students from Professor Kolman's NKVD seminar, while trying to persuade my own beloved, if mostly unintelligible, teacher - the distinguished phenomenologist Dr Patocka - to get the hell out of the country. (In those days a battle-dress adorned by WWII medals still conferred some immunity on a Jew). He didn't, and his subsequent thirty-year long via dolorosa was terminated by presumably violent death at the hands of the thought-police, his crime being the launching of Charter 77. For a long time the "primary material" of my occasional dreams was a unified compound of personal experiences and bits from *1984*. The personal and ideal-typical nightmares had fused into one. What a distance from a happy outlook of the author of an advertisement in the Economist, just arrived in today's mail, which implies, that *1984* was a book against – computers!

1984 whilst not being, and not being intended as a historical prophecy or negative utopia, is prophetic in another sense, for it anticipates thinking in social theory, which was at the time virtually unknown. Thus Gramsci's ideas, on the link between power, the hegemony of certain psycholinguistic conventions and habits, and prevailing beliefs are developed in the last and intellectually most original chapter of *1984* with a lucid simplicity and sophistication, sufficient to secure for Orwell a distinguished place among sociological classics. It links up with Wittgenstein's notion of language-games as aspects of different 'ways of life', which, unlike the pseudo-Wittgenstein of the Oxford influenza zone of the 'fifties, is now beginning to make headway among English social theorists.

The crucial role of the proletariat in any effective insurgency against the regime is anticipated, and the reasons for it are spelled out in some detail: The prognosis is the obverse of classic Leninism: for the proletariat will revolt *because* it has no 'consciousness' in the dialectical (doublethink) sense, and cannot be got at. It lives in unavoidable poverty irremovable from the system, and can therefore unlike the intelligentsia not be bribed, at least not permanently. How the proles will shake off Big Brother is not anticipated: Orwell did not live long enough to witness Solidarity. It seems also that in Poland, and presumably in many places to follow, Oldthinkers and Newthinkers alike unbellyfeel Sovsoc. Orwell's basic trust in the common people and his distrust of the intelligentsia remained with him to the end.

Concerning the non-totalitarian industrial democracies, the UK Airstrip One included, *1984* is of little relevance and there is no evidence that the author intended it to be. Prophets of gloom to the contrary notwithstanding, life in the industrial democracies, and throughout the anglomorph world is incomparably freer and better for everybody than it was at the time when Orwell took the road to Wigan Pier. Cultural pessimism remains what it was when Spengler popularized it: a squalid Teutonic racket, which can be excused as a symptom of personal disappointment and ageing (I suffer from it myself, and it determines the choice of about fifty percent of my music consumption, the other fifty percent being Mozart), but if indulged publicly by people who obviously know the facts and figures, it must be condemned as a vice, as willful persistence in error, of which particularly Catholic moral theology used to be very unforgiving.

Orwell, the man with a fascist bullet in his throat (a real, nonsymbolic bullet) would never have re-visited Brideshead, for in places which never existed, there is no air to come up for. The snob who betook himself from Golders Green where he lived among the Jews, to Highgate which is classier, whenever he posted a letter so as to disguise his true abode (Evelyn Waugh) has little in common with the man, Orwell, who wrote thus in praise of materialism:

> The damned impertinence of these politicians, priests, literary men, and what not who lecture the working-class Socialist for his 'materialism'! All that the working man demands is what these others would consider the indispensable minimum without which human life cannot be lived at all. Enough to eat, freedom from the haunting terror of unemployment, the knowledge that your children will get a fair chance, a bath once a day, clean linen reasonably often, a roof that doesn't leak, and short working hours that leave you with a little energy when the day is done. Not one of those who preach against 'materialism' would consider life livable without these things.

Until about twenty-five years ago, Orwell had to be defended mainly against the calumnies of the KGB socialists. Nowadays, one has to protect his heritage against grave-snatchers from all sorts of 'smelly little orthodoxies' hunting for Orwell as a cult-figure. True, *1984* may yet come upon us, but hardly from within: only if we are conquered.

Our main problem is the loss of our capacity to face and fight wars, induced originally and indelibly by 1914-1918. And the related incapacity to understand books such as *1984*, which are written by people whose life has taught them that the risk of war, even of nuclear war, is preferable to Ingsoc as a certainty, if only because nuclear war will be part of it. For unlike our liberal Oceania, neither Eurasia under Moscow, nor Eastasia under Peking will tolerate nuclear protestors. And they are already fighting and aiming rockets at one another!

25

The Multicultural Enterprise and Its Consequences

A Personal Perspective
(*Quadrant,* May, 1984)

I got involved in the multicultural debate, more or less by accident. On my return from my sabbatical in England, in August 1980, I read in *The Age* that the ethnic broadcasting station 3EA had run into trouble with the Polish community in Melbourne. I rang a reliable Polish acquaintance in Melbourne to find out more. It seemed that whoever was running the Polish program at the time had put an interdict on reports of the nascent Polish uprising, thereby extending to Melbourne the policy of radio-silence then practised by the dying Gierek regime in Poland itself. I then contacted two people I knew on the management or whatever of 3EA. One tried to evade answers by bureaucratic nonsense, and the other attempted to pull rank by asking (in a mixture of several Levantine accents with a bit of Bavarian twang): 'Do you know who I am?' Before hanging up on him, I concluded with the obvious rejoinder: 'I wish I knew'.

I wrote a letter of support for the Poles to *The Age* (published) pointing out that whatever broadcasts may do for ethnic minorities here, they should not give aid and comfort to their enemies. In the upshot, the affair seems to have reached a satisfactory conclusion, due largely to the toughness and solidarity of the local Poles. This incident, and some rather odd recollections which started to make sense in retrospect, made me curious about what appeared to be a new emergent racket in the rapidly expanding quango gardens of the expiring Fraser government. This one, judging by some of the types it attracted – like a dead cat attracting blowflies – was more likely than any other to do serious harm to Australian minority groups, and ultimately, perhaps, jeopardise the security and stability of the country.

As a survivor, against overwhelming odds, of some of the worst ethnic catastrophes of this century, I am rather sensitized and trained to smell trouble in this area. After catching up on neglected homework concerning Australia in this field, I gave a few radio talks on the ABC, wrote a piece in *The Bulletin* and published a chapter of a more detailed kind in Robert Manne's *The New Conservatism in Australia* (1982), which I also presented to seminars in my university.

The following is a summary of my analysis.

The dividing line between ethnics and non-ethnics in Australia is not based on where a person was born, but on whether he is an anglomorph or not. Anglomorphs are defined as persons either born from Australian born parents, or immigrants from anglomorph countries where they were born (which means in practice, almost entirely from the UK and Eire). Australia is an anglomorph country, in that her institutions, habits, political structures, and ways of life, both secular and spiritual, are transplants from the British Isles where the English enjoy cultural and political hegemony. Non-anglomorph immigrants and Australian-born children from at least one non-anglomorph parent are defined as ethnics, respectively first and second-generation ones. The breakdown is 78.3 percent anglomorphs and 21.7 percent ethnics. Of the 9.3 percent non-Australian anglomorphs 8 percent are from the British Isles. The shift from anglomorphy to ethnicity between 1945-78 was 12 percent. The largest ethnic groups are, in rank order, Italian, Greek, German and Yugoslav.

The de facto ethnic policy of all Australian governments since 1947, when the mass immigration program started as one of eminently successful benign neglect, fostering assimilation in the second and third generations into the hegemonial anglomorph culture of the country. I concluded that this policy is a good one and ought to be continued, for the alternatives are separatism, apartheid, and ghettoes. The record of 'multiethnic' societies in this century is catastrophic, and we should, therefore, not tamper with the Anglomorph cultural homogeneity of Australia, which the overwhelming majority of Australians wish to see perpetuated.

The following extract from *The New Conservatism in Australia* (Manne, op.cit. pp.50-60) summarises my views on immigration:

> The third option, advocated here, favours the continuation of a substantial immigration program, more widely open to fleeing victims of communism from South-East Asia, and as a general rule a policy of intelligent but remorseless assimilation of ethnics into the hegemonial anglomorph culture of the country. If a ceiling on immigration has to be put, the criterion of inclusion ought to be flexibly biased in favour of those whose alternatives to entry are unjust imprisonment or death. This would clearly increase the proportion of South-East Asians at the expense of Continental Europeans and, perhaps, of immigrant anglomorpshs, without damaging the economic interests of Australia. The evidence that the quality of immigrants from Indo-China compares favourably with Australia's most numerous ethnic and Anglo-morph groups is already considerable. There is no evidence that the social distance between the anglomorphs and people from Southern Europe, the Levant, and the Balkans is less than that between anglomorphs and the type of Indo-Chinese who are likely to reach Australia. A history of ethnic bigotry against Asians,

among immigrants, should disqualify for residence in Australia, and incitements to aggression against ethnic immigrants on the part of people living here ought to be made a criminal offence. There is anecdotal evidence that some new immigrants from the UK have a disposition towards aggressiveness against Asian immigrants; appropriate screening tests should be incorporated into selection procedures in London to weed them out. Membership of the National Front and related organizations should disbar UK emigrants automatically from entry into Australia. Those who nevertheless slip through should be dealt with firmly by deportation, if only to discourage others. English racism is merely a nuisance in the mother country. In Australia, an anglomorph enclave in an alien sea, where assimilation of diverse ethnics is, literally, a matter of national survival, it is the political analogue of Bubonic plague. Criminalisation of intolerance between different ethnic groups would, however, be unwise (as against criminalization of anglomorph racism), if only because it does not, by the nature of things, represent a threat to Australia's anglomorph national cohesion, and it is very hard to enforce. The 'legal difficulties' created by this distinction can be overcome in various ways.

The law is an ass only when the rulers in collusion with lawyers want it to be one. The issue is not a hypothetical one, for the 1972-75 Australian government singled out for program-like attention what was then the most deprived ethnic group in Australia: the Croats. The same government conducted a campaign of defamation against the most tragically stricken, resilient, gifted, and adaptable immigrants this country has ever received, in terms which would not be tolerated in any other industrial democracy.

Had appropriate laws against racism and group libel been in existence in 1972-75 this would have made such conduct impossible, and saved many lives of abandoned and betrayed allies in a war we helped to lose. For even if anti-racist laws and legal provisions against group libel (like libel laws in general) can be misused to stifle free speech, and may at times lead to vexatious litigations by or against harmless eccentric individuals and groups, their presence on the statute book would act as a deterrent against delinquent governments.*

The torrent of stupid abuse which greeted what is, after all, little more than a justification and explication of current de facto Australian ethnic policy, very decent by world standards (except perhaps during the Whitlam years) indicated that important economic interests felt threatened, namely those of the new multicultural quangocracies, benefiting almost entirely either anglomorphs or a few totally emancipated ethnics.

The following is a prize exhibit, penned by A J Grassby:

> 'My two Australian godchildren of Chinese origin shouldn't have to apologise for being Australian to Michael Barnard, or Frank Knopfelmacher or the recently arrived Geoffrey Partington (who as far as I know is not a citizen)'. (*The Age*, Letters, March 3, 1984).

The Age behaved very decently over this and promised to print a reply. My letter, pointing out that I am not really worried about the IQ of the two Sino-Australians since godfatherhood has no genetic implications, was never sent, because the inevitable and predicted happened in the meantime and a backlash against Asian ethnics, the first since my arrival here from England in 1955, was unintentionally triggered off by Geoffrey Blainey's comments about the Australian tolerance threshold for Asian immigrants. The comments themselves are not really borne out by statistical evidence, but they are legitimate and entirely without malice.

The victims of the fraudulent 'multicultural' antics will be the most vulnerable, deserving, and competent immigrants this country has ever received, the Indochinese refugees from the Hanoi Gulag. The Left is in a bind on this: they hate the refugees for political reasons, whilst having to oppose racism. And the Right (outside the NCC) will find the appeal of racism irresistible. The outbreak will be contained, though some Vietnamese and Khmers will die as a result of it, since the Indochinese migrant intake is already being reduced, and it will be harder to protest against the reduction since the Minister of Immigration, Mr West, has behaved quite decently in trying to defuse the backlash on the media.

By identifying a policy of assimilation through upward mobility, advocated here, with racism (e.g. in Jupp's *Ethnic Politics*), the multiculturalists have destroyed the climate for rational debate on a crucial policy issue. The resulting exchanges of incivilities will henceforth be confined to the traditional Australian categories of White Australia racists, now released from their cupboards, to self-serving quango bureaucrats, recruited from the predominantly anglomorph ranks of the parasitic non-entrepreneurial bourgeoisie, and moles or just plain racketeers working for the guilt-peddling self-haters of the pro-communist left, located mainly in the universities.

The following passage, from a book published by a former Minister of Immigration in an Australian government, is self-explanatory:

> Willesee is a compassionate human being who felt a sense of guilt over the Government's apparent lack of concern for those Vietnamese who had been caught up on the wrong side in a civil war that was drawing to a sudden end. He had never worn his religion on his sleeve but deep down he was a devoted son of his Church and a Christian who tried hard to practice what he had been taught. He wanted Whitlam to recognize the realities of war and ease the restrictions applicable to other migrants.
>
> Whitlam refused and I supported him, saying that I saw no reason why we should take the risk of opening our doors to war criminals. But Willesee argued that this was not the proposition he was putting and stubbornly refused to budge in his fight for what he regarded as a humane approach. Finally, Whitlam

stuck out his jaw and, grinding his teeth, turned to Willesee and thundered, 'I'm not having hundreds of fucking Vietnamese Balts coming into this country with their religious and political hatreds against us.' Poor Don looked pleadingly towards me for help but I replied, 'No Don. I'm sorry mate, but I agree with Gough on this matter'. Indeed, not only did I agree with what he had said but I could have hugged him for putting my own view so well; unemployment had already risen to a very high level and my job was to foster migration policies that would not make the unemployment position any worse. Willesee gave up, but he continued to press his other recommendations.

(Clyde Cameron *China, Communism and Coca-Cola,* 1982, p.230)

26

Second Thoughts on Muggeridge

(*Nation Review*, 1984)

Critical comments about a social commentator Dr Knopfelmacher usually admired.

> There are two interiors which scarcely seem to have changed through the centuries, brothels and anterooms of ecclesiastical dignitaries, both expressing in their heavy hangings and upholstery, a certain continuity, a relationship with what is changeless in us and our lives; in the one case sensual, in the other, spiritual.

One wonders if Father Patrick Murray is at all familiar with Muggeridge's two autobiographical volumes (*Chronicles of Wasted Time,* 1972-73) – his supreme literary achievement – from which the above is quoted. The manner in which Murray confronted Satan in Claudia Wright at a recent talk-back programme, invoking Muggeridge's authority, indicates that he isn't. (May I hasten to add that I regard the Fathers Murray in our society, despite severe reservations, as unconditionally preferable to Claudia Wright, Bettina Arndt et al. both morally, and aesthetically). It is, incidentally, yet another symptom of the Catholic Church's present decadence that it permits its clerical officials and lay notables to consort with the creeps of the Festival of Light, the 'little people' of Muggeridge's resentment fodder.

The bond between Muggeridge and most of his devotees is that of a communion of hatred. Muggeridge more than anyone else I know, and better, expresses one's loathing, frustration, and contempt against a large variety of powerful and flawed people and institutions with definitive mastery. His treatment, for example, of the Webbs, of Kennedy, Eden, CP Scott and countless others, are character-demolition jobs of unsurpassed deadliness. Nobody singled out by Muggeridge can be resurrected. Like that of Calvin's God, Muggeridge's damnation is totally deadly as well as irreversible. The culprit's character – and I am using the term in its Reichian sense for a mask-like personality armour grown into the soft tissues and protecting them against reality – once dissolved reveals fleshly loathsome and sometimes pitiable creatures; Hobbesian human interiors, prompted by cupidity, fear and lust. True, not all of Muggeridge's character-operations succeed. I don't think he really brought it off with Churchill or Bertrand Russell, perhaps because they did not deserve such punishment. His occasional attempts at celebration (e.g. of an English prelate or Mother Teresa) sound unconvincing. When Muggeridge praises *anybody* one finds oneself asking unwittingly what he is really up to, or whom he is trying to spite by upstaging somebody else. There is a sense in which those he praises are his only truly innocent victims, exploited in a cause which is not their own.

Muggeridge's spirit moves me profoundly and I am a glutton for his writing, but I know that the spirit is not of Christianity. It is not Christ driving out the money-changers, but Thersites[29] mocking the great. Muggeridge is neither savagely indignant like Swift, nor wrathfully prophetic like Solzhenitsyn. He is like a faintly ghoulish surgeon revelling in the discovery of yet another tumour beneath a seemingly healthy surface, and wielding his scalpel with accuracy and gusto. The patient, meanwhile, dies and one does not quite

---

[29] A Greek god in Homer who abuses the powerful.

know whether the cause of death is the tumour or Muggeridge's surgical ministrations. Muggeridge's impulse is not a variant of Solzhenitsyn's holy anger, but its psychological inversion in a weak person, a process termed by Nietzsche *ressentiment*. (Nietzsche is a man whom Muggeridge grossly and deliberately misrepresents, misrepresentation being a vice not entirely foreign to him.)

Muggeridge purports to feel profoundly ill at ease in the modern world and he is capable of articulating this unease on behalf of millions. True one does sense very strongly that the times are out of joint. The feel of contemporary Western societies is bad. The doings of the media, both electronic and printed, the swinish intelligentsia and their cynical power and money-holding patrons have finally turned contemporary reality into a satire of itself, as prophesised by Karl Kraus fifty years before Muggeridge. Yet there is a catch in Muggeridge's 'despair'. We are told not only that the world is awful but that it is rapidly *getting worse* and that despair is *spreading*. The devil is actually *on the march*. We are regaled with true as well as unconvincing stories about the sinfulness of lust, materialism, sodomy, atheism – as if the message were new – as a sort of news-commentary. Muggeridge has managed to turn original sin into a permanently red-hot serial without boring anybody, a feat for which a Nobel Prize in creative journalism is surely overdue. In fact, of course, the chiliastic prophet of doom is a standard figure throughout the ages. And he is usually suffering from what Seymour Martin Lipset calls the 'quondam complex'[30] – that once, in one's youth perhaps, or in Periclean Athens, Republican Rome or under the universal rule of Pope Innocent III things were good, wholesome. The 'quondam complex' is the Right-wing psychological equivalent of the Leftist 'cities of the mind' in the USSR, Cuba, etc.

The comparative study and measurement of happiness through the ages, a sort of eudemonology,[31] or, worse, eudemonometry, are

---

[30] 'Quondam' - 'former' - the attitude of a group who feel they have been passed over and targeted, with no means of redress.
[31] *Eudaimonia* ancient Greek word for happiness.

unviable sciences. The reason why this must be so is demonstrable, technical and outside the scope of a column. Muggeridge castigates lust made safe by hygiene and pharmacology as soulless. He attacks 'hedonism' brought within the practical reach of the common people not by the 'first atheist state in history' as he misleadingly labels the USSR – they are producing Christians, we are told truthfully but with malicious glee – but by the unparalleled mass affluence spread across the Western world by the multinationals, and, therefore, ultimately by the hegemony of American style capitalism. Welcoming inflation as the means of 'dissolving our earthly treasures' and presumably helping us to bridge the gap between ourselves and Christogenic Gulag territory, Muggeridge is only being consistent.

How can Muggeridge be so sure that the quondam world - in which infanticide and abandonment performed the function of abortion, and where the combined effects of dissolution by terminal syphilis and 80 per cent infant mortality added the thrills of tragedy to soulless copulation, whilst making contraception socially harmful – was a better, more wholesome world? Were the religious wars of the 17th Century fought by sword, torch, musket and the plagues less horrible than contemporary conflicts? Was the very real impact of the Black Death less horrible than a rather hypothetical danger of future nuclear exchanges? Are we really sure that the world was a better place when the galley-slave spat his lungs out at his oar, propelling human sardine-boxes filled with freshly captured African slaves to the colony of an island empire where God blessed the squire and his relations, and kept us (for an average living span of 30 years) in our proper stations?

As I said, I too am a Muggeridge addict. It is an unhealthy addiction, like Wagner's music or sado-masochistic voyeurism which is quite at variance with the Christian vision. The orthodox Christian message, so one is told, is one of hope and *agape*, not of *ressentiment* camouflaged by hysterical exhibitions of television piety. The Church teaches that men are confused, disordered creatures, fallen from divine grace yet redeemable by acts of will guided by educated reason and assisted by the grace of God. The earthly society into which they are born is a naturally good institution, the government of which it is their moral duty to improve. And improvement is attainable, albeit imperfectly, on earth. Such was the teaching of St Thomas Aquinas, who, until the advent of Professor Charlesworth, held his place as the statutory keeper of political orthodoxy in the Roman Church.

I am not a Christian. Neither am I a Thomist. Muggeridge titillates me. Aquinas bores me. Yet my professional commitment as a social scientist forces me to concede that as *doctrine*, or 'social theory' if you wish, Aquinas contains a lot of sense, Muggeridge almost none. Cultural despair, no matter how wittily expressed, cannot replace a political doctrine though it may serve as an incitement to one.

27

Boring For Women

(With apologies to Malcolm Muggeridge)

(*Quadrant*, October, 1984)

Speaking up for moderate, rational feminists as opposed to radical ones.

Among the discussions into which I drifted by accident and against my better judgement, the present 'debate' on feminism pretty nearly tops the list. Yet having got into it, the only decent way of getting out, is to summarise my position as coherently as I can, and leave it at that. The linguistic ambiguity of the title is deliberate, and logicians will recognize that it does not exclude men.

The issue has now become a complex topic. The basic proposition of the feminists seems to be stateable thus:

> Seemingly, gender-determined modes of division of labour and of social roles oppress women. They are a device of maintaining masculine hegemony. Whether the latter is a by-product of a particular class structure is disputed within the movement, and a bone of contention between the Marx sisters and the rest.

The following, more or less testable problems follow:

1. Are biological sex differences partly or wholly determinants of female roles in society and their ensuing disadvantages, or are they more or less contrived biological pretexts for social oppression by men?

2. Do technological revolutions and intellectual changes introduce new variables which make gender-rooted structures of the division of labour and privileges redundant; therefore, clearly oppressive without redeeming social functions?

The ensuing sub-problems (e.g. gender-differences in things such as mathematics, resistance to stress, persistence, etc). are being investigated. The quality of the research is variable and not below the quality of that in other areas of the social sciences. Some of it is very good. Pot boilers such as the Greer stuff are becoming increasingly *passü*, which may make her recent outbreak of prodigal sonmanship in the direction of the Moral Majority intelligible. Startling conversations, particularly of merely the altar-teasing variety, are notorious as attention getters. For, to use Greer's own vocabulary, carezza - with coitus interruptus up one's sleeve in case one went too far - lasts longer than the average... and can be profitably serialized. This fact is not unrelated to the recently reconfirmed finding that romance will always beat porn in sales figures among women. I am deeply sceptical (on the basis of introspection and participant observation) that this is not so also among males.

I believe female disprivilege of an unjustifiable kind exists in our society, but it does not top my concerns for three reasons:

1. I am not a woman and I have a clean conscience on how I have treated women in my personal life. Also for a Middle European of my generation the stuff is *passü*.

2. I am not a specialist in this increasingly technical field, and do not intend to become one.

3. Other things – refugees, racism, totalitarianism, the Jewish question and social philosophy turn me on much more. One lives only once.

Why, then, do I write on this?

Yes, you have guessed it. Feminism, particularly in Australia, has unintended political consequences and *they* do turn me on. That does not mean that I am not really interested in the topic, using it merely as a pretext for political concerns elsewhere. I wouldn't argue, knowingly, a *bad* case, but I am prepared to argue a good case which does not greatly excite me, because of its political implications which *do* excite me.

There are about 50 percent women in the Australian population. Those in the work force are relative newcomers to industry, and, hence, vulnerable to radical or radical-ethnic demagogy and somewhat less amenable to constructive reformist unionization, a bit like the first-generation peasantries elsewhere inducted into industry. The middle-class part of the work-force tends to be formed in the ideology-producing parts of the tertiary education bureaucracies (e.g. in the 'Arts' faculties) where the hegemony of the Left can no longer be seriously disputed. (Another reason by the way, why female expansion into other parts of the tertiary system ought to be fostered).

If feminist demands in Australia were to be formulated and verbalized exclusively by enemies of the open society – hiding the appalling fate of women in communist countries or for that matter in enemy countries dominated by Moslem clerical gangsters such as Libya or Iran – the interests of the free world will suffer and the totalitarians and their accomplices will profit.

The political subversion of the feminist movement is already clearly apparent, particularly here and in the UK. Feminist activists are in the forefront of actions against US military installations, they promote vigorously luddite campaigns against the free world's industrial and defence development (anti-uranium) and, in Victoria, they attempt to exclude moderate trade unions from membership of the ALP. The dishonest and cynical way – from their own *value standpoint*, that is – in which feminists were drawn into these campaigns (women are too gentle for war, as mothers they suffer more with dying uranium babes in arms etc., all standard male chauvinist garbage, to use their own language) indicates unmistakably bolshevik-style leadership, quite apart from direct evidence.

It is, therefore, essential for defenders of the open society not to drive women into the networks of totalitarian cadres, by denying rational discourse on women's legitimate grievances, in the name of so-called 'conservative values'. (I believe that this is what Mr Michael Levin is in fact doing, however unintentionally, at least in Australia.) These things are happening in Australia and in America due to two different historical accidents, involving respectively Irish Catholics and East European Jews.

The most organized and effective opponents of feminism in Australia tend to be Irish Catholics, particularly those who have stuck to their fundamental beliefs despite the theological ravages of Vatican II and social mobility. They are also the people who, in the post-war years and later, have been in the forefront of the struggle against communism in the ALP. Since they are deeply committed to their religious beliefs they will fight for them from the standpoint of an ethic of conviction, rather than from an ethic of political responsibility. This is an honourable standpoint, vastly preferable, on both aesthetic and moral grounds, to Catholics of the Tiflis syndrome, who are very much more dangerous to the open society for other, more fundamental reasons. Yet the theological commitments of the conservatives will, indeed they must, conflict with intelligent strategies designed to wrest control of feminism from totalitarian agents. I concur that this is, in a way, a tragic (or rather mini-tragic) situation. But then life and politics frequently are tragic.

The situation in America is quite different and the hidden agenda there is Jewish, rather than Catholic. To the many eponyms which Jews of my generation had to suffer to prettify or uglify their pseudoethnicity (Israelite, mosaic, Hebrew, non-aryan, etc.) the term 'neoconservative' has now been added (yes, yes, I know, there is, or rather *was*, Patrick Moynihan). That American Jews have been overwhelmingly on the Left including the extreme Left; that they made up most of what was the American Communist Party and 80 per cent of the Vietnik cadres in the American academy throughout the 'sixties until 1973, is common knowledge and no longer passes as dirty linen not to be washed in public (cf. S. Rothman and S. R. Lichter: *Roots of Radicalism: Jews, Christians and the New Left*, OUP, 1982).

It is also no secret that the present Jewish march to the Right in America is the hidden agenda behind the 'neoconservative' movement. The principal reasons for it apart from genuine conversion to a decent respect for the opinion of mankind are the following factors: (1) the disappearance - in the third and fourth generation - of East European hangups from the political consciousness of American Jews, and their political integration into American political 'normality'; (2) the total dependency of Israel on American military and economic protection; and (3) the growing conflict between the Blacks and the Jews, aggravated last but not least by the fact that the Jesse Jacksons of this world no longer depend on money from American liberal Jews, but get it increasingly from the Arabs.

The problem with the American Right-ward marching (neo-conservative) Jews – unlike people such as Sidney Hook, a social democrat virtually his whole adult life, as I am –is that whilst they have altered the content of their beliefs, they have retained the same political style, illustrated by the following ancient joke: On 21 June 1941 a group of New York intellectuals, all CP sympathizers, were sitting in a café discussing the iniquities of the imperialist war and the threat of American participation in it on the more dangerous – British - side. One of them had to go to the lavatory, and whilst there, the radio announced in a special news-flash that Hitler had just invaded the Soviet Union. On his return (ignorant of the new turn of events) he took up the conversation where he left off, attacking 'the war'. His companions promptly denounced him as a German Nazi agent, and marched out of the café singing 'God bless America'while giving Churchill's V-sign. It is a style I call 'Comintern conduct'.

Having turned to the Right on foreign policy and defence, the 'neo-conservatives', like the chained prisoners in Plato's cave, have to turn their whole persons. One by one *Commentary* and allied publications have proceeded to demolish *all* elements of the 'liberal' syndrome, not only its blameworthy anti-anti-Communist aspects, but aspects of *Kulturpolitik* unrelated to Marxism - one of which happens to be the social emancipation of women. That sort of thing will do 'us' (I mean Jews) or for that matter anybody else, no good. If exported to a provincial backwater such as Australia, it may, actually, do a lot of harm. A former denizen of New York bohemia preaching to an uncomprehending Australian public the blessings of Irish-Catholic fertility cults will confirm the addicts in their loyalties and annoy some of the brighter pagans, and make them wonder why American Jews should be shipping coal to Newcastle.

To borrow a bit of cominternese myself - the conservatism *a l'outrance* of former radicals, including former Marxist-Leninists is, unlike a participation in the defence of freedom, 'objectively harmful'. Its only unintended innovation – in the light of modern Israeli realities – will be the growth, already noticeable, of anti-Semitism, in places where it has been politically extinct or virtually unknown as a significant political variable.

The 'former denizen of New York bohemia' is most likely Norman Podhoretz, who visited Australia.

28

The Vietnam Debate Revisited

(*Quadrant*, October, 1989)

Why it was a just war to begin with, why it was a total defeat for the West and the continuing consequences of the debacle.

The Vietnam War resulted in an unmitigated and total defeat – military, political and moral – of the United States by a small and immeasurably weaker communist state. The only vague analogy of such a debacle one can think of in modern times was the defeat of the Soviet Union (disguised as a pyrrhic victory) by Finland in the winter war of 1940. Still winnable before 1 April 1968, the date of President Johnson's initiating capitulation speech, the actual defeat was the work of the Nixon-Kissinger regime, eventually paralysed by Watergate, but not only for this reason. The fury with which a group of liberal *frondeurs* set about to destroy Nixon, a man psychologically disabled for the function of an American president – despite the genocidal cost of such an undertaking – which must have been foreseen – had its roots within the Ivy league of the American East Coast rather than in South East Asia. For Nixon was the Hiss-killer, the man who caught – it seems ages ago – the old WASP establishment with their pants down, or so they thought, and he had to be punished.

Kissinger's role seems to have been that of a defeat-manager, immortalized by the then novel and now sadly established contributions to American political prose such as 'elegant bug out' and 'decent interval' (the time span between deceiving your ally and delivering him for conquest), as well as unguarded reiterations of false but clearly obsessive analogies between Central Europe of pre-1848 and post-1918. With Kissinger cast first in the garb of Metternich and then allegedly Walter Rathenau, yet one knowledgeable of the need to ward off *die Dolchstosslegende* (the German myth of attributing defeat in the Great War to the subversive social-democratic enemy within, rather than to official incompetence). Alas, what was myth in Germany became sober truth in America. In England, Central European refugee intellectuals desirous of gaining academic or political influence had to submit to a painful process of housetraining. Not so in the USA where the market ('of ideas') remains the sole arbiter. Hence the emergence into prominence of charlatans such as, say, Marcuse on the trans-Atlantic side, and outstanding men like, say, Popper, Koestler, and Labedz on the cisatlantic. The late Professor Hugh Seton-Watson once quipped that the rush of German professors to America was Germany's revenge on America for two major defeats in war.

The actual sequence of events can be stated with a minimal resort to *personalia*. The post-war world emerged polarized between the USA and the Soviet Union. The latter was committed to world conquest by way of spreading across the planet communist regimes modelled on the Soviet Union, ultimately controlled by Soviet military and police power. This fact was at first not understood by the US elites, then predominantly WASP. A realistic understanding of the Soviet regime in America was, at the time, virtually restricted to small, marginal and rather down-market groups of foreign-born or just not foreign-born labour activists, mainly of Jewish origins, and a few academic associates of theirs. The first important debate took place between such an academic moving rapidly from a Trotskyite position towards conservatism – James Burnham, an Irish-American – and George Kennan, an almost ideal-typical WASP.

Kennan was aware of the malignant nature of Stalinism and proposed to 'contain' it by a defensive strategy of plugging the holes wherever and whenever a Soviet tentacle tore through the fabric of a Western possession. In his book *The Struggle for the World,* Burnham opted for a preventive offensive strategy, the object of which would be American hegemony over the planet. The time to act was soon, preferably in the rapidly expiring time of US nuclear monopoly. The target of Burnham's polemic was explicitly George Kennan.

Burnham's strategy seemed more realistic if one ignored (in the manner of economists rather than people of Burnham's stamp) psychosocial variables. The dominant American tradition in foreign policy is isolationism, which was bound to reassert itself after a world war, along with the baby-boom. Kennan's push-meets-shove strategy, stopping short of an all-out brawl, is obviously more closely compatible with isolationism than the doctrine of *attaque a l'outrance*[32] applied globally. Containment won out – in practice – though political propaganda continued to be dominated by a 'roll-back Communism' rhetoric, particularly among Republicans. This was so throughout the first presidential campaign and subsequent presidency of Dwight Eisenhower. It was ended by the Soviet suppression of the Hungarian revolution in 1956 when the American realities were re-symbolised by Ike's alleged comment (from a golf course), 'I did not ask them to rise.' He actually did, in a way: for example, by the tone and content of Radio Free Europe). From that time onwards, but particularly after the accession to power of President Kennedy, the containment policy won out in the ideological sphere as well, embellished by congenial theoretical props.

It seemed then to many that the American Right talked loudly but carried only a frail golf-stick, whereas the Democrats, America's

---

[32] *Attack to excess.*

traditional war party, talked softly, more intelligently, and their economic outlook, at least, did not preclude the acquisition of a big stick. The emergent Kennedy-containment ideology, churned out at the time in thousands of volumes and papers in very many government or near-government subsidized outfits (the word think-tank was not yet in general circulation) can be summarized thus:

(1) Communism in its Stalinist form is unquestionably malignant, not livable-with.

(2) Hem it in, contain it, and it will change. Growth of managerial power at the expense of apparatchik power; loss of apparatchik-sustained chiliastic beliefs; the devolution of power inside the Soviet bloc and within the USSR as a result of liberalization; loss of empire by diversification of communism and polycentrism, and, finally, convergence – an ideological rapprochement, followed by mutual systemic interpenetration of Communist and American style executives – these factors must corrode and eventually dissolve communism.

(3) Western societies, safe under the American nuclear umbrella, are immune from internal communist takeovers because of (a) a high level of education and a tradition of peaceful conflict management among the populace; (b) the accomplished *embourgeoisement* of the workers; (c) the absence of a revolutionary intelligentsia as a result of a complete and gainful integration of educated people into the economic, administrative, and cultural systems of the open society; and (d) because of the near total internalization of the pluralist democratic, capitalist ethos among the general population.

(4) The premises under (3) do not hold in underdeveloped, ex-colonial or 'dependent' countries, which must, therefore, be regarded as the proper arenas of contest (including warfare) between communism and the West. The USA must hold this 'third world' by a combined policy of economic development and counterinsurgency, the latter being facilitated by communist polycentric disunity.

Looking back at the above program today, it is evident that the Indochinese debacle falsified the feasibility of (4) in a catastrophic manner, and thereby the overall feasibility of the Kennedy-style containment strategy. The actual debacle in Vietnam was brought about by the interaction of several minor factors and one major one. The minor factors were the absence in America of 'old hands' and special units familiar with colonial administration and warfare, of the kind the British had at their disposal, say, for the Malaya Emergency; the partition of the country into two at the Geneva conference of 1954 which provided the guerillas of the NLF with a privileged sanctuary in the already bolshevized North, and finally the lack of firmness (as against brutality) in the conduct of military operations - which was due to a manifest absence of clear goals and clear overall intent on the part of the US leadership. Which brings up the last and major cause of defeat: the collapse through subversion, treachery and psychological warfare of the principal home-front which wasn't at all in Indochina, where the Tet offensive brought about a near complete defeat of the NLF insurgency, but the USA.

In two world wars, propaganda techniques were developed, particularly by Britain, designed to undermine the morale of the enemy. An aspect of these, named 'black propaganda', was based on the correct assumption that the more disguised the hostile source of the propaganda, the more effective it will be. In the case of America's Indochinese war, the resources of the American Republic related to knowledge and ideology, and wielded by 'symbolic knowledge' sections of the middle classes in the Schelsky-Berger sense of the term, were almost fully mobilized to paralyse America's war effort in Indochina. No 'disguise' was required, for the effort did originate in authentic American institutions, public and private, and was conducted by the most powerful and prestigious parts of the American population: the upper-middle classes.

The social, religious and ethnic breakdown of the 'Vietnik community' has not yet been carried out in detail. The nature of the anti-American *fronde* was visible mainly through the (misnamed) student movement which did produce one useful contribution to knowledge. It undermined whatever rationally grounded trust there is in the right of the humanities social science segment of universities in our type of society to administer themselves without some kind of effective invigilation or to cohabit institutional space with scientific and professional faculties, whose nature and market preclude the type of delinquent conduct evident in the humanities and social sciences, tolerated if not encouraged by its elites. Throughout the war America was assisted by allies. The known military contribution of Australia was a mere segment of the total Australian effort, particularly in the field of counterinsurgency. The enemy propaganda effort here in Australia was, unlike the American, opposed by counterorganization throughout the universities. What made the local propaganda war comic was the fact that the material came almost entirely from top prestige institutions of our principal ally. Not even specific American spelling conventions and gimmicks (the latter not really understood here) were altered, such as 'defense' for 'defence' or 'Amerika'.

After the Kampuchean massacres – and the present looming horrors of the Final Solution of the robbed, raped, but still non-devoured and non-murdered 'non-political' refugees in our area – it is impossible to absolve from guilt those who were in positions of authority during the Vietnam war and who refused to stand up to the local saboteurs. The fact is that our environment is now in part dominated by regimes of which the inhabitants, irrespective of class and wealth, regard - in the most literal sense (and increasingly so) - as less endurable than slow martyrdom and death. At the time these regimes were being imposed we were still among the masters of the earth. We co-imposed them. For once, in an ocean of fake, simulated or fraudulently avowed 'compassions' and 'guilts', largely for nothing, we have copped a real one: it is our responsibility, *nostra culpa*, that children are devoured by famished mothers, or fed to the sharks by rampaging pirates, that human beings of many cultures (yes, for once truly multicultural) live under conditions of permanent crucifixion. And we tolerate among our representatives abroad a man who not so long ago exhorted our victims 'not to jump the queue' – presumably from *stabat mater* and *pieta* – amidst blood, excrement and shallow mass-graves.

Two events mitigated the dire consequences for us of the Vietnam debacle. One was the Sino-Soviet conflict which diverted the energies of our two global totalitarian enemies from external aggression to the pleasing process of mutual devouring. And the other, more recent, is, of course, the apparent disintegration of the Soviet empire, both within and outside the Soviet Union proper, under the eccentric baton of conductor Gorbachev. As for America, its value as a straight military ally remains dubious, but of less serious consequence, for the Soviet crisis has probably removed the Soviet Union as a likely military threat in the near future and perhaps for good. The totalitarian restoration in China has as yet unpredictable consequences in the field of strategy, though it brought us nearer in time to an event predicted long ago: masses of Chinese refugees heading to our shore from Hong Kong. What does one do with a million or so Chinese who shout: give us landing permits or give us death?

With America as the hegemonial power of the West, her internal techniques (perfected during the Vietnam war, of sabotaging a just war by fighting a legitimate American government) have been briefly available for export-chic and have contributed to moral decline in fields not directly related to patriotism, such as intellectual honesty in schools and academies, in family life, in politics and business. The use of TV as a near irresistible tool of instant disinformation is yet another consequence. When the practical implications of Ho-Ho-Ho-Chi Minh worship became painfully apparent, particularly in Cambodia, a revulsion against 'socialism' led to 'capitalist' chic, which replaced Ho by Ivan Boesky[33] – a revolutionary Socialist by a monetarist folk-hero. Having trained myself, following Weber, to respond to nausea by

---

[33] An American stock trader infamous for his insider trading activities.

objective analysis, I have to concede that even Boesky for Ho is an improvement, but I don't want to be in it.

As for the neoconservatives, they are, individuals apart, bad news as a movement. Originally marxist-leninists of stalinist or trotskyite denomination, they converted to anti-communist liberalism around the McCarthy period. During the Vietnam War many of them joined the Vietniks and advocated a Vietcong victory as a suitable basis for a settlement. During the deepening crisis following the Yom Kippur war they made the 'discovery' that without American military power Israel is doomed. Their presence around the Reagan administration made the Reagan presidency accident-prone, particularly in the Middle East.

To sum up: I supported the American (and Australian) military efforts in Indochina for strategic reasons linked to the defence of the Free World and of Australia in particular. It was a just war, as the alternative was predictable genocide; and it is just to support the tolerable against the intolerable. My support did not waver and would be the same were I given the impossible option of reliving the past. The effluxion of time has altered the general global situation, the main new variable being the crisis of the Soviet regime. At the time of Vietnam this crisis was unpredictable as an event calculable in space and time for practical purposes. By hindsight it just may be argued that the actual American debacle in Indochina, rather than a possible victory, might have weakened the forces which brought this crisis about. The totalitarian restoration in China, another factor which was hard to predict in time and space for practical purposes, will increase the already terrible pressures against Indochinese refugees, by turning three million Chinese residents of one of the most prosperous cities on earth into potential boat-people.

29

Bangs and Whimpers: The Soviet Crisis

(*Quadrant*, March, 1990)

I am quite sure, when the cracks in the Bolshevik edifice brought about, at last, a clear process of collapse, that I was not the only one who muttered to himself, questioningly, the appropriate Eliotry: 'bang or whimper'? And when less than a minute later I picked up my *Economist* from the mailbox there it was printed: 'neither bang nor whimper'. Lit. crit. Clichés, rather than the Navy, seem to be replacing whatever bond remains holding the Empire together. The *Economist's* application of Eliot's poesy may have been somewhat premature, for it was printed before the Bucharest-Temesvar massacres, when the Ceausescu couple died riddled with 120 bullets, yet sharing a single *rhesus sardonicus* (grin of death).

For all one knows, the beginning of the end happened in Poland, a country with an old tradition of saving Europe from Lenin's abomination. For, as Joseph Schumpeter has pointed out almost sixty years ago, there was next to nothing between Trotsky's war machine and the Rhine, except Polish manpower, capable of putting up a fight when the Bolsheviks invaded Poland in 1920. To understand the significance of the Polish events of 1980, it is necessary to recapitulate the way Bolsheviks think about revolutions. (It is now, of course, no longer a matter of fervent beliefs but of pretty 'automatic' linguistic or conceptual habits.) Lenin's theory of revolution is as totally elitist as Aristotle's, though intellectually corrupted by Hegel. The plebs, mob, the masses, the proletariat – call it what you will as long as it designates social underclasses – are disabled by deprivation, fatigue, booze, superstition (e.g. religion) or sheer lack of intelligence, and incapable of planning a revolutionary alteration of their misery. The best they can do is an occasional riot or acts of real or threatened labour-withdrawals. To transform this sort of spontaneity (*stikhiinost*)[34] of disaffection into political activism of a systematic kind, political consciousness (*soznatelnost*) has to be woven into their spontaneous fury by professional social philosophers of an activist bent of mind, organized in a conspiratorial manner. These revolutionary apostles are usually of middle or upper-class origin, highly educated and perhaps oedipally motivated against the generation of their parents. However critical one is in relation to this 'Freudian' interpolation into Lenin (known as the Feuer Thesis), the 'student politician' character of most of the Old Bolsheviks (as against the 'Stalin-bandit' type) stands out.

Unlike Aristotle, Lenin 'hegeled' himself into believing that the projects of the revolutionary intelligentsia 'belong' in some dialectical sense to the dim-witted proletariat, that the interaction is not just a rather one-sided political collusion between upper-class frondeurs and available proletarian foot-soldiery. The helpless rage of the poor and the scheming of the plotting clever ones have formed a dialectical unity. I prefer Aristotle's simpler language in which nobody 'really is' somebody else. The masses are the incarnated *matter* of the revolution, the brainy cadres in its incarnated *form*. Yet my favourite language remains purely

---

[34] Naturalness

empirical assessment of actions between interacting empirically identifiable distinct groups, without metaphysics.

The almost century-old tragic-comedy of errors, unintended consequences and very much intended knaveries, transformed the Bolshevik project into a now at last expiring system of human bondage unparalleled in history. There are, roughly, three historicist models of Bolshevism. The first 'Polish' one, emanating from basically Polish intellectual sources, defines Bolshevism as just another (probably the most unlovable) form of customary Russian mis-governance, marked by savagery, *chamstvo*,[35] and Asiatic despotism. The Polish version exists in many sub-varieties. It is based on the conviction that the Russian mental and social climate is likely to deform and ruin any system, however attractively delivered by the donor. Conversely the 'Russian' version sees Russian culture as benign, at worst slothful, symbolized in many ways by Goncharov's figure of Oblomov and presented most strikingly in Dostoievsky's *Brothers Karamasov*. Bolshevism is the result of intrusion, by fierce Westernisers, of cold-edged ideologies into the vast innocence of the motherland. The carriers are either foreigners – such as Germans, Letts, deracinated Jews - or westernized illuminati in general.

The third version denies Bolshevism at the present time any ethnic or ideological character, though an ethnic or ideological association in its early days is not disputed. On this view, the system benefits a group of criminal racketeers and exploiters, and their hangers-on, a colluding list of names – the *nomenklatura* – whose residual 'ideology' is an almost totally empty jargon traceable to the gang-syndicate's remote do-gooding historical origins. The sole object of the *nomenklatura* is to hang onto power and privilege indefinitely. This is achieved by policies calculated to keep their captives in a state of apathy born of helplessness, resembling in this respect Calcutta pavement dwellers, and maintain the outside in a state of insecurity and turbulence, thereby decreasing such residual hopes

---

[35] Boorishness, nastiness.

as it may still evoke in the system's victims. This Al Capone model of contemporary Moscow Bolshevism is nearest to my own, and it seems to prevail, generally, among Czech dissidents trapped, before 19 November 1989, within the Bloc. The Bolshevik system is totally devoid of legitimacy in the satellite ex-empire and largely also within the Soviet Union proper. The best known ideal- type of the system, anglified in detail, is of course Orwell's *1984*. Some features of President Havel's literary work are mellower attempts to come to grips with the way the system 'worked'.

The acquisition of the satellite empire after world war two weakened the homogeneity of the Soviet bloc. For, whilst the Bolshevik system was imposed by Soviet agents on the satellites, backed by the Soviet army and the KGB, its internalization was very much milder and superficial in comparison with the home country. For the combined effects of two colossal acts of genocide following in close succession, the collectivization disasters of 1928-33 and the ensuing *Yezhovshchina*[36] of the middle and late 'thirties, had the effect of transforming into a huge amorphous porridge, formless matter bereft of history making elites and traditions and at the mercy of an omnipotent *Vozhd*.[37] Nothing nearly as catastrophic happened to any of the satellites though the Polish record was pretty grim; yet not grim enough to obliterate, as in the Soviet Union, the nation's nervous system and bone structure.

The casualty rate of Sovietisation in Eastern and Central Europe was not a matter of millions but at worst of thousands, mostly four-figure numbers. It tends to be forgotten that the pre-war record of Nazism pampered us in matters of cultural pessimism related to slaughter. The worst 'peace-time' act of terror in Nazi Germany, the notorious 'Rohm purge' of 1934, yielded altogether 150 corpses, very much less than a daily yield of murders during the Great Terror in the Soviet Union or, for that matter, a daily train-load of gas-chamber fodder for a minor German extermination

---

[36] Stalin's great purge of the1930s, carried out by the Soviet secret police chief Yezhov.
[37] Leader.

camp during the Final Solution. As a result of the 'moderate' Bolshevik encrustation of the satellites, the pre-Bolshevik elites, family structures, customs and other political characteristics have been almost fully preserved beneath a mocked and despised alien facade. As a consequence of this 'uneven' distribution of Bolshevism, the satellites became a near permanent source of instability. Yugoslavia, shielded by massive Anglo-American sea power, was the first to bolt, and uprisings in Germany, Hungary, Poland and Czechoslovakia followed. In developing a strategy of counter-insurgency, Moscow defined an 'intervention threshold' by applying its own originally Leninist theory of revolution. As long as either the masses only – or else the intelligentsia - played up, Moscow grumbled, ordered a purge or two but did not send in the troops. When the two events, spontaneous disaffection among the underclass and ideological or dissidence among the intelligentsia, *coincided* in time and space, the Soviets marched in and replaced for a time indirect government by themselves, as in Hungary and Czechoslovakia.

And then, in 1980, within the key satellite of Poland, notorious for its reckless heroism, the intervention threshold was reached and vastly overreached. The masses were not only in spontaneous uproar but effectively organized in a trade union which represented the Polish *pays reel*. The intelligentsia, never really quiescent in Poland, acted as a brains-trust for Solidarity. To top it all, the undefeated Church, headed *urbi et orbi* by a Polish prelate, provided organizational and ideological counter-structures of unique firmness to the Bolshevik apparatus. And the Soviets did not march. They cursed, leaked and televised threats of imminent invasion, and in the end an internal manoeuvre, transparently doomed - replacing one satrap by another – was all they could do or would cause to be done.

The Soviet failure to march when the intervention threshold was clearly reached in the key area of the satellite empire marks the first visible beginning of the present Soviet crisis. Its origin is to me not clear. Economic difficulties cannot be a sufficient condition for the fall of a regime generated entirely by terror and unique in Europe for having transformed (and having emerged from it strengthened) the breadbasket of Europe – Ukraine - into an area of protracted famine and cannibalism. Once Poland was allowed to happen, Roosevelt's gift to Stalin – the Soviet bloc beyond the Soviet Union – was doomed and is no more.

There is no evidence that Gorbachev assumed leadership with a specific plan in mind. It is also unclear whether he realized that the Bolshevik system is unreformable. If he is a nominalist, in the scholastic sense of the word, that is, one who believes that apart from concrete, perceivable things we cannot refer words to anything, it does not matter much. For the medieval struggle between nominalists and realists had a highly political dimension. The realists insisted on evidence for the validity of abstractions (e.g. transsubstantiation) whereas the nominalists restricted evidence to perceptible data and invoked the authority of the Church as the only support for abstract notions. Thus, a nominalist General Secretary may redefine the supreme moment in the leading role of the Party as self-abolition, and Adam Smith's free market as socialist distribution among technological literates under conditions of high-tech. Conversely, realists will squabble about the true meaning of 'vocal farts', the robust nominalist word for abstractions. Let us hope that Gorbachev, or his successors, will be nominalistically disguised liquidators of the Bolshevik regime.

It seems that since the failure of the *apparat*, glaringly revealed in Poland for the first time, competent Sovietology has ceased to be a soothsayer's paradise. The old reliable models, based on the work and thought of the grand masters, such as Borkenau, Schapiro, Labedz, the New York Jewish Mensheviks such as Nikolayevsky, Abrahamovich, Dan, Levitas, et al., as well as imaginative and compelling essayists and novelists of the Orwell and Koestler kind, have all now been superseded by a huge J or U turn of history. Never since August 1914 has such a drastic shift in the political landscape of the world taken place.

In the many debates about this truly new deal, the effect of the Soviet crisis on the West is neglected. Some points are worth considering:

(1) *The vanished enemy.* Most of our politics depends on coalitions. This includes the big and small ones on which our statecraft is based; from NATO to the LCP-NCC combination of Australia's Menzies years and the many mini-coalitions in the plurality of our industrial and cultural institutions. It is a common fallacy to assume that the stability of coalitions depends on shared ideals and objectives. If anything, shared ideologies and aims, both material and ideal, are divisive, for they generate factions, infighting about 'truth' and dissolution. The long history of Christianity bears witness at least to this if to nothing else. A shared, lethal, clear and present enemy, however, can always be invoked to stabilize a shaky coalition. The enemy must be a kind of Hell which *really* burns, which has a really real presence. For example, the Gulag. And such an enemy was, since roughly the outbreak of the Greek civil war in 1944, Soviet Russia. Not Communism as such, certainly not since the Tito defection in 1948 *a fortiori* the formation of a de facto Sino-American alliance against Moscow in the late sixties.

With the growing decrepitude and dissolution of the Soviet Bloc, statecraft will glide into some disarray, both on macro and micro-levels. And even the enormous majority of people among us unaware of the fact that Kohl is German for cabbage will find it hard to see a new Hitler on the horizon, though a new Metaxas[38] is already alive and well (my closely guarded secret who he is). Statecraft may be on the way back to pre-1914 normalcy, which is no claim that normalcy is not at times bloodstained and awful and a quite legitimate territory of our Vale of Tears.

(2) *The new fifth column.* The victims of glasnost least deserving of sympathy are not the dead genocide chiefs such as uncle

---

[38] Authoritarian Greek Prime Minister from 1936 to 1941.

Koba (my improvement on Roosevelt's idiotic uncle Joe), and the assorted two or three generations of Chekists, the worst of them dead or totally senile. (Even my favourite candidate for a Ukraine-inspired war crime trial, comrade Kaganovich, died recently at the age of 90 or something). The real villains are the westerners who knowingly supported the Bolshevik regime. The least culpable among those are the 'true believers', who include the party-members and fellow-travellers, most of them impeccably well-intentioned though very foolish. The real danger comes from very powerful men whose career expectations are based on détente. For they need the enemy to détente with.

Those who denied what the Soviet regime was like, often quite knowingly, will be in the position of the well-known British savants who recognized Hitler's fake diaries as genuine a few years ago. Yet with one difference: they *saw* the plastic. The preservation of the Bolshevik regime in *some form* is a vested interest of very powerful men. They include, incidentally, 'indispensable' allies whose unpleasant embrace would become dispensable with the disappearance of a hegemonial foe against whom their presence is 'vital'. And so on. If a full restoration of the Cheka regime is no longer possible, less strident modes of *glasnost* combined with the kind of profitable *perestroika* (known in small quantities as bribery) might do. It is no accident – as uncle Koba would not have said on this occasion – that Dr Kissinger's first response to the undeniable signs of a major Soviet crisis was the proposal of a modified Sonnenfeld solution; that is, the negotiation of a new division of Europe to make us all happy again.

(3) *Quadragesimo anno*. The future of decency. 'Decency' was Orwell's favourite word of moral approbation. In his view it was virtually synonymous with socialism. Forty years later, during which many of our distinguished universities named their courses on the cheka-states 'Socialist societies', the equation has become a terminological inexactitude. Replacing socialism by social democracy will do me. An essay on this topic would simply *have* to be called *Quadragesimo Anno*. The struggle with the Soviet

bloc was not a contest between economic systems, though the latter differed. They also differed within and outside Auschwitz. Yet whether a planned economy, or rather a partially planned economy, must lead to Sovietism is an empirical problem which can be tested only by way of empirical hypotheses, forever open to refutation. Trying to avoid the hard labours of empirical enquiry by the moral blackmail of pointing one's finger to the Cheka state is — indecent.

I do not accept the proposition that the only answer to Bolshevism which is safe against its insidious re-emergence is a society of political-equals under 'commercial freedom', in which the rich and poor alike are forbidden to steal bread and to sleep under bridges. I abhor acquisitiveness, envy and greed. And ambition, other than of my own kind (to be right in argument on a number of fairly esoteric topics and being acknowledged to have been right if I was). With Ronald Hingley, I am aware of a dreadful moral paradox. In his Stalin biography of 1974 Hingley argued that whilst living within Stalin's realm was a fate worse than death, it bought benefits to outsiders not within his grip. For those ruling in the pluralistic West realized that, unless the conditions of the disprivileged are maintained at a tolerable level, Stalin's agents may weasel into power by seducing the miserable into support-fodder for themselves. In this manner the martyrdom of the *zeks* (the political inmates of Soviet camps) became part of the price we paid for Western welfare states. Replace *zeks* by coolies and you get Lenin's theory of imperialism in inverted form.

Not being an economist (an understatement), I have to rely on secondary or oblique sources. Peter L Berger's *Capitalist Revolution* is such a source, and a splendid one in my opinion. Its major thesis that capitalism, unlike all actually attempted forms of socialism, tends to produce more material well-being under most conditions strikes me as clearly indicated, even without much economic expertise. Yet I also wish to emphasize another key thesis of Berger's: unlike other systems, capitalism cannot be celebrated and glorified. It resists uplifting myths about itself. It seems to be intrinsically *unattractive*.

It is unlikely that from now on a fraudulent attractiveness will significantly compete with capitalism's overt unattractiveness. From now on decency in one country must never again depend on the martyrdom of *zeks* in another.

30

The Crown in a Culturally Diverse Australia

(*Proceedings of the Second Conference of the Samuel Griffith Society: Upholding the Constitution* 30 July-1 August, 1993)

A swan-song summary of Dr Knopfelmacher's views on Australian society.

It is more helpful in a paper such as this to alter the title from 'Crown' to the more verbose expression 'English system of government', for this is what we must be, essentially, dealing with; unless we desire to regurgitate trivialities, and eventually confirm Karl Marx's famous quip, that it is the mark of fools to analyse social and political systems on the basis of their formal constitutions.

It would be both tedious and by now vacuous, to repeat in a paper such as this the long history which culminated in the present English system of government (in which Australia also participates) and which is generally known as 'The Queen in parliament'. Also, it must be firmly asserted that not only the word 'Crown' but the very term 'English' is now inaccurate and 'foreign' in use. Continental Europeans use it for all inhabitants of the British Isles and often also for their clearly identifiable overseas offspring (e.g. the German term 'Englander'), irrespective of whether they refer to Cockneys, Glaswegians, Dubliners or, indeed, Melburnians, without being aware of possible ethnic slights. Among those slights, the linguistic annexation of Celts to Englishmen appears to some particularly obnoxious.

To avoid such naming issues, not without importance in a paper on ethnic culture and politics, we have coined the term *anglomorph* for all native inhabitants of the British Isles and their overseas descendants. Anglomorphy thus refers not only to the institutionalized population of a few offshore European islands, but also to the more or less powerful 'antipodean' and otherwise distant colonial offspring of those islands, whose men, guns and ships exported anglomorphy – both the human stock and the cultural and political structures – to form a mighty global 'colonial' set of establishments. The present Australian state ('Commonwealth') is one such anglomorph establishment i.e. politically and culturally 'English'.

A more realistic title of this paper would, therefore, become a query: 'Can ethnically diversifying Australia remain anglomorph?'

Before analysing the problem as it looks at present, an important empirical distinction has to be made. The most notorious and culturally influential factor in Australian politics, historically linked to ethnicity, has been the presence of the Irish in this country. And yet in the light of present analysis the Australian Irish are 'anglomorph'. Their politics, culture, religion, etc. are colonial co-importations from the plural mother country to Australia. Without their contributions, 'English' literature, religion, and, yes, warfare would shrink to little. And this applies, of course, very much to 'trade unions' in the often proudly self-proclaimed 'most unionised' country in the world. The Anglo-Irish conflicts, seminal to Australian politics, are, therefore, not locally generated provincial problems but co-imported mother-country issues, along with football, cricket, pudding and almost all varieties of grog. And, and of course, religion - yes, particularly Catholicism.

The Irish Catholics of anglomorphy may share with baroque continentals their trust in the mysteries and invisibles, but anything that can be seen, sensually appreciated and socially assessed is of a different world. Sceptics are advised to visit, say, Prague, for testing this pseudo-heretical proposition.

The overall conclusion about the effect of Irishness on Australian ethnic diversity is only seemingly paradoxical: the presence of a powerful Irish element in Australia not only does not enfeeble this country's homogeneity, but it decisively strengthens its cultural and political unity by bringing into Australian politics and culture the decisive formative influence of home-country rooted organic Irishness, almost totally linked to this colony's distant origins. Few things are more anglomorph than an Anglo-Irish conflict within an anglomorph Commonwealth. It is, therefore, essential to separate Irish politics from other ethnicities, such as they are.

Until the end of World War II, the more or less unspoken population policy of Australia was the retention of anglomorphy. The term 'white Australia' was a partial misnomer of this policy, the underlying assumption being that coloured Asians such as the Chinese must be more different from anglomorphs than, say, Slovaks and Serbs. Yet the emotive impetus was the proposition that colours cannot mix, that those who look like colonial 'natives' ('coolies') cannot co-exist with Sahib material, however well disguised. The underlying economic motives of 'white Australia' were perhaps not more but equally important.

The policy of exclusive anglomorphy as a necessary condition for immigration was given up in stages, and after a period of admitting growing quotas of European whites, the 'white Australia policy' was given away, at first verbally and eventually, at least in part, seemingly altogether. The differences thereby visibly generated to the character of the country seemed greater than the reality. Before the post-war immigration programme was launched, Australia was about 90 percent anglomorph. By 1975 anglomorphy dropped to 77 percent, the principal 'intruders' being Southern Europeans. The 'coloured' quota remained virtually unchanged. At present there seems to be a shift from anglomorphy to 'ordinary' Europeans and a distinct shift to Asians.

The 'racial origin' of immigrants – any immigrants – is overrated. The real question is this: can and will the offspring of non-anglomorphs, both Asian and European, coloured and white, become 'normal' Australians: that is, anglomorphs?

This writer strongly believes that they 'ought to', for the alternatives are, inevitably, ghettoized cultures, permanent strife and eventually civil wars. This writer is one who does not 'theorize' (in the pejorative sense of the word, for many theories are necessary and some are good) on matters of 'multiculturalism'. A (sole) survivor of a holocaust family, a mature witness of the Sudeten crisis and the outbreak of World War II in Germany, with subsequent months in the Palestine Police under British rule, and four years as a front-line combat soldier in Libya and Normandy under Montgomery, he literally *knows* what he is talking about, in the English sense which traditionally since Hume links the term 'knowing' with 'perceiving'. A near miraculous survivor, now of declining years (past three score and ten), he has only one remaining duty: to warn.

So far there is no evidence that the post-World War II intake of non-anglomorph immigrants generates opposition to our hegemonially anglomorph culture and political system. The occasional ethnic islands such as those of the Greeks in the Victorian ALP are ethnic 'accidents', sometimes exploited or exploitable by ethnic operators who might actually not clearly belong to the culture which they claim to represent. And then there will always be the 'Wiener Schnitzel' symptom (already Australianly misspelt by virtually all butchers), linked to the vanishing palates of the founder generation, and hopefully improving globally for ever the notoriously frightful gustatory appetites of the anglomorphs.

Love of the old country does not vanish with emigration, induced by poverty, general disadvantage, and persecution as almost all of our immigrations are. Some deviant ethnicity is bound to remain, passing itself on with the young generations and forming more or less attractive regional fashions. They are minor culture innovations quite independent of the major culture-political system.

Occasionally such ethnic diversions can be exploited to subvert our general system. Such attempts ought to be opposed prudently and intelligently. The main supporters of 'multiculturalism' i.e. the desire to disrupt the anglomorph structure of Australia, are our own, mostly ethnically anglomorph self-haters (Blainey's 'Black armbanders'). They must be fought, politically, to the death.

With our victory in the Cold War against Communism (and like all victories this one bears also bitter fruits), the strategic situation of our Continent may become precarious in hitherto not fully predictable ways. And for that kind of contingency there is only one, the oldest, device of statecraft: military power, the sword enmeshed in flexibly intelligent alliances.

Let us, by all means, subject to economic inevitabilities, take any immigrants we can. Let us not discriminate against the best and ablest ones (I mean, of course, the Chinese) in the tradition of our bogus egalitarianism. Let us admit as many refugees from Indochina, and in the near future from Hong Kong, for our honour (and not only or even mainly our interests) dictates it. If they come as political resistance fighters, the otherwise strict requirement of induction into anglomorphy may be relaxed, balanced by interests of the Australian State.

A good symptom of a correct policy is that it is being enacted before becoming official. A destructive policy is usually being urged by bogus elites in places such as the world of certain Arts faculties. This simple fact makes Patrick Moynihan's celebrated phrase 'benign neglect' for the optimal way of assimilating strangers such a powerful, for so obviously truthful, phrase.

Our non-anglomorph intake breeds Australians. It has done so in the past and it will continue to do so in the future. No threats or bribes from ethnic fuehrers can alter it. There can be no reason for de-anglifying a country such as this, and this includes the bogus striving for a 'true Australian culture'. There is no such thing and cannot be. Anglomorphy as a dominant way of life is good enough where a country is marked or Crowned by it.

www.ingramcontent.com/pod-product-compliance
Lightning Source LLC
Chambersburg PA
CBHW052105230426
43671CB00011B/1939